Research in Comparative and
Global Social Policy

Series Editors: **Heejung Chung**, University of Kent,
Alexandra Kaasch, University of Bielefeld,
Stefan Kühner, Lingnan University

Through a unique combination of comparative and global social
perspectives, this series questions how nation states and transnational
policy actors deal with globally shared challenges.

Also available

Women, Welfare and Productivism in East Asia and Europe
By **Ruby Chau** and **Sam Yu**

Compulsory Income Management in Australia and New Zealand
More Harm than Good?
By **Greg Marston, Louise Humpage, Michelle Peterie, Philip**
Mendes, Shelley Bielefeld and Zoe Staines

Welfare Reform and Social Investment Policy in Europe and East Asia
International Lessons and Policy Implications
Edited by **Young Jun Choi, Timo Fleckenstein** and
Soohyun Lee

Minimum Income Standards and Reference Budgets
International and Comparative Policy Perspectives
Edited by **Christopher Deeming**

Local Policies and the European Social Fund
Employment Policies Across Europe
By **Katharina Zimmermann**

Find out more

policy.bristoluniversitypress.co.uk/
research-in-comparative-and-global-social-policy

Coming soon

Welfare Attitudes in East Asia
The Case of Beijing and Singapore
By **Trude Sundberg**

Editorial advisory board

Find out more

policy.bristoluniversitypress.co.uk/
research-in-comparative-and-global-social-policy

VARIETIES OF PRECARITY

Melting Labour and the Failure to Protect Workers in the Korean Welfare State

Sophia Seung-yoon Lee

First published in Great Britain in 2023 by

Policy Press, an imprint of
Bristol University Press
University of Bristol
1–9 Old Park Hill
Bristol
BS2 8BB
UK
t: +44 (0)117 374 6645
e: bup-info@bristol.ac.uk

Details of international sales and distribution partners are available
at policy.bristoluniversitypress.co.uk

British Library Cataloguing in Publication Data
A catalogue record for this book is available from the British Library

ISBN 978-1-4473-6925-7 hardcover
ISBN 978-1-4473-6926-4 ePub
ISBN 978-1-4473-6927-1 ePdf

Cover design: Andrew Corbett
Bristol University Press and Policy Press use environmentally responsible
print partners.
Printed and bound in Great Britain by CPI Group (UK) Ltd, Croydon, CR0 4YY

FSC
www.fsc.org
MIX
Paper | Supporting
responsible forestry
FSC® C013604

Contents

Series editors' preface

Heejung Chung (University of Kent, UK)
Alexandra Kaasch (University of Bielefeld, Germany)
Stefan Kühner (Lingnan University, Hong Kong)

In a world that is rapidly changing, increasingly connected and uncertain, there is a need to develop a shared applied policy analysis of welfare regimes around the globe. Research in Comparative and Global Social Policy is a series of books that addresses broad questions around how nation states and transnational policy actors manage globally shared challenges. In so doing, the book series includes a wide array of contributions, which discuss comparative social policy history, development and reform within a broad international context. The book series invites innovative research by leading experts on all world regions and global social policy actors and aims to fulfil the following objectives: it encourages cross-disciplinary approaches that develop theoretical frameworks reaching across individual world regions and global actors; it seeks to provide evidence-based good practice examples that cross the bridge between academic research and practice; not least, it aims to provide a platform in which a wide range of innovative methodological approaches, be it national case studies, larger-N comparative studies or global social policy studies, can be introduced to aid the evaluation, design and implementation of future social policies.

In this regard, we are delighted to have Sophia Seung-yoon Lee's contribution on precarious labour in Korea as a part of our book series. This book brings together a unique collection of case studies of different scenarios of labour market preciousness or fissured workplaces in Korea. This includes Ssangyong Motor Industry plant workers, call centre cleaning workers, to Korean platform workers. Together they tell the story of the rise of precarious and 'melting labour' in Korea and the failures of their welfare state development in protecting workers.

The highlight of this book is its unique and innovative theoretical contribution of the concept of 'melting labour'. Melting labour entails the dismantling of various boundaries surrounding traditional forms of work and workplace – namely the rise of non-regular and atypical work, subcontracted and outsourced work and bogus self-employment like dependent or disguised self-employed individuals, freelancers and platform workers. Through the use of the concept, Lee aims to provide a better conceptualisation of the increased new forms of work that deviate away from standard employment, and better understand the common features of changes in work and workplace forms that enable this. What is more, Lee examines policy drift and policy makers' failure to adapt existing institutions to these new labour market contexts, to show how institutional inconsistencies are created that fail the social contract of protecting its citizens. These contributions allow us to understand the case studies provided in this book not only as something limited to that of South Korea, but something happening and applicable globally, of interest to labour market and social policy scholars alike.

Much of the work Lee presents here is based on numerous policy and activism work she has conducted over the years in addressing issues of labour market precariousness in Korea. As part of the South Korean government taskforce on youth and precious labour, she has been the leading voice in exposing the issues of rising precariousness in the labour market in Korea. Her work has highlighted the inadequacies of the welfare state in providing security – or in her words 'decommodifying' these workers. This is why, as the readers will find out, her stories are real, true and fresh, as they are told by the narrator who has been fighting this field for a long time and has heard numerous stories told directly by the workers experiencing this melting labour first hand. Again, her stories are not limited to the Korean experience, but resonate to a wider audience across the world experiencing the melting labour phenomenon.

In sum, we are confident that anyone who is interested in understanding the wider societal changes happening to the labour market with regards to the erosion of employment and social contracts will appreciate the contribution this book makes. We are incredibly pleased to be able to include this book in our series and we hope you enjoy the book.

List of figures and tables

Figures

Tables

Acknowledgements

This book represents a culmination of my decade-long research on social policy and precarious workers in South Korea. I aim to offer a comprehensive examination of the complex relationship between the evolving landscape of precarious labour with the concept of 'melting labour' and the inadequacies of institutional protections in the Korean welfare state. Through my exploration of Korean precarious workers, including dismissed workers, subcontracted and outsourced workers, cleaning workers, call centre workers, freelance workers, and platform workers, I investigate why the compressed institutional development of the welfare state has failed to protect these workers in Korea. I argue that the mismatch between the institutional combination established during the compressed welfare state development and the melting labour, which has increased precarious work, is at the core of this issue. I will explain how this mismatch renders the old institutions obsolete, employing the concept of policy 'drift'. Rather than repeating the narrative that despite the development of Korea's welfare state and economic growth, workers are struggling, I discuss what I have learned about the reality of the institutional and social structures surrounding precarious workers. Ultimately, I hope that my research will contribute to a better understanding of the reality of precarious labour in our society.

I want to express my heartfelt gratitude to all those who have contributed to the creation of this book. I owe a special debt of thanks to my dear friend and colleague Seung-sup Kim, whose thoughtful contribution to Chapter 3 was crucial to shaping my ideas. I am also deeply appreciative of the contributions made by Ko-eun Park, Eun-ji Kim and Hyukjin Cho to Chapter 4, as well as those made by Hyo-jin Seo to Chapter 5, and Kyoung-jin Park and Gyu-hye Kim to Chapter 6. The dedicated efforts of Jae-wook Nahm and Seung-ho Baek in contributing to Chapter 7 were also indispensable. Your insightful perspectives and collaborative spirit have significantly enriched the analysis and discussions in this book, and I am truly grateful to have had the opportunity to work with such excellent research collaborators.

This book project was supported by the Laboratory Program for Korean Studies through the Ministry of Education of the Republic of Korea and the Korean Studies Promotion Service of the Academy of Korean Studies (AKS-2018-LAB-1250002). I am grateful for this support. My deepest gratitude goes to the members of the Korea Inequality Research Lab, including Jong-Sung You, Frederick Solt, Stephan Haggard, Timo Fleckenstein, Byung You Cheon, Cheol-Sung Lee, Jun Ho Jeong, Sung Ho Park, Nak Nyeon Kim, Woo Chang Kang, Eun-Young Ha, Namhoon Kang, Jung Wook Son and Seung Ju Lee, as well as Soohyun Lee. Without their unwavering support and insightful comments, I would not have been able to publish this book. Their contributions have been invaluable in shaping my research and providing critical feedback that has helped to strengthen and clarify my arguments. I am truly fortunate to have had the opportunity to work with such a talented and dedicated group of scholars, and I look forward to continuing our collaboration in the years to come.

My next gratitude goes to the dedicated and hardworking research assistants at the Precarious Work and Social Policy Research Lab at Chung-Ang University, including Eunbyeol Kim, Heejeong Shim, Ji-won Kim, Sungjun Park, Gyu Hye Kim and Tae-Hwan Kim. Your tireless efforts and commitment to this project have been invaluable and greatly appreciated. I would also like to express my gratitude to my students at Chung-Ang University who have inspired me with their passion for learning and their willingness to engage with important social issues. Your enthusiasm and dedication have been a constant source of motivation and inspiration for me. Furthermore, I would like to thank my colleagues at Chung-Ang University who have provided support and encouragement throughout the course of this research. Special thanks go to Sung-Chun Kim, Yeon-Myung Kim, Sun-Hae Lee, Sung-Ho Moon, Kyo-Seong Kim, Sul-Ki Chung, Young Choi, Young-Eun Chang and Yeon-Jung Lee in the Social Welfare department, as well as Kwang Yeong Shin, Byoung-Hoon Lee and Jin-Wook Shin in the Sociology department. I have learned how and why it is important to be in a community of wonderful people, and I only wish I could be as good a colleague to them as they have been to me.

Also, I would like to express my heartfelt appreciation to the members of Labour Forum NAMU and the Korean Social Policy Research group, as well as Jong-jin Kim at Union Center, for their invaluable contributions to this book. I am especially grateful for the insightful comments and feedback provided by Seung-ho Baek, Robert Walker and Guy Standing, which were instrumental in shaping my thinking and understanding of the complex issues surrounding precarious workers and the Korean welfare state. Their exceptional guidance and support have been a source of inspiration to me, and I am truly grateful to have had such outstanding mentors and colleagues throughout this research journey. I would also like to express my warm appreciation to my partner, Junbeom, and my two children for their patience, support and understanding of my passion for this work. Your unwavering support has been a source of strength and motivation for me, and I am forever grateful.

Finally, I want to express my sincere gratitude to all workers themselves who have shared their stories and experiences with me, even in the face of difficult circumstances. As a researcher, I recognise that my position has both enabled and limited my perspective on the realities of precarious workers in Korea. I am grateful for the opportunity to engage with this topic, and I have approached this research with a critical and reflective mindset, constantly questioning my own assumptions and biases.

I am deeply inspired by the workers who have persevered in the face of adversity and continue to fight for their rights and dignity. It is my hope that this book will contribute to a deeper understanding of the challenges faced by precarious workers not only in Korea but in all inhumane capitalist labour markets and ultimately lead to a more just and equitable society for all.

Introduction: Melting labour and institutional inconsistency

The precariat in South Korea

The combination of the Korean welfare state and its labour market is puzzling. In this book, I embark on a journey to unravel the complex relationship between the evolving landscape of melting labour and the inadequacies of institutional protections in the Korean welfare state. South Korea (hereafter, Korea) is often recognised as the most typical case of the East Asian miracle, characterised by broadly fair income distribution without prominent welfare politics representing income, wealth redistribution or labour. The puzzle lies in understanding why, despite achieving economic affluence and rapid institutional development in welfare institutions, Korea has witnessed a distinctively high rate of new forms of precarious work since the 2000s. Why and how does the compressed institutional development of the welfare state fail to protect precarious workers in Korea? In this book, I argue that the mismatch between the institutional combination established during the compressed welfare state development and the melting labour, which has increased precarious work, is at the core of this issue. I will explain how this mismatch renders the old institutions obsolete, employing the concept of policy 'drift'.

As the traditional boundaries of work disintegrate and give way to fissured workplaces, the Korean welfare state's reliance on the standard employment relationship proves increasingly insufficient in addressing the challenges of the modern labour market. The central thesis of this book is that the inconsistencies between institutional decommodification and the evolving nature of labour contribute to the expansion of diverse forms of precarity.

In Korea, economic growth led to a rapid expansion of wage workers and increased real household income. Without the welfare politics of wealth redistribution, Korea achieved compressed development in its welfare institutions within 30 years, creating a social insurance system set in most major risk areas and adopting a universalistic family policy. The social insurance system started as loyalty incentives given to the ruling group of state institutions, such as bureaucrats, professional soldiers and police officers (Lee G.C., 2009). The modern Korean social insurance system stems from the social security laws introduced in the 1960s (Won S.J.,

2013). The first of such laws is the Civil Service Pension Act, enacted in 1960, followed by these laws in 1963: the Military Pension Act, Industrial Accident Compensation Insurance Act (enforced in July 1964) and Medical Insurance Act (Yoon J.D. et al, 2008). The Medical Insurance Act came into effect in 1977 and was preferentially applied to employees as a 'cooperative medical insurance'. Similarly, the National Pension Act, enacted in 1973, was first applied to employees in the formal sector in 1988. The Private School Teachers and Staff Pension Act was passed in 1973 and enforced in 1975. The National Pension Act was implemented in 1997 and 1999 as a system covering rural and urban residents, respectively (National Pension Service Compilation Committee, 2015). The medical insurance by cooperatives/unions was enacted in the National Health Insurance Act in 1999; the medical insurance by organisations, including employee unions and the Medical Insurance Association, were also fully integrated (Lee G.C., 2009). The Employment Insurance Act was passed in 1993 and enforced in 1995. The early employment insurance system, which pays unemployment benefits to workers, has expanded continuously, covering workplaces with 30 or more employees (Yoon J.D., 2008) (see Table 1.1).

The statutory minimum wage system is a crucial institutional mechanism designed to contribute to the sound development of the national economy by guaranteeing a minimum level of wages for workers, thereby improving their livelihoods and the quality of the labour force (Minimum Wage Act Article 1). While Korea's minimum wage system was initially specified in the Labour Standards Act enacted in 1953, it did not have a significant impact (Lee J.A., 2013). However, after the 1997 Asian financial crisis, the minimum wage system began to evolve and gain prominence in society. This progression coincided with the rapid polarisation of the labour market, characterised by the expansion of non-regular workers. Prior to this, the proportion of workers eligible for the minimum wage was so low that it was challenging for the minimum wage to become a significant social issue (Jeong Y.H., 2013). The minimum wage, which began at 462.5 Korean won (KRW) in 1988, increased annually and reached 8,720 KRW as of 2021. While most European welfare states took over 100 years to develop their advanced welfare institutions, Korea's welfare institutions have managed to catch up with them in less than 40 years (see Figure 1.1).

Korea has achieved significant institutional development of welfare following its economic growth. However, it stands out among the countries in the Organisation for Economic Co-operation and Development (OECD) for two reasons: first, the comparatively low level of government welfare spending; and, second, the high proportion of non-regular workers, low-paid workers, small-sized business owners, and more recently, platform workers, who are all commonly referred to as precarious workers.

Despite rapid institutional development, the growth of Korean welfare spending has been modest. This achievement of economic growth has strongly influenced the formation of the policy paradigm. Social expenditure accounts for only about 13 per cent of the total general government expenditure. While there was substantial progress in institutionalising social security schemes during the compressed economic developmental period (as illustrated in Table 1.1), population coverage and benefit levels remained minimal, and state intervention and financial commitment were limited. The state's financial burden on the fund was minimised since employers and employees contributed to a social insurance system, as shown in Figure 1.2.

Korea has experienced a sharp increase in atypical and non-regular workers since the late 1980s; these workers now constitute more than a third of the country's total number of employees (Eun S.M., 2011; Lee S.Y., 2011; Kang S.T., 2014; Seo J.H., 2015). While the OECD average temporary employment rate is continuously around 12 per cent, the share of temporary employment in Korea has been well above most of the OECD countries, reaching approximately 30 per cent (see Figure 1.3).

Table 1.2 shows trend of the percentage of non-regular workers (temporary, part-time and non-typical workers) to total wage workers in Korea. The proportion of non-regular workers stood at 36.3 per cent in 2020, close to the previous year (36.4 per cent) but increased by 2.5 per cent from 33.8 per cent in 2008. As of 2020, the proportion of non-regular workers among women (45 per cent) was higher than that of men (29.4 per cent); this gender gap has continued since 2008. By age group, the proportion of non-regular workers was high, in the order of 15–19 years old (84.1 per cent), 60 years or older (71.0 per cent) and 20–29 years old (37.7 per cent). The proportion of non-regular workers increased among these groups between 2008 and 2019.

The puzzle at hand is understanding why, despite achieving economic affluence and rapid institutional development in welfare institutions, Korea has experienced such a distinctively high rate of new forms of precarious work since the 2000s. What factors contribute to the failure of the compressed institutional development of the welfare state to protect precarious workers in Korea? In this book, I argue that the mismatch between the institutional combination established during the compressed welfare state development and the melting labour, which has increased precarious work, is at the core of this issue.

To further elucidate this argument, I employ the concept of policy 'drift', an academic term that refers to a gradual and often unintended change in the effects or outcomes of a policy due to the interaction of changing social, economic or political conditions with existing policy structures. Drift is of particular interest as a mode of policy change because it involves a distinctive kind of politics. When a policy is drifting, political actors can

Table 1.1: The early employment insurance system

	Social insurance			
	National pension	National health insurance	Employment insurance	Industrial accident insurance
1960s–1970s	**1960** Introduction of Public Officials Pension **1963** Introduction of Military Pension **December 1973 (January 1974)** *National Pension Welfare Act* enacted (implementation postponed due to oil shock)	**December 1963 (March 1964)** *Medical Care Insurance Law* enacted **December 1976 (January 1977)** Application of obligations to business establishments with at least 500 employees excluding public officials, faculty, and soldiers		**November 1963 (January 1964)** Act No. 1438 *Industrial Accident Insurance Law* enacted. Large-scale mining and manufacturing industry with more than 500 full-time employees
1980s–1990s	**December 1986 (January 1988)** Amendment bill Act No. 3902 *National Pension Act* for businesses with 10 or more full-time employees **January 1995 (July 1995)** Expansion of obligatory application to farmers, fishermen and the self-employed in rural areas	**January 1988** Health insurance for local residents in farming and fishing villages **July 1989** Urban residents, self-employed health insurance (realisation of national health insurance) **February 1999 (January 2000)** Act No. 5854 *National Health Insurance Law* enacted • Initiate integrated health insurance (run by a single insurer of the National Health Insurance Service) • The purpose includes medical examination, rehabilitation, and prevention	**December 1993 (July 1995)** Act No. 4664 *Employment Insurance Law* enacted **1998** Expand application to all business establishments with one or more workers (except for some industries, such as agriculture, forestry, hunting, and so on, with less than four regular workers)	**1989** Expansion of application to 'any business or place of business' **December 1999 (July 2000)** • Expansion of application to small and medium-sized business owners • Application of business establishments for more than one person and expansion of all business establishments

Table 1.1: The early employment insurance system (continued)

Social Assistance	Labour law		
National Basic Living Security Act	Labour Standards Act	Temporary Workers Protection Act	Dispatched work act
December 1961 *Livelihood Protection Law* enacted			
1982 Complete revision. Principles of ensuring minimum living, clarification of national responsibility, and priority of kinship supporting **September 1999 (October 2000)** Act No. 6024 *National Basic Living Security Law* enacted	**March 1997** Act No.5309 *Labour Standards Act* enacted **February 1999** Restrictions on dismissal during the period of closure due to work-related injuries, medical treatment, prenatal, postnatal, and so on, and for 30 days thereafter		**February 1998 (July 1998)** Act No. 5512 *Act on the Protection of Dispatched Workers, and so on*, enacted

(continued)

Table 1.1: The early employment insurance system (continued)

	Social insurance			
	National pension	National health insurance	Employment insurance	Industrial accident insurance
2000s–	**2003** Expansion of obligatory application to businesses with fewer than five employees **2009** Revision of Special Occupational Pension Act **2012** Expansion of obligatory application to working social assistance recipients who were only allowed to join voluntarily **May 2014 (July 2014)** Act No. 12617 *Basic Pension Law* enacted **March 2018 (September 2018)** Basic pension benefits increased from 200,000 to 250,000 KRW **January 2020** Support for pension insurance premiums for locally insured person	**July 2008** Introduction of National Long-Term Care Insurance **May 2009 (January 2011)** Unify the collection of social insurance premiums (National Health Insurance + Long-Term Care, National Pension, Employment Insurance, Industrial Accident Insurance) into the National Health Insurance Corporation **January 2018 (July 2018)** Employees who have worked for more than one year are recognised as voluntary continuous subscribers	**December 2002 (January 2004)** The requirements for receiving job-seeking benefits applied to daily workers are determined **2010** Allow self-employed people to voluntarily subscribe to unemployment benefits and establish a system to support the creation of short-term jobs **2012** Allow self-employed people who employ less than 50 workers to receive unemployment benefits **July 2021 (January 2022)** Included in the subject of employment insurance obligations for special employees	**December 2007 (July 2008)** Expand the target to four special types of workers (golf caddies, home-school teachers, cargo drivers, and insurance planners) **December 2016 (December 2016)** State the prohibition of disadvantage treatment and penalty provisions to prevent employees who apply for industrial accident compensation insurance benefits from being dismissed **October 2017 (January 2018)** As a type of industrial accident, new content that recognises accidents that occur while commuting to and from work in the usual route and method

Table 1.1: The early employment insurance system (continued)

Social Assistance	Labour law		
National Basic Living Security Act	Labour Standards Act	Temporary Workers Protection Act	Dispatched work act
2014 Reorganisation into customised benefits (livelihood benefits, medical benefits, housing benefits, education benefits, dissolution benefits, funeral benefits, self-help benefits, and so on)	**March 2008** Restrictions on paid holidays, overtime work, and pay for holiday work for short-time workers	**December 2006 (July 2007)** Act No. 8074 *Temporary and Short-Time Workers Protection Act* enacted	**December 2006** • Dispatched business owners specify that employment conditions should be announced when dispatching workers
	June 2010 State employers' obligation to notify employees of dismissal 30 days in advance State restrictions on labour contracts against minors	**April 2007** Specify limitations on overtime work for short-term workers	• Restriction of the work of the worker dispatch business to those prescribed by Presidential Decree other than manufacturing
	February 2012 State maternity leave for female workers during pregnancy	**February 2012** State applications for correction of discriminatory treatment. Revision of the contents such as suspension of discriminatory acts, improvement of working conditions such as wages, appropriate compensation, and so on	• State that the dispatch period does not exceed one year
	May 2020 State disclosure of the list of overdue business owners. Specify the obligation to devise a wage preservation plan so that existing wage levels do not decrease if workers are employed according to the flexible working time system within three months		**April 2007** Specification of special cases related to the application of the Labour Standards Act
		May 2020 In the case of a contract for conversion to an indefinite period or to a regular worker, it is specified that workers of the same type or similar type of work in the relevant workplace should be hired first	**April 2019** State investigation and research on major issues related to the worker dispatch project
			May 2020 In the case of childbirth, illness, injury, and so on, specify that the duration of dispatch may be adjusted for the period necessary for the elimination of such reasons

Source: National Legislation Information Center: https://www.law.go.kr/LSW/main.html

Figure 1.1: Changes in statutory minimum income in selected OECD countries

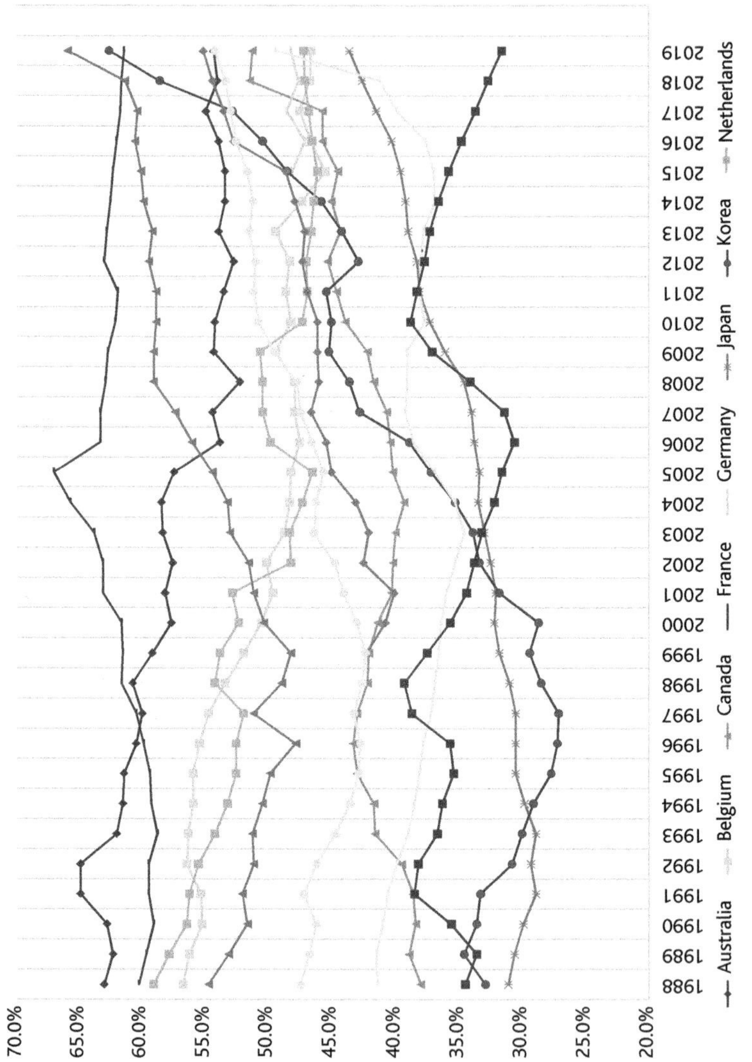

Source: https://stats.oecd.org/index.aspx?DataSetCode=RMW

8

Figure 1.2: Public social expenditure as percentage of gross domestic product

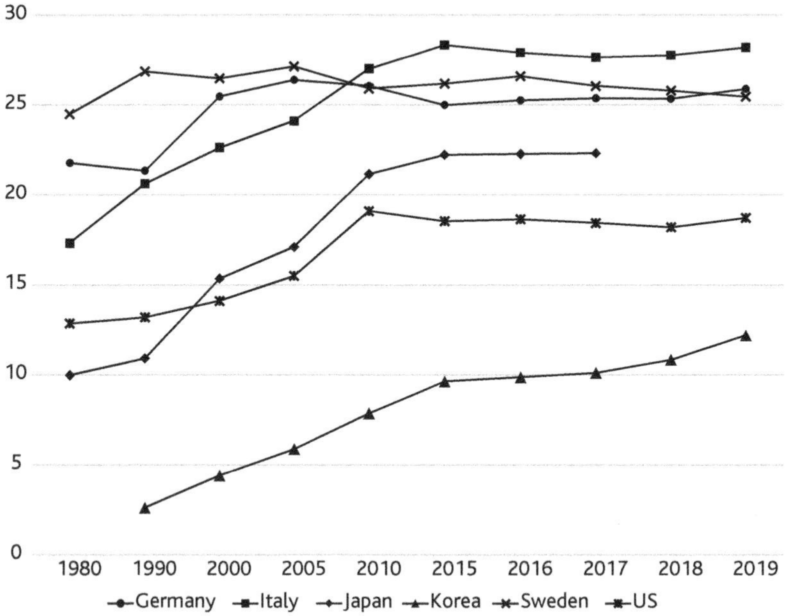

Source: https://www.oecd.org/social/expenditure.htm

achieve major changes simply by doing nothing, or more precisely, by failing to update a policy to keep pace with changing external circumstances. This distinguishes drift from other forms of subterranean policy change, such as conversion (the adaptation of a policy to achieve new purposes) and layering (the addition of a new policy on top of an old one that changes the latter's operation) (Hacker, 2004).

In the context of Korea's welfare state, policy drift helps explain how the mismatch between the institutional combination established during the compressed welfare state development and the evolving nature of labour renders the old institutions obsolete, unable to address the contemporary challenges faced by workers in the Korean labour market. Drift does not require active blocking; given the difficulty of updating policies, policy makers may simply lack a sufficiently large support coalition to overcome the many hurdles thrown up by political institutions or may prioritise other policy changes, leading to deferred maintenance.

By examining the intricacies of policy drift and the implications of the mismatch between the welfare state's institutions and the shifting labour landscape, this book seeks to provide a comprehensive understanding of the factors contributing to the prevalence of precarious work in Korea since the 2000s.

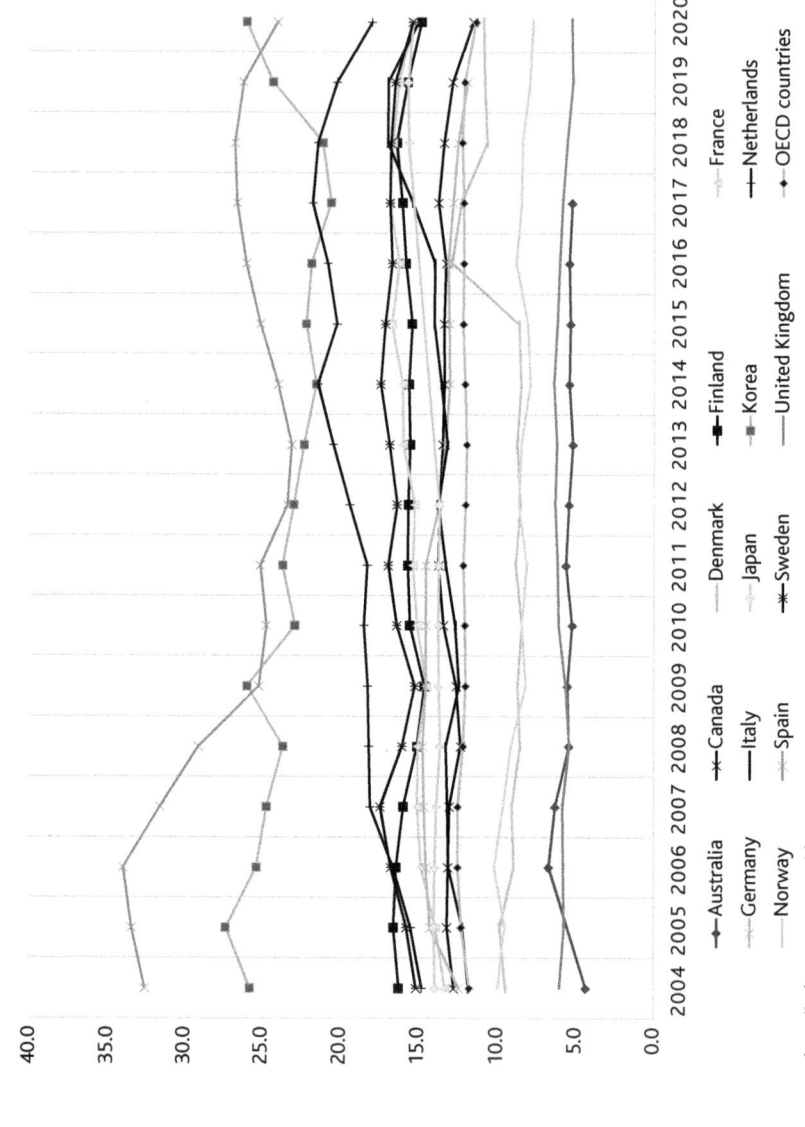

Figure 1.3: The share of temporary employment

Source: https://stats.oecd.org/index.aspx?queryid=54750

Table 1.2: Percentage of non-regular workers among total employees in South Korea by gender and age group

		2008	2009	2010	2011	2012	2013	2014	2015	2016	2017	2018	2019	2020
Total		**33.8**	**34.8**	**33.2**	**34.2**	**33.2**	**32.5**	**32.2**	**32.4**	**32.8**	**32.9**	**33**	**36.4**	**36.3**
Gender	Male	28.8	28.1	26.9	27.7	27	26.4	26.4	26.4	26.3	26.3	26.3	29.4	29.4
	Female	40.7	44	41.7	42.9	41.4	40.6	39.9	40.2	41.1	41.2	41.4	45	45.0
Age group	15–19	64.9	75	69.6	69.6	76.1	74.8	70	74.3	75.2	73.4	74	77.8	84.1
	20–29	31	31.6	31.1	31.6	30.5	31.1	32	32.1	32.2	33.1	32.3	38.3	37.7
	30–39	26.8	25.2	23.4	24.4	23.1	22.2	21.8	21.2	21.1	20.6	21	23.7	22.8
	40–49	31.6	32.3	29.7	30.5	29.1	27.2	26.6	26	26.1	26	25.3	27	26.7
	50–59	39.8	40.6	39.3	39.7	37.5	37.1	34.6	34.6	34.2	33.9	34	35.5	34.3
	60–	65.7	72.6	69.7	70.6	70.4	67.3	68.5	67.2	67.9	67.3	67.9	71.6	71.0

Note: Ratio of non-regular workers = (number of non-regular workers/total number of wage workers) × 100

Source: Statistics Korea (2021)

Explaining the Korean welfare state and labour market

The Korean welfare state and functional equivalence

In understanding the economic development accompanied by a comparatively low inequality rate, the East Asian 'productive welfare state' literature has gained popularity. This strand of literature focuses on the importance of the functional equivalent of other policy domains to social protection policies (Estevez-Abe, 2008; Kim P.H., 2010; Lee S.Y., 2016). It explains that Korea used industrial policy as a social policy. Korea has achieved its economic development within about 20 years of the compressed period through export-led growth strategies during the 1970s and the 1980s. Until the Korean financial crisis in 1997, the average annual growth rate had been around 9 per cent, and household income growth had continued to play a role in enhancing individual welfare (Goodman and Peng, 1996; Kwon H.J., 2005; Kim H.K., 2008; Lee S.Y., 2016). Kim Pil-Ho (2010) and Kim Do-Hyun (2018) provide an excellent viewpoint of how the Korean and Japanese government promoted savings-oriented programmes for both public and private welfare; they also explain how such state control of capital provided financial capacity that its small tax revenue would otherwise have not allowed. Estevez-Abe (2008) highlights the concept of decommodification, referring to the degree to which the welfare state makes citizens more independent from the wage earned in the market and, using this concept, she explains how a whole range of industrial policies are, in fact, functionally equivalent to (social democratic) social policies that attenuate the effects of market forces. The literature on Korean productive welfare states and welfare production regimes (Estevez-Abe, 2008; Lee S.Y., 2016) provides theoretical explanations on how Korea accomplished the compressed economic development without a real increase in social spending and the lack of welfare politics from the trade union or left party. Most studies have highlighted such functional equivalence by focusing on the low level of social expenditure and referring to Korea as a small welfare state; however, introducing a series of welfare institutions is often not emphasised. Although the actual spending seemed to lag, major social protection schemes and legislations were introduced in a short period. Korea introduced the national pension in 1988, with a funded system with 20 years of mandatory contribution. There were 'pensioners' only since 2008. Therefore, the state's financial burden on the fund was minimal since it was a social insurance system to which both employers and employees contributed. The immaturity of the social security systems, as well as funding through insurance, resulted in a low level of Korea's social expenditure. Social expenditure was only about 3 per cent of the gross domestic product (GDP) in 1990 and reached 10 per cent of GDP after 2010 when the ratio of the population of people aged over 65 years exceeded 10 per cent of the Korean population. The composition of welfare expenditure is shown in Figure 1.4.

This study aims to examine the implications of the early compressed development of social protection institutions focused on employees in the formal sector through a social insurance scheme, and how these institutions reveal inevitable limitations in protecting precarious workers engaged in new forms of work.

New risk and non-regular workers

The other strand of literature associated with this puzzle concerns the expansion of non-regular workers in post-industrial Korea. The literature on 'new risk' (Bonoli, 2006) and post-industrial transition (Lee S.Y., 2016) posits that the shift towards a service economy has led to an increase in low-skilled, low-paid workers, thereby creating non-regular and atypical workers. By introducing the concept of new risk, the literature successfully sparks a discussion on precarious workers and the need for a new welfare state. The new risk literature suggests that certain demographic groups, such as women, the young, and lower-educated or low-skilled workers, face new risks and that the welfare state does not sufficiently support these groups.

Although the literature on new risk makes a distinguished contribution to understanding welfare states and labour market transitions, it has some limitations. In contrast to the explanation offered by the new risk literature, labour market risks in Korea are shifting more quickly towards men and higher-educated workers than towards women and lower-educated workers (Lee S.Y., 2011). While it is still valid to argue that women, the less educated and the young are more exposed to risk, describing them as the new risk groups may be inaccurate, as these three demographic groups might have always faced precarious labour situations. For instance, in Korea, where non-standard employment is dominated by women, the less educated and the young, the risk of working in a precarious job is also shifting to men, the higher educated and the elderly. This leads to the need for a concept of precarious work that is more specific to the Korean context.

Dualised labour market thesis

Next is the literature on dualisation. Dualisation has gained considerable attention in explaining the discriminative gap between standard and non-standard employment. Gorz (1999) explains that in 1986, Wolfgang Lecher predicted that the proportion of stable, full-time jobs would fall to 50 per cent by 1996, and France and Britain would follow a similar path (Gorz, 1999). Gorz (1999) describes the dual labour market of standard and non-standard employment as 'the ... split into two major categories: a central core made

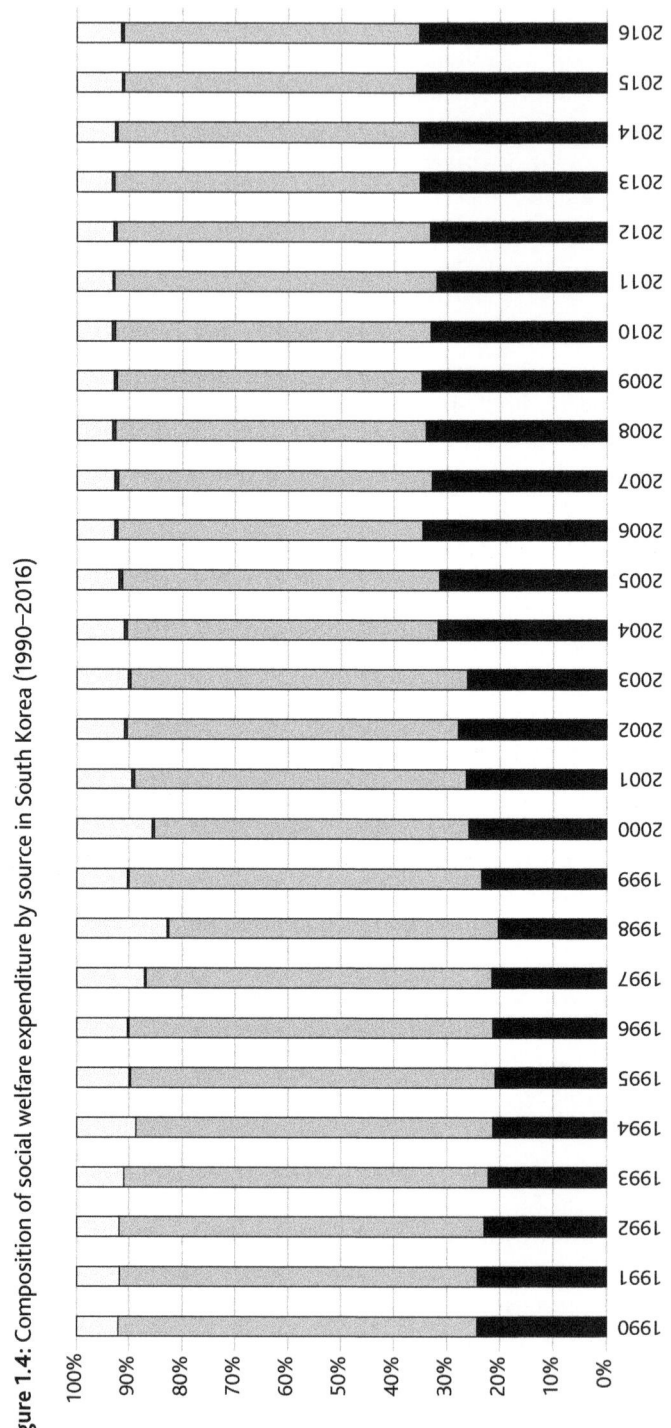

Figure 1.4: Composition of social welfare expenditure by source in South Korea (1990–2016)

Source: https://stats.oecd.org/index.aspx?DataSetCode=RMW

up of permanent and full-time employees, who are occupationally versatile and mobile, and around that core, a sizeable mass of peripheral workers, including a substantial proportion of insecure and temporary workers with variable hours and wages' (Gorz, 1999: 48).

The literature on varieties of capitalism explains that the labour market and the composition of complementary welfare systems are closely related to economic growth and income inequality (Hall and Soskice, 2001; Baek S.H., 2005; Lee S.Y., 2016). Esping-Andersen (1990) also emphasises the stratification effect of social policies through the analysis of three types of welfare capitalism (Esping-Andersen, 1990). The labour market dualisation argument, which underscores the role of social policy as an independent variable, explains the dual structure of the labour market using the concept of 'institutional dualisation' (Emmenegger et al, 2012). The dualisation thesis critiques existing discussions on polarisation, fragmentation and marginalisation; it only focuses on the outcome of labour market segmentation and overlooks the politics of change (Emmenegger et al, 2012).

This theory begins with an understanding of the socioeconomic mechanisms and processes by which non-regular workers are produced, and how employment protection (Rueda, 2005; Emmenegger, 2009) and labour market policies (Rueda, 2006) contribute to the formation of the dual labour market.

According to the dualisation thesis, most 'insiders' in the primary labour market are regular workers, and the 'outsiders' in the secondary labour market are mostly non-regular workers (Kalleberg, 2003; Baek S.H., 2014; Lee S.Y. and Kim S.S., 2015). The 'insider' belonging to the internal labour market is characterised by job security, high wages, opportunities for skill formation within the company, and a promotion system. The external labour market is characterised by precarious employment, low wages, limited opportunities for skill formation, and the absence of a promotion system (Doeringer and Piore, 1971; Jeong I.H., 2013; Baek S.H., 2014; Kim S.H., 2015).

Studies have mainly divided insiders and outsiders into belonging to the primary and secondary labour market, respectively, based on employment type (regular and non-regular workers) and company size (large companies and small- and medium-sized enterprises) (Jeong I.H., 2001; Lee B.H., 2004; Jeong Y.H., 2013; Baek S.H., 2014). Due to the low mobility between the two types of labour markets (Piore, 1980), the segmental structure becomes more entrenched. As such, although the segmentation of the labour market has been observed in industrial societies (Doeringer and Piore, 1971; Gordon et al, 1982), the structural change to the service economy has resulted in a new form of labour market segmentation or dualism (Esping-Andersen, 1993; Oesch, 2006; Standing, 2009; Emmenegger et al, 2012).

The status of outsiders tends to be fixed mainly in low-skilled service occupations working as non-regular workers (Emmenegger et al, 2012); such status is closely related to the change in the industrial structure to a service economy. Deindustrialisation, globalisation and the increase in female workers have made the segmented structure of the labour market more likely to persist.

Emmenegger et al (2012) focus on the process of dualisation of social policy. They explain how social policies within welfare states apply different rights, eligibility and social services to workers with different statuses, thus widening the gap between outsiders and insiders in the dual labour market. Dualisation arises from the differential application of social policies to insiders and outsiders, mainly represented by regular and non-regular workers. In other words, the dual labour market is further deepened by the existing dual institutional arrangement of the welfare system. This dualisation of the labour market is particularly prominent in the corporatist welfare state (Lee S.Y., 2018).

In the corporatist welfare state, it is difficult to introduce a system that allows for wages to be commensurate with productivity, as in liberal countries, or increases public employment, as in Nordic welfare countries, due to high tax burdens and social insurance contributions. Additionally, institutions protecting the internal labour market (regular workers) have a strong path dependence; in this situation, continental European welfare states adopt a dualisation strategy (Saint-Paul, 1996; Pierson, 2001; Emmenegger et al, 2012). The dualisation of the labour market proceeds without dismantling the internal labour market-related system, while achieving partial deregulation that modifies existing regulations, resulting in non-regular workers (Lee S.Y., 2018).

The living and working conditions of non-standard workers in Korea align with the characteristics of 'outworkers' described by Gorz (1999). Non-standard workers are excluded from income and employment security. Furthermore, in Korea, where the welfare production regime has been shown to be persistently geared towards large firms (Lee S.Y., 2016) that experience less mobility in their labour markets, these workers are likely to enter the category of non-standard employment and continue working in non-standard jobs.

The literature on dualisation offers an excellent perspective for understanding the gap between regular and non-regular workers and the increase in non-regular workers' size. However, it has limitations in capturing the large-scale self-employed workers in Korea (25 per cent), the increasing new forms of work beyond the dichotomy of standard and non-standard employment, and the formation of new employment relationships such as subcontracting or increasing disguised self-employment.

Acknowledging the contributions and limitations of the literature, this study goes further to explain precarious workers in the Korean context, while grounded in the general explanations of capitalism's evolution and its impact on work. In the following sections, I will introduce literature on changes in work by stages of capitalism and workers' precariousness based on the literature on precarious work, and I introduce a new term, the 'melting labour'.

Changes in work by stages of capitalism

Fissured workplace

It is essential to examine how the process of capitalism's evolution, by fine-tuning the capital accumulation strategy, changes the conditions surrounding workers. Existing studies have explained the spread of new forms of work as intensifying competition due to globalisation, the weakening of the membership of unions, the change in industrial structure towards a service economy, and the lack of government regulation. However, Weil uses the concept of 'fissured workplace' to explain how changes in the organisational structure of large corporations have driven changes in the overall employment structure (Weil, 2015). Since the 1970s, investors and financial institutions have demanded corporate managements to focus on core competencies and maximise profits for shareholders (Weil, 2015).

Weil (2015) presents franchising, third-party management and supply chain systems as representative organisational forms of fissured workplaces. First, franchising provides a replicable business model to other companies but is an organisational form in which the head office takes over control. A third-party management consignment is an organisational form that aims to increase efficiency by concentrating only on core competencies and entrusting the rest to a third party. Finally, the supply chain system is an additional organisational form that enables companies to implement the fissured model; in this way, expanding the scope of the supply chain improves efficiency, reduces inventory risk and demands fluctuation risk. In the supply chain, the company's detailed specifications of the technology, loading, delivery and product standards that the supply base must comply with must exist.

This management revolution refers to new management techniques introduced by companies and can be summarised as labour market flexibility. Dispersion, geographical movement and scale-up through labour market flexibility in the form of 'wiping off' tasks other than core competencies have begun to replace Fordism based on mass production systems and standardised labour. The change in the method of capital accumulation through micro-adjustment significantly impacted the instability of workers. The process of companies outsourcing all but core competencies, which expanded with globalisation, has expanded the scope of the production process geographically to a global chain; this puts pressure on lowering costs and increasing efficiencies. Large companies in developed countries have sought to accumulate capital through cost reduction by employing subcontractors in developing countries. In addition, as all competencies, except for core competencies, are outsourced within the country, the number of subcontractors expands.

These fissured workplaces make it possible for companies to shift the obligations imposed on employment to sub-organisations, such as franchising contracts, third-party management, outsourcing, subcontracting and services. Shifting these obligations reduces labour costs, social insurance premiums, labour management costs and corporate welfare costs. The shift also allows companies to avoid the obligation to comply with consistent personnel policies and the observance of labour standards and the working environment. At the same time, companies can streamline the management and control of subcontractors and perform quality management efficiently through innovation in the supply chain system, which is made possible by technological development, and so on (Thelen and Mahoney, 2015; Weil, 2015). In the end, the scope and limits of employment responsibilities become more ambiguous because of the fissured workplace.

A prime contractor seeking flexibility and low unit prices outsources various tasks and projects to subcontractors, with whom they must sign contracts. The relationship between the two parties is often asymmetric. The pressure to lower unit prices frequently results in subcontractor workers receiving low wages and being exposed to risks in the workplace. Workers often have to work long hours to keep up with contract timelines.

The employer in the subcontracting company may be passive in investing in equipment for occupational safety to profit from the fixed contract with the prime contractor. The flexibility in the production process required by the prime contractor also necessitates workforce flexibility in the subcontracting company, which is accompanied by an increase in the number of precarious workers while minimising the number of core workers (mostly standard workers) even in subcontractors.

By utilising atypical and ambiguous employment relationships, ranging from non-regular workers and special type employments to freelancers and platform labour, employers can reduce personnel management, layoff and social insurance costs, as well as investment in skills. This situation results in a fissured workplace with increased job insecurity, income inequality and limited access to social protection for workers who are part of these non-standard employment arrangements.

Platform capitalism

The fissured workplace concept explains the reasons for the proliferation of precarious workers resulting from the change in organisational forms of companies that have been required to focus on core competencies. However, it has limitations in explaining the emergence of dependent self-employment relationships, especially the expansion of platform work. In this context, the theory of platform capitalism, which explains the rise of the digital economy, is useful. This theory explains the background of the spread of dependent self-employment, such as gig work and platform work, as the growth of platform businesses.

Policies to protect the emerging precarious work, which has expanded because of fissured workplaces, have focused on regularising non-regular workers. This is a strategy to incorporate new forms of precarious work into a social protection system designed to protect formal employment by re-standardising non-standard employment forms. Since these approaches define non-regular work as a departure from the standard employment relationship, the solution to the problem tends to result in the regularisation of non-regular workers.

The reason dependent and precarious self-employment did not receive much attention in literature on dualisation and new risk is that they did not have a standard employment relationship in the first place. However, since the mid-2000s, new types of work, such as platform work, which deviate from the standard employment relationship and the wage-labour contract relationship, have expanded. This expansion has led to the discussion of the regularisation of non-regular workers entering a new phase.

New forms of work, such as platform work, do not simply deviate from the standard employment relationship but occupy an ambiguous space that does not clearly fit within standard or non-standard employment relationships (Kalleberg and Vallas, 2018). Addressing the needs of workers in these ambiguous relationships requires new approaches and policies that go beyond the regularisation of non-regular workers and consider the unique challenges faced by workers in the platform economy and other emerging forms of work.

Platform capitalism, as described by Srnicek (2017), offers a framework for understanding the growth and characteristics of platform companies in response to various crises of capital accumulation. These crises led to the shift from an industrial economy in the 1970s to a post-industrial economy after the 2008 financial crisis. The response to these crises has prompted the demand for labour market flexibility, which is reflected in the platform company business model that fosters precarious and fragmented jobs (Choi C.W., 2017).

The core of the platform business model is to reduce labour costs through outsourcing using information and communication technology (ICT) and extracting valuable big data via the platform (Srnicek, 2017). Companies have increasingly shifted their business models to maximise profits by creating platforms that utilise algorithms to extract excess profits and enable many people to work on the platform.

Platform companies can be found across various industries, including advertising platforms like Google and Facebook; cloud platforms that extract data and generate revenue by renting software and hardware; commodity platforms that generate revenue by renting company-owned assets; and brokerage platforms that generate revenue through providing services such as Uber and Airbnb. In the manufacturing sector, industrial platforms like Siemens are emerging as dominant business models that combine traditional manufacturing with platforms to extract data from production, logistics and distribution processes, control the production process, and reduce costs (Srnicek, 2017).

The expansion of platform work and platform capitalism has significant implications for the labour market, as it creates new forms of employment that are often precarious and fall outside traditional employment relationships. This calls for a rethinking of labour policies and social protection systems to better address the needs of workers in the platform economy and other emerging forms of work.

In Korea, the rapid growth of intermediary platforms like delivery apps (Baedal Minjok), surrogate driving platforms (Daeri Wonjeon) and housekeeping services platforms have significantly impacted the labour market. These platforms are part of the broader platform economy that has emerged due to technological developments and changes in economic structures. Although digital platforms have the potential to increase productivity through artificial intelligence, machine learning and automation (Kenney and Zysman, 2016), platform owners often capture a disproportionate share of the rent or excess rent (Srnicek, 2017).

The rise of the platform economy has led to a decrease in skilled jobs and the creation of new employment forms that diverge from traditional employment relationships. The gig economy is one such example, characterised by atypical labour allocation and the use of short-term independent contract workers (Huws et al, 2016). Crowdsourcing is another manifestation of the platform economy, providing employment opportunities for people with disabilities and the youth who have difficulty participating in the labour market. Crowdsourcing also enables the flexible use of working hours and allows participants to obtain additional income. However, it has similar aspects to existing outsourcing in that it facilitates the utilisation of precarious short-term labour contracts and low wages. Specifically, it brings benefits, such as reducing labour costs and avoiding regulations for companies; however, there is currently weak legal mechanism for social protection of crowdsourced workers, thereby producing precarious workers. Digital platforms also allow companies to circumvent various regulations under current laws. As a result, the instability of the labour force may be amplified, and economic benefits may be distributed asymmetrically (Scholz, 2016).

Precarious workers and melting labour

Precarious workers

In a capitalist society, workers inherently face precarious situations due to market dependence, as they must sell their labour in the market to earn a living. The capitalist mode of production primarily aims at extracting surplus value, pressuring individuals to work and increasing worker productivity through mechanisation or efficiency of the labour process. This pursuit makes it easier to replace workers, as they don't possess the means of production, and results in a structure that exploits workers. Consequently, precarious work, the proletariat and the working class are primarily synonymous when referring to the working conditions of capitalism, and precarity is a defining characteristic of workers within this system.

Many social scientists have incited discussion on the precariousness of workers, relating it to social change and economic transition. Notable studies include Polanyi's *The Great Transformation* (1944), Beck's *Risk Society* (1992), Taylor-Gooby's *New Risks and New Welfare* (2004), Rifkin's *End of Work* (1995) and others, such as Webster, Lambert and Bezuidenhout's analysis of recent change in the *Second Great Transformation* (2008). The increase in precarious work has also gained widespread attention in the fields of sociology, economics, politics and social policy (Kalleberg, 2000; Blank et al, 2006; Hacker, 2006; Houseman and Osawa, 2006; Standing, 2009).

In his book *Work after Globalization* (2009), Guy Standing brings the notion of commodification to the centre of his discussion on labour in the global transformation period. Although Standing pays little attention to structural changes in fissured workplaces with outsourcing and platforms and mostly mentions globalisation, the new class structure he suggests provides an excellent insight into the discussion on non-regular and precarious workers (Standing, 2009). He argues that the class restructuring driven by changes following the development of a global market society is causing inequality, and below the core of this class structure is the precariat.

Many scholars have argued that the commodification of labour in a capitalist economy is inevitable. However, when more than a third of the working population are non-regular workers and a quarter of the working people are working in a 'very precarious' condition in Korea (Lee S.Y. et al, 2019a), the discussion of institutions of decommodification and the new forms of work should come to the fore again, following Marx, Polanyi, Esping-Andersen and, more recently, Gorz (1999). The living and working conditions of the precarious workers in Korea match the characteristics of the 'precariat' described by Standing (2009) and 'outworkers' described by Gorz (1999). Precarious workers are excluded from income and employment security. Moreover, in Korea, where welfare institutions are persistently geared towards standard employment, precarious workers suffer from less mobility in their labour markets. This means that once workers enter the category of precarious workers or outsiders, they will likely continue working in the outside labour market.

The dissolution of the standard employment relationship leads to uncertainty, insecurity and instability (Rodgers and Rodgers, 1998) in the employment contract relationship. Precarious work is characterised by variable levels and degrees of objective (legal status) and subjective (feeling) characteristics of uncertainty and insecurity. Literature on precarious work explain it as having characteristics of uncertainty as to the duration of employment, multiple possible employers or a disguised or ambiguous employment relationship, a lack of access to social protection and benefits usually associated with employment, low pay, and substantial legal and practical obstacles to joining a trade union and bargaining collectively. Precarious work is defined as a condition in which employment is unstable, unpredictable and risky (Kalleberg, 2009). It is characterised by uncertainty about the continuity of employment, arbitrary and unstructured training, low bargaining power, and low wages (Kroon and Paauwe, 2013).

Negative aspects are mainly focused on using terms such as non-standard employment relationship, atypical employment relationship, vulnerable work, disposable work and contingent work (Green et al, 1993; Kalleberg, 2000). They mainly define precarious labour in terms of employment type. Recent attempts to define instability as a concept with multidimensional properties rather than a single property of employment form are increasing. These studies define precarious employment as a state lacking various forms of labour security. However, there is no agreement on the items of those dimensions.

One of the earliest multidimensional measures of precarious employment is Rodgers and Rodgers (1989). They measured precarious employment in terms of short-term employment contract duration, lack of control over work/wage/labour processes, lack of social security/legal employment protection, and low income. In Laparra et al (2004), it was measured by dividing it into temporal, social, economic and working condition dimensions. Standing (2014) Guy Standing categorises labour-related security into seven dimensions: income security, employment security, work security, skill security, social security, representation security, and voice security. These dimensions encompass aspects such as adequate wages, job stability, a safe working environment, access to social protection, participation in decision-making processes, and the freedom to express concerns in the workplace.

Vosko (2006) synthesises these studies. She measured instability by reflecting on the situation of the self-employed in Rodgers' dimension. She measures insecurity in terms of the degree of certainty, legal protection, control over the labour process and income adequacy (Vosko, 2006). Baek Seung-ho (2014) also divided precarious labour into three dimensions – employment contract type, income and social protection – by synthesising the existing discussion on insecurity. Whereas existing studies on precarious work measure each dimension independently, Lee S.Y. et al (2017a) measure instability by combining these three dimensions. This approach pays attention to the fact that instability has complex and multidimensional properties. Also, Yoon Y.S. and Chung H.J. (2016) examine the patterns of labour market segmentation in the UK over the period from 1999 to 2010 by using a latent class analysis model. The findings show that the labour market in the UK can be divided into three groups, including insiders, outsiders and a third group identified as the 'future insecure'. The main characteristics that divide the groups are income levels, occupational profiles and social security benefits stemming from employment. The study concludes that labour market divisions may not be generalisable, and further empirical investigations are needed to understand cross-national variations (Yoon Y.S. and Chung H.J., 2016). In that these studies constitute indicators that reflect the multidimensionality and complexity of instability, they can be an advanced discussion compared to studies focusing only on the single dimension of employment form.

Both notions of non-regular work and the precariat are indeed helpful in their own terms. This study does not aim to counter the proposed definitions. Instead, by introducing the concept of melting labour, it seeks to provide a more comprehensive understanding of the increasing ambiguity of the boundaries that contribute to the precarity of workers. The term 'melting labour' is more concrete and closer to explaining the empirical reality of the changing work process that leads to workers' precariousness. The concept of melting labour highlights the fluidity and uncertainty in the working conditions and relationships in today's labour market. It captures the essence of how traditional boundaries between regular and non-regular work, as well as between dependent and independent work, are dissolving, leading to new forms of employment relationships that are not easily classified.

Melting labour

As economies transition from industrial to service-based, the expansion of non-regular work and the externalisation of costs and risks have led to changes in the temporal and spatial arrangements of employment and jobs, as well as the individualisation of risks (Kim Y.S., 2017). In many cases, workers in these non-regular roles are excluded from the protections offered by the Labour Standards Act, the Trade Union Act and social insurance laws, as they are not recognised as employees but rather as independent contractors or self-employed individuals.

The breakdown of the standard employment relationship has resulted in increased uncertainty, insecurity and instability (Rodgers and Rodgers, 1989) in employment contracts. These non-regular forms of work have been referred to as atypical, non-standard, fissured labour or outsourced work (Kalleberg, 2000; Weil, 2015). Some studies have gone further, expanding the concept of instability to include income, social protection and employment contract relationships (Beck S.H., 2014; Lee S.Y. et al, 2017a). Additionally, works like Sargeant (2009) examine precarity by focusing on how workers are subordinate to organisational change, explaining that precarious work can also include standard employment contracts where workers are subjected to organisational changes such as restructuring, downsizing, privatisation or outsourcing (Sargeant, 2009).

However, despite the broader scope of research on precarious labour provided by these studies, they have not adequately captured the precariousness of emerging forms of work. A more comprehensive understanding of these new forms of work is necessary to address the challenges faced by workers in the evolving labour market.

Since the late 2000s, and with the accelerated shift to digital capitalism, new forms of work have emerged that are distinct from those found in industrial and service-based economies. The rapid development of knowledge, information and communication technologies has led to the emergence of economic activities in which labour and goods are traded on online platforms, and services produced and sold using these platforms have gained attention.

As economic activities previously organised in offline workplaces move to online platforms, the most significant changes observed include the rise of various platform companies and platform work. Platform work is conducted through online platforms, such as the internet and social networks, which provide specific services or act as intermediaries between service consumers and providers. These new forms of work are referred to by various names, such as 'online work', 'gig work', 'app-on-demand work' and 'platform work'.

The most significant difference between platform work and conventional labour is that in the former, workers are invited to an online platform where their labour is extracted through calls, tasks and projects. These emerging forms of work are characterised by such fluidity and liquidity that it is challenging to categorise them using dichotomous divisions like regular and non-regular workers. The labour processes in platform work, including contract relationships, work order receiving, skill formation, compensation and control methods, differ significantly from those in traditional work (Kim Y.S., 2020a; Lee S.Y. et al, 2020a).

While previous non-regular employment displayed an unstable but explicit wage-labour contract relationship, platform labour is considered entirely different from the standard or non-standard employment relationships of non-regular workers (Manyika et al, 2016b; Kim J.J. et al, 2018). The ambiguity of the employment relationship has been maximised, with sophisticated control through star ratings from multiple evaluators and algorithms. The lines between rest and work, productive and non-productive time, and workspace and private space have become increasingly blurred.

As platform work gains attention among scholars, discussions on labour and social rights surrounding it have rapidly developed. While the main focus of these discussions has been on the emergence of this new type of work, long-standing issues related to the precarity of non-regular workers, subcontracted work, fissured workplaces and the precariousness of new self-employment remain unresolved. In this book, I introduce the concept of 'melting labour' as the dismantling of various boundaries surrounding traditional forms of work and workplace, such as standard employment before the fissured workplace and pure self-employment. The concept of melting labour encompasses the increase in new forms of work that deviate from standard employment, such as non-regular and atypical work, subcontracted and outsourced work, and changes in pure self-employment like dependent/disguised self-employed individuals, freelancers and platform workers. This conceptualisation aims to capture the common features of changes in work and workplace forms from the industrial to the service and platform economies. Melting labour can contribute to our understanding of precarious work by going beyond non-regular work and focusing on employment.

A common feature of modern society, as described in Ulrich Beck's *Risk Society* (1992) and Zygmunt Bauman's *Liquid Modernity* (2000), is uncertainty. When workers cannot predict or control the future, they experience uncertainty, which is closely related to precarity. Uncertainty differs from the concept of 'risk' as it is unmeasurable and difficult to establish both private and public risk management programmes (Beck, 1992). The concern is that the unpredictability of the future can lead to the depreciation of human capital through skills, and irregular income affects workers' control over their lives. In the era of melting labour, skills accumulate at work and wages fluctuate, making future planning difficult (Bauman, 2000). Melting labour can be a useful concept to capture these diversified forms of work and workplace, as it is related to the macroscopic changes in capitalism characterised by the dismantling of the standard employment relationship of the industrial capitalist period due to fissured workplaces and the increasing ambiguity in defining standard employment.

By developing a conceptualisation that captures the changing features in work and workplace across various contexts, it is possible to move beyond the current concept of precarious work and establish reform principles for fundamental social security. These principles offer comprehensive solutions to the problems faced by each type of work that deviates from traditional forms of work and workplace. Melting labour, with its shared exposure to the vulnerability of institutional protection and precarious working environments, highlights the need for unified strategies to address these challenges.

Through the concept of melting labour, policy makers and stakeholders can develop a more holistic understanding of the evolving nature of work and create more inclusive social security systems that account for the diverse experiences of workers. By focusing on the common features and challenges faced by melting labour, it is possible to design policies that address the uncertainty and precarity experienced by a wide range of workers in various sectors, rather than just focusing on specific types of employment. This approach can lead to more robust, flexible and comprehensive social security systems that better support workers in the rapidly changing world of work.

Theoretical framework

Polanyi (1944) argues that institutions play a crucial role in shaping society. This study investigates how institutions contribute to the prevalence of precarity in South Korea by examining how the country's compressed welfare institutions are inconsistent with the concept of melting labour, resulting in a diverse range of precarious workers. Institutions matter because their organisational structure impacts political culture (Skocpol, 1985), production system formation, labour market structure and workers' precarity. By prioritising social policy, this study aims to offer an explanatory framework for labour market risks and envision a positive future for reframing work and improving the labour market in which workers can participate.

The current Labour Standards Act and Trade Union Act only provide protection to workers with contractual relationships who engage in waged work. However, melting labour is characterised by ambiguity in determining the identities of workers and employers, making it difficult to fit within the current legal framework. In addition, melting labour faces challenges in terms of weak bargaining power, income instability and being excluded from social security protection. The existing social insurance programmes are primarily designed to protect waged workers, making it difficult for workers in melting labour to access necessary protections.

Platform work is characterised by the subdivision of tasks into smaller units, which are distributed among numerous platform workers through a competitive system (Lee S.G., 2018; Lee S.Y., 2019). As a result, platform workers participate in the production process in a fragmented and intermittent manner, performing only microtasks, which increases their dependence on the platform for income activities and various costs (for example, cost of computer or vehicle purchase, fuel, repairs and insurance premiums) (Lee S.Y., 2019; Lee S.Y. et al, 2020a). The lack of control and bargaining power over the labour process also stems from the power asymmetry that occurs when platform companies monopolise information and mediate platform users (Schmidt, 2017). The information imbalance leads to a power imbalance that enables control over the platform labour process (Lee S.Y., 2019; Lee S.Y. et al, 2020a).

Moreover, the atomisation of the labour process and de-spatialised performance of microtasks makes it difficult for platform workers to collectively act and negotiate power to deal with the labour control of platform companies. As a result, platform workers are excluded from the existing labour-related laws and social protection systems, leading to a vicious cycle of income instability and low bargaining power (Lee S.Y., 2019; Lee S.Y. et al, 2020a).

This book focuses on melting labour as companies and capital evolve the mode of capital accumulation along with technological development. The forms of work have changed from the standard employment relationship in Fordism-based industrial economy to fissured workplace in the service economy and melting labour in the digital economy (see Figure 1.5). The solid boundaries that constitute the traditional form of work are dismantling and becoming tangible. I intend to concretely explain how we fail to include, protect and, ultimately, decommodify. In other words, I will explain how labour instability appears in a space where liquefied labour and institutional protection are inconsistent.

The thesis of this book is that the combination of institutions for decommodification is inconsistent with melting labour, and the number of precarious workers in the era of melting labour is expanding. The current Korean labour market overlaps with the problems observed in these newly expanding forms of work such as platform work and long-standing problems, such as non-regular workers. In other words, beyond the departure from the standard 'employment relationship', the methods and forms of work are changing differently from the existing standards. Nevertheless, the problems with these types of work are consistent with those of non-regular workers discussed thus far. Therefore, it is necessary to look at the long-standing problems of non-regular workers and those brought about by the emerging 'form' of work from a comprehensive and integrated perspective (European, 2017; ILO and OECD, 2018).

From the standard employment relationship to fissured workplace and melting labour, the solid boundaries that constitute the traditional form of work are dismantling and becoming tangible. The institutional protection for the decommodification of work is still concentrated on the standard

Figure 1.5: Changes in form of work and workplace by economic stages

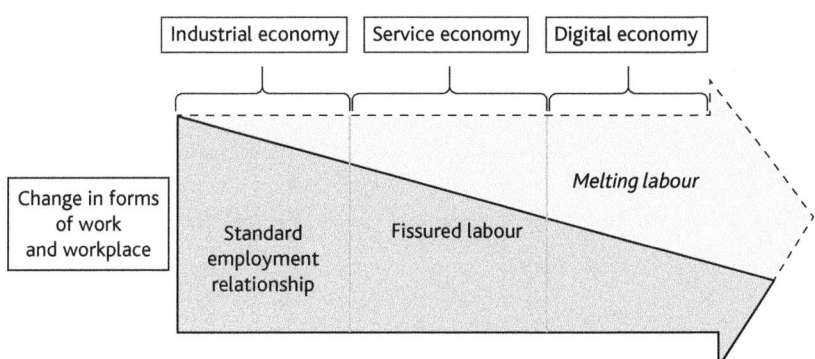

employment relationship in Korea as they were rapidly institutionalised in the 1960s and 1970s. The labour law, social security law, protection of the working environment, union law, minimum wage and working hours regulation, and education and skill system are among the components of such institutional protection. Technological innovation leads to an increase in productivity and social progress, but the feature of melting labour causes inconsistency with the existing system that is designed based on standard employment relationships.

In this book, I aim to provide a comprehensive analysis of the intersections between melting labour and existing institutional protection in South Korea. The goal is to broaden our understanding of precarious work and explore how institutional inconsistencies have resulted in a variety of precarious work. The current labour market in South Korea is experiencing a shift from the traditional form of work, from the standard employment relationship in Fordism-based industrial economy, to fissured workplace in the service economy, and now to melting labour in the digital economy. As a result, the solid boundaries that once constituted the traditional form of work are now dismantling and becoming tangible.

Specifically, I examine how existing institutional protection policies reveal inconsistencies with new forms of work brought about by the digital economy, resulting in various precarious work. To analyse this intersection, I use a two-by-two matrix consisting of low/high levels of melting labour and low/high levels of institutional consistency (see Table 1.3). The matrix consists of four cells, each representing a specific type of labour market segment. The first cell includes wage workers who are excluded from institutional protection, such as non-regular and subcontracted workers. The second cell includes wage workers who are covered by institutional

Table 1.3: Matrix of the degree of melting labour and institutional consistency

	Low to middle level of melting labour	High level of melting labour
Low level of institutional consistency	(1) Wage worker excluded from institutional protections: outsiders of the Korean labour market, non-regular workers, subcontracted workers	(3) New forms of work and excluded from institutional protection: platform workers, freelancers, dependent self-employment
High level of institutional consistency	(2) Wage workers covered by institutional protections: insiders of Korean labour market, full-time regular workers in large companies, public sectors	(4) New forms of works but included in the old institutional protection: cases not found

protection, such as regular workers in large corporations and the public sector, who are considered labour market insiders. The third cell includes melting labour but is excluded from institutional protection, such as platform workers and freelancers. Finally, the fourth cell represents high levels of melting labour and high levels of institutional consistency.

The structure of the book and research methods

In the following chapters, I will present a detailed case study of the Korean labour market to provide a comprehensive account of each of these cells and their implications for precarious work. I will begin by examining the institutional development of Korean social protection and labour market policies and then move on to analysing the empirical trend in the Korean labour market. Additionally, I will provide legal and statistical definitions of various new forms of work in Korea, including platform work, and discuss the latest legislation and empirical data on Korean platform workers. By examining these issues through the lens of the matrix, I aim to provide a comprehensive understanding of the intersections between institutional protection and melting labour in the Korean context.

Chapter 3, titled 'When "insiders" are kicked out: layoff of the manufacturing regular workers', delves into the case of SsangYong Motor, one of the largest automobile manufacturers in Korea, and examines the experiences of its regular workers after being laid off. Specifically, this chapter focuses on the process in which once labour market insiders, who are covered by institutional protection, such as regular workers in large corporations and the public sector, fall into the outsider and precarious work categories. To investigate this issue, a questionnaire survey was conducted with 187 dismissed workers of the 2009 SsangYong layoff case. The chapter analyses in detail the cases of 116 respondents who had employment experience over six years in the labour market after the layoff. The study reveals how standard manufacturing workers, who were once considered insiders in the dual labour market, fall into the outsider category due to weak institutional protection. Through this case study, the chapter highlights the issue of old precarity, where workers with stable employment status can easily slide into precarious work once they lose institutional protection.

Chapter 4, 'Same boat, different destiny: subcontracted workers in the Korean shipbuilding industry', focuses on the employment structure of subcontracting in the shipbuilding industry, which has spread in conglomerate-led manufacturing industries. The chapter reveals the disparity between the subcontracting labour market and the social safety net by analysing subcontracted workers' experience of the social safety net based on the results of in-depth interviews with 12 workers consisting of nine shipbuilders' subcontracted workers, two experts familiar with the subcontracting employment structure in the shipbuilding industry, and one tax accountant in charge of taxation of subcontractors in the shipbuilding industry in Ulsan.

The chapter focuses on the changes in the predominant employment structure of contractor–subcontractor contractual arrangements in the shipbuilding industry dominated by conglomerate manufacturing companies, which are considered the so-called Korean insider labour market. Furthermore, this chapter examines subcontracted workers' experience of Korea's social safety net, including the employment structure, wage structure, working patterns of subcontracted workers and the association between subcontracted workers' labour market and social security experiences. Specifically, the case study aims to shed light on the employment status of subcontracted workers who are excluded from institutional protection, such as non-regular and subcontracted workers.

Chapter 5, 'Outsourced young and old female workers: female workers in call centres and cleaning services', notes that the increase in female labour following entry into the service economy leads to the spread of precarious jobs through outsourcing, particularly affecting young and old female workers. This chapter sheds light on the gender gap in the Korean labour market with empirical data and interviews thirteen workers and union leaders. In addition to cleaning work, the chapter focuses on ten young female call centre workers and examines the issue of institutional protection and instability surrounding older and younger female subcontracted labour in call centres. The chapter highlights how outsourcing has become easier due to technological development. Overall, this chapter provides insights into how female workers are concentrated in precarious forms of work and experience unique challenges and issues related to institutional protection and job instability.

Chapter 6 of the book, titled 'Are freelancers really free? Korean freelance labour market and the precarity of young freelancers', focuses on the third cell, which includes melting labour but is excluded from institutional protection, such as platform workers and freelancers. The chapter presents a case study that explores the experiences of Korean freelancers, with a particular focus on young workers. First, the chapter outlines the expansion of freelancers in Korea and presents existing empirical data on the definition of freelancers. The chapter then moves on to describe the interviews conducted with nine entrepreneurial and non-entrepreneurial freelancers. These interviews help explain the precarious nature of young freelancers' working conditions and examine how they experience Korea's social protection system. Finally, the chapter positions the case of Korean young freelancers in cell 3 of the theoretical framework, which focuses on melting labour that is excluded from institutional protection. This chapter sheds light on the challenges faced by freelancers in Korea, and highlights the need for better social protection for this group of young workers.

Chapter 7, 'The digital precariat: various Korean platform workers and new work logic', examines the labour status of platform workers who are situated in cell 3 of the theoretical framework, which is characterised by a high level of melting labour but a low level of institutional protection consistency. The chapter presents official data and legal definitions of platform work in Korea and explains how Korea's platform labour market has been expanding into diverse sectors with the advancement of technology and high internet usage rates. The main aim of this chapter is to understand the specific operation of the Korean platform labour market and the inconsistency of the social security system. To achieve this, the chapter categorises platform companies and platform workers and conducts interviews with platform workers in delivery platforms, housekeeping service platforms, and high skilled freelance platforms, examining their working conditions and experiences with the social security system. This chapter sheds light on the precariousness and lack of institutional protection experienced by platform workers in Korea.

This book employs various qualitative research methods to provide a detailed account of each cell in the theoretical framework and its implications for precarious work. The studies use case study and phenomenological research methods, as well as in-depth interviews, to understand how precarious workers are included or excluded from the social protection and the inconsistencies of the current social security system. The cases were selected to explore the essence of subjective experience, and the in-depth interview method was deemed appropriate for understanding past events and memories that are difficult to observe in the present.

A case study, one of the qualitative research methods, is a methodology that studies problems explored through one or more cases when boundaries within a system exist. This methodology aids in an in-depth understanding of cases by enabling exploration of bounded system cases and in-depth data collection (Seo J.H. and Lee J.S., 2015; Lee S.Y. and Kim K.T., 2017; Lee S.Y. et al, 2017a). The studies in this book use case study research methods to understand how precarious workers are included or excluded from the public social safety net and are inconsistent with the current social security system. The phenomenological research method, which is one of the qualitative research methods used in research along with case studies, is known as a methodology that can grasp the essence of subjective experience because it describes reality as it is through phenomenological reduction (Nam K.M. and Bang H.S., 2012). All studies were conducted using the in-depth interview method because the in-depth interview is effective in understanding past events and memories that are difficult to observe at present (Kim Y.C. and Kim J.H., 2006). The experience of precarious workers with social protection was explored by asking the interviewees to recount their experiences during their period of precarious employment. This method was considered suitable for these studies, due to the importance of both current and past experiences. A questionnaire survey was also used in Chapter 3 to identify the characteristics of a population through sampling and explain the relationship between variables related to social situations or phenomena. The survey is a widely used data collection method in the social science field and ensures objectivity and accuracy through standardised questions (Kim T.H. and Kim K.H., 2022). The questionnaire items used in the study were composed through a review of existing research and interviews with laid-off workers of SsangYong Motor, and the final questionnaire items were completed through pilot tests.

The study participants were selected based on the recommendation of related experts, using a snowball sampling method. The snowball sampling method is useful for finding members of a specific population and can discover essential characteristics of the research subject. The number of participants was determined after considering subject selection criteria such as gender, age and years of service. In-depth interviews were conducted individually at the location desired by each participant, such as cafes, restaurants and conference rooms in areas frequented. The interviews were about an hour to an hour and a half, and all were recorded with the participants' permission and transcribed into transcripts after data collection was completed. Before the study, the research team explained the purpose and specific methods of participation to ensure ethical conduct, and written consent was obtained. A small reward was provided to motivate participants and compensate for their participation time.

After data collection, researchers repeated reading the transcriptions for data analysis to understand how participants in the study experience the social safety net regarding their socioeconomic status and type of work in the workplace. The aim was to understand in-depth the incongruence between the unstable labour market and the Korean social security system. Follow-up contact with interviewees was made to confirm unclear content, and the validity of the study was secured by checking the context from the study subjects. Expert interviews were also conducted separately according to the research needs, and the number of target study participants was established based on previous studies and expert advice.

Chapter 8 concludes the book by summarising the cases presented in previous chapters and referring back to the theoretical framework introduced in this chapter. The chapter highlights the academic contribution of the book and suggests policy directions for institutional protection for melting labour and restoring workers' sovereignty. It also explains policy alternatives and implications for advanced welfare states and emerging economies where the melting labour and expansion of precarious work are similarly presented. The chapter emphasises the increasing pressure on the Korean welfare state with the rise of melting labour and societal changes, such as traditional family structures being challenged and technology development. I explain the concept of policy drift and how policy makers' failure to adapt existing institutions to new labour market contexts can create institutional inconsistency, resulting in a weakened ability to achieve the goals embodied in existing social protection frameworks. Overall, the chapter emphasises the need for policy adaptations to address the changing nature of work and institutional protection. In addition, this chapter also highlights that one avenue for future research is the varieties of precarity and their contribution to the discussion of class. This chapter concludes by proposing that examining the mobility patterns of precarious workers of melting labour is a new research agenda for class analysis. This can reveal a new class structure in the post-industrial and digital economy era, which may vary depending on the presence or absence of consistent institutions. Further analysis of precarious workers' mobility can explain differences in power between classes according to the role of institutions.

2

Social protection policies and the South Korean labour market in comparative perspective

Flexibility measures and precarious workers in Korea

In this chapter, I will examine the Korean social protection and labour market policies, as well as the empirical trend in the Korean labour market. The chapter will also provide legal and statistical definitions of various new forms of work in Korea, including platform work. Furthermore, I will explore the concept of melting labour by examining the characteristics of non-standard forms of work (NSFW) and their deviation from the traditional standard employment relationship. We will examine how the eligibility criteria for social security are inconsistent with new forms of work, conceptualised as melting labour, and the level of social protection benefits is low due to low wages and contributions. Additionally, employers' non-compliance with the scheme and their ambiguous employment relationships make it difficult to determine who the employer is.

The Korean labour market underwent significant changes after the economic crisis in 1997. Measures to increase labour market flexibility led to a rise in non-standard employment and dualisation. The International Monetary Fund required restructuring of corporations, improving governance structures, privatising public enterprises and opening capital markets, leading to policies that lowered employment protection and increased the number of layoffs and non-regular workers (Peng I., 2012; Lee S.Y. et al, 2016). With this as the starting point, 'dismissal for managerial reasons' became possible through the amendment of the Labour Standards Act in 1996, and regulations and a flexible working hours system for part-time workers were added. The Act on the Protection of Temporary Agency Workers was introduced in 1998 to justify massive layoffs and increases in irregular employment (Lee S.Y. et al, 2019b). Moreover, many labour market flexibility policies were introduced with the passing of the Act on the Protection, etc. of Dispatched Workers in 1998, along with other measures. The purpose of introducing the policy was to enable the flexible operation of employment relations, provide a flexible working hours system and ensure the proper operation of workers' dispatch business, among other measures.

However, the introduction of the policies lowered the level of employment protection, allowing for an increased number of layoffs and creating more significant numbers of non-regular workers. Notably, since then, the number of non-standard workers rapidly increased as many companies have started replacing regular with non-regular workers with short-term/fixed-term contracts (see Figure 1.3 for international comparison). According to Statistics Korea (KOSIS) in 2001, the first official record of the number of non-standard workers was 26.8 per cent (3.64 million) of the total number of wage and salary earners, jumping in 2016 to 32.8 per cent and 38.4 per cent in 2021.[1] Labour unions argue that the number is underestimated; according to their estimates the non-standard workers amounted to 55.7 per cent (7.37 million) in 2001 and 44.5 per cent in 2016 (Kim Y.S., 2016). According to the Korea Labour and Society Institute, the rate has been decreasing after peaking at its highest level after the economic crisis. However, the proportion of non-standard employment is still very high, 43 per cent in 2021 (see Figure 2.1).

In response to the increasing number of non-standard workers, measures similar to those implemented by other post-industrial countries have been adopted, designed to handle the growing employment instability and related social problems. For example, throughout the 2000s, the government gradually extended the coverage of social insurance schemes, including employment insurance, national pension, health insurance and industrial accident insurance, to non-standard workers. However, despite these efforts, the poor working conditions attached to non-standard work have improved very little. The 90/10 income inequality ratio increased from 3.86 in 1990 to over 4.5 in the early 2000s, showing income gaps between waged workers increased.

Figure 2.1: Proportion of non-standard employment

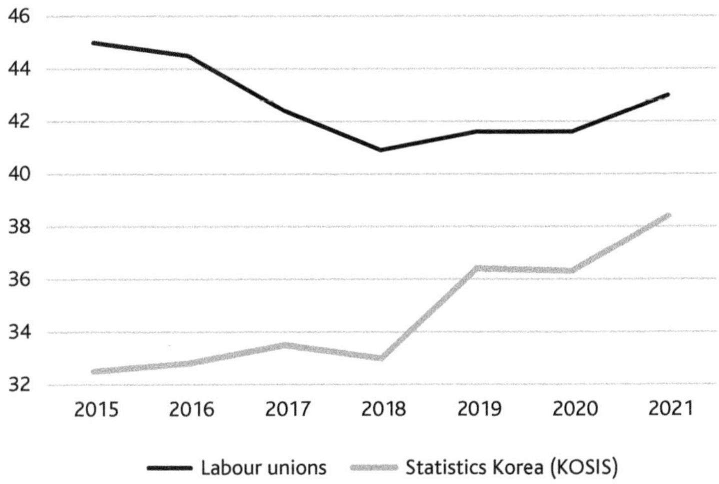

Source: Korea Labour and Society Institute (2021); Statistics Korea (2021)

In March 2008, after President Lee Myung-bak took office, a regulatory reform agenda was presented in the form of the 'Action Plan for National Issues in the Labour Sector', which included a plan to protect non-regular workers by giving them a particular form of employment insurance and providing corporate support for the improvement of non-regular workers' employment. Later in the successive Park Geun-Hye government (conservative), the September 2015 agreement of the Economic and Social Development Commission (the Korean Tripartite Commission) argues for establishing a robust employment order, strengthening the public sector's leadership role, enhancing the effectiveness of the anti-discriminatory system, strengthening the protection of non-regular workers, rationalising regulations, and strengthening the employment stability of fixed-term and dispatched workers and the regulations governing them. However, in the detailed discussion of the agreement process, opinions expressed that a limitation on the number of contract renewals for fixed-term workers would only increase short-term, fixed-term workers. Also, measures were included to expand the permissible dispatch range for dispatched employment. In other words, extending the employment period of fixed-term workers and the range of dispatched work was discussed; this was a policy direction that tolerated an increase in non-regular workers and expanded the labour market's flexibility. The expansion of conditions unfavourable to the earnings and working conditions of workers observed in these major guidelines has been interpreted as a policy direction that enhances flexibility and reduces the stability of the labour market.

In summary, in response to the legislation intended to strengthen non-regular workers' rights, employers utilised the labour practice of creating separate job groups or outsourcing work. In particular, many cases were more unfavourable towards women in this process, such as outsourcing or converting the female work to open-ended contracts and taking different approaches towards women compared to men (Lee J.H., 2008; Park O.J. and Sohn S.Y., 2011). There were limitations in wages and promotion possibilities and poor working conditions for female workers who were switched to open-ended contracts in office or sales and service-related jobs, considered women-concentrated occupations (Lee J.H., 2008; Park O.J. and Sohn S.Y., 2011). During the application process of the fixed-term employment act, there were cases in which the jobs women were concentrated were converted to open-ended contract jobs with poor conditions.

As of 2021, the Organisation for Economic Co-operation and Development (OECD)'s employment rate was 67.7 per cent, the unemployment rate was 6.2 per cent, Korea's employment rate was 66.5 per cent, and the unemployment rate was 3.7 per cent. The increase in women's employment has driven the rise in the Korean employment rate since 2010, and the rise in the unemployment rate, appears to have been caused by the increase in men's unemployment. The increase in female labour market participation is also related to the rapid rise in employment in the service sector. While the employment does not present much difference from the OECD average, it is worth highlighting the low unemployment rate, which is almost half of the OECD average unemployment rate (see Figure 2.2).

The unemployment rate is low but Korea presents a high rate of non-regular workers and also self-employment rate compared to other OECD countries. Table 1.2 in Chapter 1 also shows the trends in the percentage of non-regular workers (temporary, part-time and non-typical workers) to total waged workers in Korea. The proportion of non-regular workers stood at 36.3 per cent in 2020, similar to the previous year (36.4 per cent), but increased by 2.5 per cent from 33.8 per cent in 2008. As of 2020, the proportion of non-regular workers among women (45 per cent) was higher than that of men (29.4 per cent), and this gender gap has continued since 2008. By age group, the proportion of non-regular workers was high, in the order of 15–19 years old (84.1 per cent), 60 years or older (71.0 per cent) and 20–29 years old (37.7 per cent), and the proportion of non-regular workers increased around these groups between 2008 and 2019. Meanwhile, in 2020, the proportion of non-regular workers in most age groups decreased slightly compared to 2019. By age group and gender, young and elderly people, and women, are the main population groups of waged workers in NSFW in Korea.

According to the Survey of the Economically Active Population in 2016, the average wage (per month) of the non-standard workers was 55.4 per

Figure 2.2: Employment trends in (selected) OECD countries and Korea

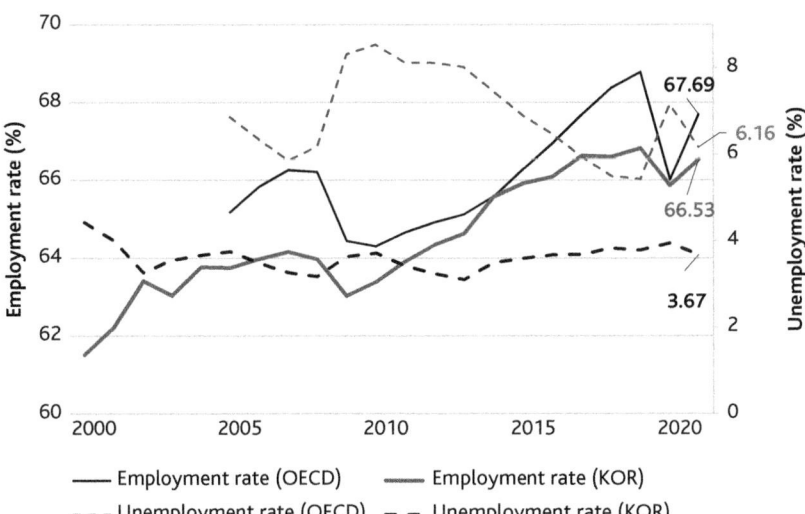

cent of that for standard workers (Kim Y.S., 2016: 16). Furthermore, the gap in social insurance coverage between the standard and the non-standard workers is equally huge: national pension coverage for the standard workers amounts to 82.0 per cent while for the non-standard workers it is only 36.9 per cent; in the case of unemployment insurance, coverage for the non-standard workers is only about half of that for standard workers (42.5 per cent and 82.4 per cent, respectively [Statistics Korea, 2016]). Also, despite the declining trend of low-wage workers in OECD countries, the proportion of low-wage workers in Korea is comparatively high. The ratio of low-wage workers in Korea was 16 per cent as of 2021, the OECD average was 14.5 per cent and 11 per cent in Japan.

The percentage of low-wage workers showed a wide gap between gender. In 2007, 18 per cent of male wage earners were low-wage workers, while 41 per cent of female wage earners were low-wage workers (see Table 2.1). This gap has been reduced to 10.2 per cent of male wage earners being low-wage workers, while 24.3 per cent of female wage earners are low-wage workers in 2021. While there has been in a reduction in the gender gap among low-waged workers, females double in the rate. Considering the higher proportion of non-regular workers among women compared to men mentioned earlier, it can be confirmed that gender differences also occur in low-wage work.

Another characteristic is the comparatively higher rates of self-employment compared to other OECD countries. The proportion of self-employed workers, including employers, own-account workers and unpaid family workers, in Korea has decreased steadily since 2009 (30.0 per cent), which is higher than that of most OECD countries. Specifically, by gender, male (26.5 per cent), and by status, own-account workers (15.5 per cent) represented a high proportion in each category(see Table 2.2). Further, own-account workers, who have been discussed to include nonstandard forms of work (NSFW) among self-employed workers, had declined until 2019, but have increased since the COVID-19 pandemic (Statistics Korea, 2020).

Expansion of various forms of work

Legal and statistical classification of varieties of work forms in Korea

In Korea's labour market, the implementation of flexibility policies resulted in various forms of employment and precarious work. These non-standard forms of waged workers are classified as workers who have an employee status but are often excluded from social protection. According to Statistics Korea (2020), wage and salary workers are classified into regular, temporary and daily workers based on the employment contract period. Temporary employees and daily workers with less than one year of employment are generally categorised as non-regular workers (see Table 2.3).

Table 2.1: Percentage of low-wage workers in total employees, by gender

	2007	2008	2009	2010	2011	2012	2013	2014	2015	2016	2017	2018	2019	2020	2021
Total	26	25.5	25	24.7	23.8	23.9	24.7	23.7	23.5	23.5	22.3	19	17	16	16
Male	18.1	17.1	16.5	16.1	16	16.5	16.6	15.4	15.2	15.3	14.3	12.1	11.1	10.6	10.2
Female	41	41.1	41	40.4	38.2	37.3	38.9	37.8	37.6	37.2	35.3	30	26.1	24.7	24.3

Source: OECD, https://stats.oecd.org, Decile ratios of gross earnings 22 August 2022

Table 2.2: Percentage of self-employed workers in total employment (%), by gender and status (KRW 10,000)

		2009	2010	2011	2012	2013	2014	2015	2016	2017	2018	2019	2020
Total[a]		30	28.8	28.3	28.2	27.4	26.8	25.9	25.5	25.4	25.1	24.6	24.4
Gender	Male	30.8	30	29.5	29.8	28.9	28.4	27.5	27.5	27.3	27	26.6	26.5
	Female	28.8	27.1	26.5	26	25.3	24.6	23.6	22.8	22.8	22.6	22.1	21.7
Status of workers[b]	Employer	6.5	6.3	6.2	6.3	6.1	6.1	6.1	6	6	6.2	5.7	5.1
	Own-account worker	17.8	17.2	16.8	16.8	16.5	16	15.3	15.3	15.2	14.9	15	15.5
	Unpaid family worker	5.7	5.3	5.2	5.1	4.9	4.7	4.4	4.3	4.2	4.1	4	3.9
Annual household income[c]	Average	–	–	–	4,985	5,294	5,506	5,544	5,589	6,232	6,361	6,375	6,519
	Median	–	–	–	3,800	4,000	4,380	4,456	4,560	4,911	4,900	5,000	5,137

Note: [a] Ratio of self-employed workers = (number of self-employed workers ÷ total number of employed workers) × 100. [b] The ratio of self-employed workers by status of workers is the ratio of self-employed workers in the relevant status among all employed. [c] In 10,000 KRW.

Source: Statistics Korea (2020)

Table 2.3: Statistical definition of employees by employment types

Employment type		Statistical definition
Regular worker		Workers who do not fall into the non-regular workers category
Non-regular workers		Employees whose types of work are temporary workers, part-time workers or atypical workers
Non-permanent workers	Fixed-term workers[a]	Workers who provide work under a fixed period of work contract (including verbal or implied promises or contracts), regardless of the length and length of the contract period, whether the contract is renewed repeatedly, or name (contract worker, part-time worker, temporary worker, seasonal worker, contract employee, and so on)
	Non-fixed term workers	Workers who do not have a set duration of the labour contract but can continue to work due to repeated renewal of the contract, and workers who cannot expect to continue working due to involuntary reasons
	Part-time workers[b]	Workers whose prescribed working hours set to work at the workplace (work) are even one hour shorter than the prescribed working hours of workers who perform the same type of work at the same workplace. This applies to cases where it is decided to work less than 36 hours per week
Non-typical workers	Temporary agency workers[c]	A person who is employed by the dispatching business owner but is dispatched to the employer's business to work. Employment relations based on wages and status are managed by the dispatching business owner, but commands and orders are received from the employer
	Contract workers	A person who is hired by a service company and works for another business owner's business. All of the wages, employment relations in terms of status, and command and orders for work are under the command and supervision of the service company
	Workers in special employment types[d]	Workers who perform work in a non-independent form without having an independent office, store, or workplace, by finding or welcoming customers on their own, providing goods and services, and earning income (commissions, allowances, and so on), and who decide their own labour provision time, and so on
	Domestic workers	A person who decides the method of provision of work and working hours, and so on; a worker who works from home is a worker spatially separated from the employer and receives a fixed salary depending on the performance of the work, and a home-based worker is a person who provides hand-made services such as processing goods as a side business, regardless of employment, and receives compensation
	Daily employees	A person who works without continuity or regularity, or who temporarily works for a short period of time when a job is created by a call from a company, association or employment agency regardless of employment or work type

Note: [a] The legal definition of fixed-term worker is 'an employee who has signed an employment contract whose period is fixed (subparagraph 5 of Article 2 of the Act on the Protection, etc. of Fixed-term and Part-time Employees)'. [b] The legal definition of a part-time worker is 'an employee

Table 2.3: Statistical definition of employees by employment types (continued)

whose contractual work hours per week are shorter than those of a full-time employee engaged in the same kind of work at the workplace concerned (Article 2 (1) 9 of the Labour Standards Act)'. [c] The legal definition of temporary agency worker is 'a person employed by a temporary work agency (a person engaged in temporary work agency business) to be assigned to work for a user company (a person for whom a temporary agency worker works under a contract on temporary placement of workers) (subparagraphs 3, 4 and 5 of Article 2 of the Act on the Protection, etc. of Temporary Agency Workers)'. [d] The official legal term is 'Special Case concerning Persons in Special Types of Employment': the legal definition of workers in workers in special employment types is 'persons who engage in jobs prescribed by Presidential Decree, among the persons who are not subject to the Labour Standards Act, etc., even though they offer labour service similar to that of employees regardless of the type of contract, and therefore need protection from occupational accidents, and who also meet all the following requirements (hereafter in this Article referred to as 'persons in special types of employment'); 1) They mainly provide one line of business with labour service necessary for the operation thereof on a routine basis, and receive payment for such service and live on such pay; 2. They do not use other persons to provide such labour service. (Article 125 (1) of the Industrial Accident Compensation Insurance Act)'.

Source: Statistics Korea (2020)

In Korea, waged workers are classified as regular and non-regular workers, with non-regular workers defined as 'non-permanent workers, part-time workers, or non-typical workers' (Statistics Korea, 2020). Non-permanent workers can be further categorised into fixed-term workers who can continue to work through repetitive contract renewals, and those who cannot expect to continue working due to factors beyond their control. Part-time workers are defined as those whose prescribed working hours are one hour shorter than those of full-time workers performing the same job at the same workplace, and whose working hours are less than 36 hours per week. Additionally, among part-time workers, there are 'very short-hour part-time workers' whose average contractual working hours per week over a period of four weeks are less than 15 hours (Article 18(3) of the Labour Standards Act). These workers are excluded from legal entitlements such as paid holidays and annual paid leave, but their status is not identified in statistics due to classification issues (Cho D.M. et al, 2015).

Non-typical workers in Korea are another category of non-regular workers, which includes workers in particular employment types, domestic workers, temporary agency workers, contract workers and daily workers. They are a significant group that faces exclusion from the Korean social security system due to their low wages, employment instability and irregular income, making it challenging to make regular contributions to social insurance. According to research conducted by Lee et al, these workers are excluded from social protection due to their non-standard employment arrangements (Lee S.Y. et al, 2019a).

Workers in particular employment types are identified based on the concept of economic dependence, which refers to dependent self-employed workers in Korea (Cheong H.J., 2019; Sung J.M., 2020). They are characterised by the fact that they are dependent on a specific employer or a limited number of employers for their income, which makes it difficult for them to exercise control over their working conditions and negotiate better terms of employment.

Studies of NSFW until the mid-2000s mainly focused on waged workers and on identifying the types of waged employment contracts (Wayne and Green, 1993; Lee B.H. and Yoon J.H., 2001; Kalleberg, 2009; Kim Y.S., 2014; Seo J.H., 2015). However, with the increase in platform work since the mid-2000s, dependent self-employment has emerged as the main subject of research interest (Eurofound, 2018).

Workers in dependent self-employment and disguised employment relationships are legally regarded as self-employed because they sign a contract rather than a wage labour contract. Specifically, dependent self-employment refers to a worker who autonomously and independently provides labour or services to others through a civil contract. However, it means that a worker is dependent on the company that paid for their labour or service (ILO, 2003). Dependent self-employment, like traditional self-employment, entails business risks on its own and provides work independently through civil contracts. However, unlike self-employment, it is not autonomous, and actual income tends to be subordinate to the order of contracts concluded with contractors. This economic dependency is because the income of the dependent self-employed mainly comes from only one contracting party providing work. Further, subsidiary self-employment is dependent because it is difficult to choose working hours, location and content freely (Böheim and Mühlberger, 2009; Mühlberger and Pasqua, 2009). In most countries, they are classified as self-employed, not employees, which leaves them in a blind spot of labour law and social protection.

Here, the disguised employment relationship is a concept that emphasises that a dependent self-employment is a subordinate group misclassified as independent and autonomous self-employment. Recently, disguised employment relationships have attracted attention because of the spread of platform work in international organisations. Further, in a disguised employment relationship, employers tend to avoid the responsibilities of social protection and employment protection by transferring labour costs to third parties or workers through civil, commercial and cooperative contracts instead of labour contracts (Weil, 2014; ILO, 2016). In the traditional bilateral employment relationship, the employer is conceived as a singular person who coincides with the enterprise. However, transformations in enterprises' business organisations have also impacted the concept of the employer. This is evident in employment relationships involving multiple parties, where it is more difficult to identify the actual employer or where responsibilities are distributed among a group of employers.

Platform work is also another new form of work which occurs in various areas such as personalised services based on digital technology, accommodation, transportation and delivery, housekeeping and personal assistance, design and marketing projects, and law and accounting. The main characteristics of platform work include an online platform, a third-party system (platform-worker-user), a contract method, work divided into tasks, and on-demand services (Eurofound, 2018). As such, the nature of platform work varies from one case to another. Platform work is temporary work that can be equated to casual work or zero-hour contracts. It may also be considered a triangular or multiple-party employment relationship. The relationship between the worker and the intermediary, the platform, is governed by a contract, which is difficult to determine. This can be seen as an extension of NSFW, which began to expand in the second half of the 20th century (Friedman, 2016). Platform workers are found to work mainly as a form of freelancer(s) or independent business at the boundary between waged and self-employed workers. This type of labour is theoretically discussed as having no human organisational dependency or economic dependency. However, it has been revealed otherwise for actual platform worker(s) (Friedman, 2016; Katz and Krueger, 2016; Eurofound, 2018; Muntaner, 2018). Because of the ambiguity of employment patterns, platform workers classified as independent contractors while working are excluded from labour laws and social security systems (Harris and Krueger, 2015; Garben, 2017; Lenaerts et al, 2017). Platform is hired and dismissed within a short period. Independent business workers prepare equipment and tools by themselves, invest in skills at the individual level, take risks and responsibilities in work, and are excluded from social security protection (Schmidt, 2017; Kim C.S., 2019). Platform workers have a heterogeneous characteristic of being distributed in online and offline networks. This makes it difficult to coordinate them, and there is no institutional device to protect them from low pay, long hours and dangerous labour.

Meanwhile, estimation of the size of the dependent self-employed workers has been based on self-employed workers, freelancers and workers in special employment types (Jeong H.J. and Jang H.E., 2018; Kim J.J. et al, 2021b). Freelancers were defined as own-account workers and workers in special employment types combined. Meanwhile, Jeong H.J. and Jang H.E. (2018) estimated the number of "special employment" workers by considering two categories: 1) employees engaged in self-employed work with high economic dependency, and 2) self-employed workers excluding those who have a high level of autonomy in their labour process. Their study revealed that the number of "special employment" workers was estimated to be 1.66 million, indicating an underestimation of 506,000 compared to the figures reported by official government statistics.

Workers in special employment types can be regarded as Korea's representative dependent self-employed workers. Because of its low validity, this has been discussed as a concept that has limitations of underestimation (Jeong H.J. and Jang H.E., 2018; Jung H.J., 2019; Sung J.M., 2020). Further, legal definitions have a narrower scope than statistical definitions, while limiting economic dependence and occupation (Sung J.M., 2020). As of 2021, there are a total of 14 types of workers in 'special employment types' covered by industrial accident insurance (Article 125(1) of the Industrial Accident Compensation Insurance Act,[2] Article 122(1)2 of the Enforcement Decree of the Industrial Accident Compensation). Meanwhile, international economic dependence is discussed as the most important feature of dependent self-employed workers. In addition, some workers fall into special employment types among own-account workers who are not self-employed, working on their own. Compared with workers in special employment types, they have weaker economic dependence and a stronger self-employed character but are not fully self-employed workers. For example, translators and platform workers(s) can be included in this group.

On the other hand, freelancers are representative types of worker between employees and self-employed workers. Since there is no official statistical definition in Korea, it has been defined by various concepts such as independent workers, one-person creative companies, workers in 'special employment types', and own-account workers in previous discussions (Lee S.R. et al, 2013).

Platform workers

In general, platform labour is defined as a job in which unspecified organisations or individuals provide services and earn income through online platforms (OECD, 2018b; ILO, 2019). In Korea, platform worker(s) are defined in various ways, and accordingly, the size is estimated differently from 0.9 per cent to 2.0 per cent of the total employed (Kim J.Y. et al, 2018; Jang J.Y. et al, 2020; Nam J.W., 2020).

To date, there have been few accurate surveys on the scale of platform labour. A recent report by the McKinsey Global Institute (Manyika et al, 2016b) confirmed that platform labour is spreading widely through a current status survey of independent workers. This report defined the characteristics of independent workers as 'high degree of autonomy, compensation based on work or sales volume, and short-term contractual relationship with consumers' and investigated independent workers in the UK and other countries. As a result of the survey, 26 per cent in the US, 30 per cent in France, 25 per cent in Germany and 28 per cent in Sweden were using online platforms. According to the Freelance Union of the United States, 34 per cent of the total workforce in 2014 reported that they were independent contractors and self-employed such as gig workers, daily workers, temporary workers and contractors for on/offline labour companies including Uber drivers. It is predicted that 40 per cent of the total annual labour force will be filled by independent contractors and freelancers.

In Korea, Kim J.Y. et al (2018) estimate the size of platform labour as 2 per cent of the employed (Kim J.Y. et al, 2018), and Jang J.Y. (2019) 2.7 per cent. The scale of platform labour does not appear to be a large proportion of the current employed, but it is expected to increase in size due to the increase in demand for home delivery and food delivery due to the COVID-19 pandemic (Jang J.Y., 2019). Lee S.Y. et al (2020a) focused on the features of inviting workers to a digital platform and extracting labour by call, case and project as the greatest difference between platform labour and existing labour. Further, the types of platform labour were classified into web-based cloud work and region-based gig work according to Schmidt's (2017) classification criteria (Lee S.Y. et al, 2020a). To reflect the concrete work method of platform work, it was categorised by considering the workplace where platform work is performed, the type of service provision (subject), and the method of using the platform. The classification revealed that platform companies that have expanded to various fields commonly mediate service providers and service purchasers and generate profits through fees. Emergence and expansion are closely related to information and communications technology development.

Further, in the case of Korea, unlike Schmidt's (2017) classification, there have been cases with both online-based and regional-based characteristics. In addition, it was shown that there are cases where the merchants that use the platform and the platform workers that provide services do not use a single app (platform). One example is working as a freelancer through multiple platforms (Schmidt, 2017).

Due to these various platform companies and types of labour, employment relationships and worker dependencies may vary among platform workers. For example, there is a difference between online-based crowd work and local-based gig work in determining whether workers are dependent. In the case of using multiple platforms, and when a single platform is used, depending on the case where the platform is only performing the role of intermediary and the case where it performs personnel management and even work order functions, the employment relationship of workers, the exclusivity of work and the degree of dependence may differ. However, various types of platform workers have weakened employment relations in common. They perform tasks, projects and split tasks rather than work based on traditional working hours and provide labour through ambiguous contractual relationships.

Nam J.W. (2021) argues that in the sense that among the various definitions of platform labour, the attribute of 'labour mediated through a digital platform' appears in common in the definitions, the method whereby work is performed is more important than the kind of work performed by platform workers (Nam J.W., 2021). That is, platform labour is a concept that encompasses various types of labour that are completely different, with only 'task' and 'intermediary through digital platform' in common (Nam J.W., 2021). Accordingly, it was suggested that Korea's platform workers could be categorised through the definition and conditions of platform labour proposed by the Korean Jobs Committee (2020), an advisory body directly under the president. First, the Korean Jobs Committee (2020) refers to the platform as 'a digital network that algorithmically coordinates transactions', the digital platform as 'a structured digital space where goods and services (labour) are exchanged' and platform labour as 'a service that is traded on a digital platform'. There are four conditions for platform labour that meet this definition:

1. labour for producing services (services) or virtual goods traded through a digital platform;
2. seeking temporary jobs, projects, and tasks through a digital platform;
3. the digital platform mediates payment; and
4. the work/task will be open to the majority, not to specific people (Korean Jobs Committee, 2020).

The number of platform workers in Korea according to the central government is 0.92 per cent of the total employed as of 2020, or about 220,000 people (Korean Jobs Committee, 2020). In the survey, 'platform worker(s) in a narrow sense' was defined as 'a person who provides labour through a platform that affects the assignment of work, etc.'. For platform economy workers (customers or among those who are looking for work), the size was estimated as a case of not a simple job application user or e-commerce worker.[3] On the other hand, a 'platform worker in a broad sense' is 'a person who provides labour through a platform', which was estimated by combining a simple job search app user and a platform worker(s) in consultation. The number of workers in this case is approximately 1.79 million, or 7.46 per cent of the total working population. An actual condition survey was conducted, focusing on consultation of platform workers as a policy target. Specifically, the survey defined the digital platform as a 'structured digital space in which goods and services (labour) are exchanged', and platform labour as a 'service traded on a digital platform' (Jeong H.J. and Jang H.E., 2018). Here, using a simple job search site, the case where the platform does not have a coordinating role in the connection process and simply acts as a bulletin board was excluded. In Korea, 86 per cent of platform workers in a broad sense answered that they use a specialised app for job hunting. However, Jang (2020b) argued that if all labour providers' workers using such online platform job matching are classified as platform workers, the adequacy of the concept of 'platform labour' is limited. On the other hand, when using a simple job search site, there was also a case where platform workers were defined by including unstable workers matched for jobs through the platform, such as short-term, part-time work (Kim J.Y. et al, 2018). In response, Jang (2020b) argued that the platform acts as a bulletin board rather than coordinating the process of connecting work and does not have a record of where and what the users of the platform workers do (Jang J.Y. et al, 2020). Moreover, supposedly because fair contracts or responsibilities cannot be requested as universal conditions cannot be imposed, it was argued that they cannot be defined as (in a narrow sense) platform workers having a homogeneous character. Next, the case of e-commerce or leasing business, that is, the case where the platform does not trade labour but trades products or leases assets, was excluded. This is because the people who earn income by selling goods through the platform are more like workers in the broader platform economy than platform workers.

The institutional inconsistency of social protection in Korea

Disguised self-employed workers, referred to as freelancers, dependent self-employed people and other self-employed people(s) under the ambiguous employment relationship, and lastly platform workers, are placed between employees and self-employed people in the informal sector in the grey area (Jang J.Y. et al, 2020; Lee S.Y. et al, 2020a; Nam J.W., 2021). These are a group of workers who do not enter into formal employment contract relationships and are not covered by the social security system as they have various contract relationships that prevent employers from contributing to social insurance (Lee S.Y. et al, 2020a). Further, among the types of contracts that form an ambiguous employment relationship, the triangular employment contract is mainly used to avoid the responsibilities of labour and social laws through civil or commercial contracts. Representative contract types that constitute dependent self-employed are dispatched work and contracted work. These contract methods and multilateral employment relationships are accelerating further through platform labour.

Until the Korean financial crisis in 1997, the average annual economic growth rate was still around 9 per cent, and household income growth was still playing its role in enhancing individual welfare (through private provision). During this period of rapid economic growth, redistributive social policy was regarded as profitable as long as it contributes to economic growth, and full employment has been perceived as the best means for social protection. However, after 2000, as a response to the problem of increasing non-regular workers was needed, attempts to alleviate the dual structure of the labour market began. From the early to late 2000s, the criteria for insurance coverage were gradually relaxed to extend coverage to non-regular labour workers. In 2008, the Labour Standards Act was improved, and the scope of industrial accident insurance was expanded. Then, in January 2012, a guideline for transition to an open-ended contract was introduced for the improvement of non-regular workers' employment in the public sector based on the 'guidelines for promoting improvement of non-regular workers employment', and the protection was later expanded to include dispatched workers as well. In this manner, policies developed in response to the problem of non-regular workers from the mid to the late 2000s.

However, the Korean social protection system faces challenges in aligning with the evolving nature of labour, which has led to difficulties in providing comprehensive social security coverage. The social insurance system operates on a contribution-based model, assuming that workers are formally enrolled in the system. However, the expansion of NSFW has created blind spots that are either specified by law or voluntary, yet substantial. These voluntary blind spots arise due to disadvantages in social insurance contribution(premium) arrangements, payroll issues, complexities in the subscription procedure, and the transition costs associated with joining the system, which contribute to workers avoiding enrolment in what can be considered a "missing middle" of coverage. The details of each system are as follows.

The national pension

The blind spots specified in the National Pension Act are based on employment status, working term contracts, working hours and labour provision method, excluding the prevention of salary overlapping and the prevention of enrolment of persons exceeding the pensionable age. Pursuant to subparagraph 1 of Article 2 of the Enforcement Decree of the National Pension Act, 'daily employees or workers who are used for a period of less than one month' cannot join the national pension scheme. According to Article 3(1) of the National Pension Act and Article 2(4) of the Enforcement Decree of the same Act, 'part-time workers with less than 60 hours of working hours for one month' cannot join the national pension. Daily employees, part-time workers and short-term workers, who are non-regular workers, were excluded from the application. In Article 2 subparagraph 2 of the same Act (workers whose location is not constant) there is the provision that regulates blind spots according to the labour provision method; unlike industrial accident insurance, the national pension system does not recognise workers in special employment types as workers (see Table 2.4).

The issue is that the blind spots stipulated by law are not only that NSFW by itself is not consistent with the increasing labour market changes, but also that these exclusions are deliberately used by obscuring employment

Table 2.4: Workers and grounds for exclusion from the national pension

Excluded type	Excluded workers	Grounds
Old age/social assistance recipients	Workers 65 years of age or older	Article 8(1) of the National Pension Act
	Workers who are recipients of the National Basic Livelihood Security (living benefits, medical benefits recipients)	Article 8(3) of the National Pension Act
Atypical workers	Daily employees or workers with a deadline of less than one month	Enforcement Decree of the National Pension Act, Article 2, No. 1
	Short-term workers with less than 60 working hours per month	Article 3(1)1 of the National Pension Act Article 2, No. 4 of the Enforcement Decree of the National Pension Act
	Workers in workplaces with irregular locations	Article 2, No. 2 of the Enforcement Decree of the National Pension Act
	Workers in special employment types	There are no provisions to recognise them as workers

Source: Reorganised data from Lee S.Y. et al (2020b)

contracts. The national pension system does not sufficiently cover forms of ambiguous self-employed workers, such as short-term workers, fixed-term workers, seasonal workers, daily employees with limited contract terms and workers at workplaces with different locations. In addition, in the case of multiple employers or high income volatility, it is difficult to include some in the national pension scheme (Ryu G.S. et al, 2017).

As a result, there is a significant difference in the national pension enrolment rate between regular and non-regular workers. Regular workers had a 98.0 per cent joining rate in 2019, while non-regular workers had a mere 61.0 per cent in fixed-term workers (85.9 per cent), short-term workers (73.7 per cent), daily workers (17.5 per cent), and others. According to Article 1 of the National Pension Act, the national pension system targets the 'people'. Therefore, it appears that fixed-term workers and short-term workers have higher subscription rates of 85.9 per cent and 73.7 per cent, respectively, than daily workers (see Table 2.5). However, it should be interpreted that the enrolment rate for these forms of labour is rather low considering the institutional targets of the national pension.

The national pension subscribers are classified into workplace, local subscribers and voluntary continuing subscribers. In the case of subscribing to a business site, the insurance premium is borne by the subscriber and half of the business users at 4.5 per cent each. Otherwise, the subscriber is responsible for paying all 9 per cent of the total amount. A worker in

Table 2.5: National pension subscription rate and growth rate by employment status

Division	National pension		
	2018	2019	Rate of increase
All	89.7	91.9	1.4
Regular workers	97.9	98.0	0.1
Non-regular workers	56.5	61.0	4.5
Fixed-term workers	86.5	85.9	−0.6
Short-term workers	69.9	73.7	3.8
Daily workers	11.2	17.5	6.3
Dispatched workers	90.4	92.0	1.6
Subcontract workers	89.4	92.3	2.9

Source: Reorganised data from Lee S.Y. et al (2020b)

NSFW is highly likely to be classified as a local subscriber or a discretionary subscriber rather than a workplace subscriber, but the premium burden is higher than that of a workplace subscriber, thus acting as an incentive to avoid joining the system. Effectively, institutional efforts to include self-employed workers as well as those who are employed provide a perverse incentive for workers to avoid the system.

Employment insurance

The provisions for exclusion from the employment insurance system are similar to those of the national pension system. The blind spots specified in the Employment Insurance Act are based on the size of the workplace, working hours and labour provision method, excluding age restrictions and workers of small-scale construction. In Article 10(1) of the Employment Insurance Act, similar to Article 3(1) of the National Pension Act, short-term workers with less than 60 working hours are restricted for one month to subscribe to employment insurance. In addition, workers in the domestic service industry (in-house employment activities) cannot subscribe to employment insurance pursuant to Article 2(1) of the Enforcement Decree of the Employment Insurance Act, and just as in the case of the national pension, legal discussions for workers in special employment types have not been conducted in the same way (see Table 2.6).

Employment insurance policy comprehensively implements other social protection and labour market policies such as employment security programmes and vocational skills programmes, which are active labour market policies. Specifically, the maternity protection programme, employment security programmes and vocational competency development programmes

Table 2.6: Workers and grounds excluding employment insurance

Excluded type	Excluded workers	Grounds
Old age/ small-sized construction workers	Workers 65 years of age or older	Article 10(1) of the Employment Insurance Act
	Workers of construction with a total construction cost of less than 20 million KRW	Employment Insurance Act Enforcement Decree Article 2(2)
Non-standard forms of work	Workers in a business in which a non-corporate person among agriculture, forestry, fishery or hunting uses four or less workers at all times	Employment Insurance Act Enforcement Decree Article 2(1)
	Short-term workers with less than 60 working hours per month	Article 10(1) of the Employment Insurance Act Employment Insurance Act Enforcement Decree Article 3(1)
	Workers in the domestic service industry (in-house employment)	Employment Insurance Act Enforcement Decree Article 2(1)
	Workers in special employment types	There are no provisions to recognise them as workers

Source: Reorganised data from Lee S.Y. et al (2020b)

are included, in addition to traditional unemployment benefits. That is, the exclusion of employment insurance means that it is excluded not only from unemployment benefits but also from a number of integrated benefits.

Workers who have subscribed to special occupational pensions such as military pensions, public employee pensions and private school teachers' pensions are exempt from employment insurance and industrial accident insurance. These accounted for 5.4 per cent of all employed as of 2019. Special occupational pension subscribers cannot be regarded as blind spots of employment insurance because the contents of employment and industrial accident insurance are covered in each system. Of the 27,358,000 employed people in 2019, 13,528,000 employees of employment insurance were covered by employment insurance, which was only 49.4 per cent of the total employed. The number of non-subscribers was 45.2 per cent of the total employed. Even when limited to waged workers, the non-registration rate reached 27.1 per cent. The blind spots at this time can be classified into legal and actual blind spots (see Table 2.7). The legal blind spot refers to a worker who is excluded as an object of exclusion under the Employment Insurance Act. Substantial blind spots refer to workers who can subscribe to employment insurance but choose not to subscribe.

Legal blind spots include those who are subject to voluntary subscription and those who are excluded from the application. Those subject to voluntary enrolment can subscribe to insurance with the approval of the Korea Labour

Table 2.7: Legal blind spots and practical blind spots of employment insurance

Self-employed workers	Employees				Employed
	Exclusion from employment insurance	No subscription to employment insurance	Sign up for special occupational insurance	Employment insurance subscription	
6,799 (24.9%)	1,781 (6.5%)	3,781 (13.8%)	1,469 (5.4%)	13,528 (49.4%)	27,358 (100.0%)
Legal blind spot		Practical blind spot	Not a blind spot		

Source: Statistics Korea (2019)

Welfare Corporation if they wish. The legal blind spot includes workers who can voluntarily apply for and subscribe to employment insurance but have not voluntarily subscribed. Employment insurance is defined as 'businesses and workplaces that employ more than one employee' as the subject of subscription. Therefore, employers of all businesses and workplaces are explicitly subject to employment insurance. However, as mentioned previously, workers with short-term employment contracts, special type workers and so on, by workplace size according to the type of business, are excluded from the employment insurance coverage. In all, 1.7 million special-type workers and 5.1 million self-employed and unpaid family workers fall under the legal blind spot. Self-employed workers account for the largest percentage of all employed workers among the blind spots of employment insurance.

Factors causing voluntary avoidance of employment insurance include paying insurance premiums (ILO, 2019). Even if the workers are not eligible for a subscription, they can apply for insurance as a voluntary subscriber, as in the national pension plan. However, this also results in a difference in the ratio of insurance premiums to those insured at the workplace. For example, in the case of unemployment benefits, workers and employers pay 0.8 per cent of insurance premiums, while self-employed people receive 2 per cent. In the case of employment security programmes and vocational competency development projects, the business owner pays insurance premiums on its own, while the self-employed pay it directly. As in the case of the national pension, the difference in the method of paying insurance premiums acts as an evasion factor for subscribing to social insurance (ILO, 2019).

Blind spots also exist in terms of eligibility requirements for unemployment benefits. Two requirements must be satisfied in order to be eligible for unemployment benefits: the person must be employed as the insured for a certain period of time or longer; and must not voluntarily resign without justification or be dismissed for serious reasons such as misconduct in the workplace. Requirements must also be satisfied, such as having a willingness to find employment, not being able to find a job, and having to prove that they have made efforts to find a job. In addition, self-employed persons must prove that their insured period is at least one year. It is highly likely that temporary employment contract workers will not be able to meet the qualifications for the insured period. Even when one is enrolled in employment insurance, the premium earned from enrolling in employment insurance actually decreases if one does not qualify for unemployment benefits. Therefore, considering the blind spots related to eligibility for benefits, the consistency between employment insurance and NSFW is even worse than the statistical figures. In addition, in the case of classification of special type employment workers and freelancers, there are many types of work that are difficult to define between unemployment and job turnover. For example, freelancers' search for or solicitation of work are such that it is difficult to clearly distinguish whether they are income, job search or non-economic activities (Kim G.H. et al, 2020). In addition, since workers who work at several workplaces can obtain insured status only in one 'main job', unemployment in the 'non-main job' is not granted insured status and is not protected (Kim G.H. et al, 2020). This is because employment insurance does not recognise partial unemployment. Since ultra-short-term jobs are one of the main forms of NSFW, employment insurance shows a high level of inconsistency for workers in NSFW.

Taken together, the legal blind spots of employment insurance generate exclusions and voluntary subscribers. All of these pertain to melting labour. Although self-employed workers can subscribe to employment insurance in the form of voluntary insurance, they are still voluntarily uninsured because of the institutional characteristics that are advantageous to employees. Employees pay only 0.8 per cent of their income, while self-employed workers pay 2.25 per cent. As of 2019, the number of self-employed persons enrolled in employment insurance accounted for only 0.38 per cent of all self-employed persons (Park C.R., 2020). In addition, considering that most of the non-regular workers dominate even in the case of real blind spots (Lee S.Y. et al, 2020a), it can be seen that the blind spots of employment insurance largely belong to NSFW. Several studies have pointed out the inconsistency of employment insurance for the detailed types of NSFW, and these studies have raised questions about legal blind spots and exclusions (Seo J.H., 2015; Lee A.Y. et al, 2019; Lee S.Y. et al, 2019b, 2020a). First, ultra-short-term workers who work for less than 60 hours per month are excluded from the employment insurance system, but ultra-short-term workers who continue to work for the purpose of living are subject to the Employment Insurance Act. However, it can be regarded as an impractical clause because there is no legal definition of the meaning of 'work for living' (Seo J.H., 2015). Special employment-type workers engage in the type of work that is not discussed in the Employment Insurance Act and are misclassified as self-employed.

As described previously, self-employed persons tend to avoid enrolling in employment insurance due to the excessive burden of insurance premiums. Further, even if they subscribe to employment insurance by paying a higher premium rate than employees, the application of insurance benefits may be limited depending on the type of labour provision. For example, in the case of freelancer(s), which has special employment types, it is difficult to apply the concept of 'unemployment' in its exclusive meaning, because task contracts dominate rather than labour contracts, and oral contracts dominate over formal contracts. The inadequate definition of unemployment leads to difficulties in receiving and receiving unemployment benefits (Lee S.Y. et al, 2019a).

Industrial accident compensation insurance

Industrial accident compensation insurance (hereinafter referred to as industrial accident insurance) shows relatively high inclusiveness compared to the national pension or employment insurance. From a legal perspective, industrial accident insurance has a higher inclusiveness than the national pension scheme and employment insurance because there is a special system (Jang J.Y. and Park C.I., 2019).

Compared to the national pension and employment insurance, industrial accident insurance shows a somewhat better rate of enrolment, even among non-regular workers. In particular, fixed-term workers (98.5 per cent), daily workers (98.3 per cent), dispatched workers (98.8 per cent) and service workers (98.2 per cent) also showed higher rates than regular workers (97.8 per cent). However, it still forms a blind spot because the inclusion of self-employed workers is low (see Tables 2.8 and 6.3).

As of May 2020, only 16.84 per cent of the total 503,306 special employment type workers (legally classified special type of self-employed workers) who had the requirement to subscribe to workers' compensation insurance were found to have subscribed to industrial accident insurance, that is, the remaining 83.16 per cent of 418,546 people voluntarily applied for exclusion, despite the fact that they could subscribe to industrial accident insurance through the special case system.

In other words, some institutional efforts to include workers in NSFW through the special case system for special type workers are observed, but self-employed people are excluded because of the fundamental limitations of the system focusing on wage work. According to the Statistical Korea (2019), the percentage of self-employed workers who subscribed to industrial accident insurance was only 55.5 per cent. Considering that the self-employed without any employees make up close to 75 per cent of all self-employed persons, it can be assumed that the blind spot for industrial accident insurance related to NSFW is large. The reason for the low enrolment rate of self-employed

Table 2.8: Industrial accident compensation insurance subscription rate by employment status (%)

	2018	2019	Increase rate
All	97.4	97.7	0.3
Regular workers	97.5	97.8	0.3
Non-regular workers	96.7	97.3	0.6
Fixed-term workers	97.9	98.5	0.6
Short-term workers	94.4	94.9	0.5
Daily workers	98.3	98.4	0.1
Dispatched workers	94.2	98.8	4.6
Home/domestic workers	97.3	98.2	0.9

people is the same as that of the national pension or employment insurance as discussed previously.

Conclusion

Existing studies have focused on work that deviated from the standard employment relationship, expressed as non-standard employment when discussing precarious work (Rodgers and Rodgers, 1989; Kalleberg, 2000). Since the mid-2000s, interest has not been limited to non-standard work and atypical work, as platform work has spread rapidly in recent years. The focus on non-standard employment among waged workers tends to lead to fragmented solutions to the old problems related to non-standard work and increasing new NSFW. Another stream of the discussion focuses on how these new forms of work deviate considerably from employees and workers' traditional definitions and encompass dependent self-employment workers and platform workers (ILO, 2016, 2017, 2018).

The specific change in the labour market after the economic crisis of the 1970s was the dissolution of a standard employment relationship. The dissolution of the standard employment relationship led to uncertainty and instability in the employment contract relationship (Rodgers and Rodgers, 1989). However, since the late 2000s, with the accelerating transition to digital capitalism, new forms of work that are entirely different from the industrial or service economy have gained popularity. At the same time, international organisations such as the ILO have paid increasing attention to the future of work as a key agenda (ILO, 2016, 2017, 2018). Characteristics of 'melting labour' make it difficult to conceptualise work with a fixed and solidified dichotomy, such as standard and non-standard work. These features of work show a completely different labour process in work, such as work order and skilled formation, and compensation and control methods such as the price of work, working hours and labour control (Lee S.Y. et al, 2020b).

The newly emerged NSFW and new contractual relationships can provide greater flexibility for workers and employers, but they create a very large gap in the inclusiveness of the social security system and are difficult to cover in the social security system. Melting labour contributes to lower bargaining power and anxiety by increasing dependence on market income. Therefore, it is necessary to adjust and reform the social security system along with changes in labour so that the social security system can function as income security and inequality relief.

In this chapter, we examined the legislations related to the new forms of non-standard work, dependent self-employed and platform workers in Korea and some of its empirical aspects. Melting labour captures the characteristics of NSFW that deviate from the traditional standard employment relationship because uncertainty and insecurity are commonly found among these workers. These new forms of work may create new opportunities for workers by providing flexibility in location and time, but they experience limited social protection coverage and unstable working conditions. They are not guaranteed an adequate income level and are exposed to instability due to the currently limited legal boundaries for paid workers. The eligibility criteria for social security are inconsistent with melting labour, and the level of social protection benefits is low because of their overall low wages and contribution. In addition, employers' non-compliance with the scheme and their ambiguous employment relationships make it challenging to ascertain exactly who the employer might be.

3

When insiders are kicked out: layoffs of regular workers in manufacturing

'Even if you climbed all the way up to be a Meister in a large company if you are fired, that's the end of the world.' (A temporary worker dismissed from a large company)

The dual labour market in Korea

This chapter presents a case study on SsangYong Motor, one of the largest automobile manufacturers in Korea, to examine the experiences of its regular workers after being laid off. The study reveals how standard manufacturing workers, who were once considered insiders in the dual labour market, fall into the outsider category due to weak institutional protection. The case study represents cell 2 in the two-by-two matrix explained in Chapter 1, which includes wage workers who are covered by institutional protection, such as regular workers in large corporations and the public sector, who are considered labour market insiders. Victims of the 2009 SsangYong Motor layoffs experienced a sharp decrease in their income immediately after the layoff and were drifting from one unstable job to another, such as outsourcing, daily labour and micro-scale self-employment. In this chapter, I highlight the issue of old precarity, where workers with stable employment status can easily slide into precarious work once they lose institutional protection.

The dual structure of the Korean labour market has been discussed since the mid-1980s in Korea, mainly driven by the dual labour market theory (Lee H.S., 1984). A significant body of research has pointed out the dual structure of the Korean labour market in various ways. The related studies can be largely divided into three categories according to the criteria for classifying the dual structure of the labour market.

Studies in the first category have examined the formation of a dual structure in job stability and wage level (Lee J.H., 1992; Jeong E.H. and Jeon B.Y., 2001; Jeong E.H., 2002; Beck S.H., 2014; Lee S.Y., 2016). According to these studies, there exists a dual structure in the Korean labour market in terms of wage and employment protection depending on employment status and company size.

Studies in the second category have dealt with the dual structure in social security dimensions such as social policy (Beck S.H., 2014; Lee S.Y., 2016). These studies have brought up the institutional dualisation of Korean society by revealing that the dual structure in the labour market exists not only in the employment pattern and wage structure but also in the area of social protection (Lee S.Y., 2016).

Studies in the third category have analysed the dual structure of the Korean labour market from a gender perspective (Geum J.H., 2004; Kim J.S. et al, 2005; Kim Y.O., 2010; Lee S.Y., 2016; Lee S.Y. et al, 2016). These studies have delved into the dual structure of the Korean labour market associated with gender discrimination, the social rights of female temporary workers and various policy combinations.

In recent years, however, an increasing number of studies have investigated the instability of the labour market from an integrated perspective, including the dual structures concerning employment status, wage level and social insurance (Lee S.Y. et al, 2017a). These studies classify the dual structure of the Korean labour market taking into account not only employment status, but also company size, gender, wage level and social security, either collectively or individually. Nevertheless, the mainstay of all these studies is the employment status dichotomised into regular and temporary employees, superimposing the insider and outsider positions of the dual structure of the Korean labour market.

The dual labour market, consisting of stable workers and precarious workers, is a common trend in capitalist economies to varying degrees. However, for a labour market to be considered dual, a dual structure must be the predominant characteristic. Therefore, while the dual labour market theory was developed in the US, the US labour market is not classified as dual as it does not exhibit a dominant dual structure (Jang J.Y., 2019). To determine if the Korean labour market is predominantly dualised, two aspects need to be considered. First, the extent of the gap between insiders and outsiders needs to be examined, and second, the size of the segmented labour market needs to be determined (Park S.J., 2022). These two dimensions are important because even if there is a significant gap between insiders and outsiders, if the size of the segmented worker group is relatively small compared to the overall labour market, it is only a small group within the larger neoliberal system. Therefore, to establish the presence of dualisation, both the degree of segmentation and its statistical significance must be evaluated.

The aforementioned studies can be categorised as empirical research on quantitative and qualitative differences. Looking at the wage gap, as a typical example, if the mean wage of regular employees of large companies is 100, that of their temporary counterparts was found to be as low as 63.2. The wage levels of regular employees of small- and medium-size enterprises are only 58.2 for companies with 1–4 employees and 64.2 for companies with 5–9 employees, and those of their temporary counterparts are 31.0 and 37.8, respectively (Kim Y.S., 2019).

Table 3.1: Wage gap between regular and temporary workers in Korea (2019)

Company size (N)	Monthly wage (10,000 KRW)		Wage gap 1 (%) ≥300 Regular=100			Wage gap 2 (%) By size Regular =100	
	Regular	Temp.	Total	Regular	Temp.	Regular	Temp.
1–4	240	128	159	58.2	31.0	100	53.3
5–9	265	156	206	64.2	37.8	100	58.8
10–29	293	168	241	70.9	40.8	100	57.5
30–99	323	191	287	78.4	46.3	100	59.0
100–299	345	221	318	83.7	53.7	100	64.2
≥300	412	261	391	100	63.2	100	63.2
Total	321	163	256	77.7	39.4	100	50.7

Note: Wage gap 1: The percentage of the wage level by employment status (regular or temporary) and company size (number of employees), with mean the wage (4,120,000 KRW) of large companies (≥300 employees) set at 100%; Wage gap 2: The wage level of temporary workers relative to that of regular employees by company size.

Source: Kim Y.S. (2019: table 2), reconstructed by the author

In all categories, the mean wage of irregular employees was reduced towards the half level of regular employees (see Table 3.1). The wage levels of both regular and irregular employees of small companies (1–4 employees) were close to the half of those of large companies (≥300 employees). That is, the wage gap is formed between regular and irregular employees as well as between large and small companies. Similar patterns also appear in the ratio of workers receiving less than the minimum wage, proportion of the low-wage groups, social insurance rate and the union organisation rate, with the tendency the most apparent for the employment status (Kim Y.S., 2019). Along with the employment status, the company size significantly contributes to the wage gap, which is ascribed to the fact that the segmentation of Korean labour market has traditionally taken place mostly by large export and heavy industry companies (Jeong M.K., 2007). These companies, which have played a locomotive role in Korea's rapid economic growth, need a skilled labour force and an institutional alignment prioritising regular male employees has long been established in individual companies to provide them with employment incentives (Lee S.Y., 2016). Such dual structure is the dominant aspect of the Korean labour market. Lee H.Y. and Yang J.J. (2017) differentiated between core and peripheral features of the labour market under the three criteria of wage level, social insurance coverage and regular employment, and reported that an absolute majority (75.94 per cent) of the total labour market consisted of insider and outsider labour markets (Lee H.Y. and Yang J.J., 2017). Even when the same criteria were applied to younger employees only, a similar percentage (65 per cent) was obtained (Lee S.Y. et al, 2017a).

The dual labour market theory classifies regular male workers of large manufacturing companies as insiders in the Korean labour market. However, this chapter shifts the focus from the gap between insiders and outsiders to the process of how insiders degrade to outsiders in the dual labour market structure. While previous discussions have mainly centred on the differences in labour market status or social security, this chapter highlights the process of losing institutional protection and sliding into precarious work in the dual labour market.

As outlined in Chapter 1, the shift from an industrial economy to a service one has resulted in the expansion of non-regular work and the individualisation of risks. This transition has led to the dissolution of the standard employment relationship and has caused uncertainty, insecurity and instability in the employment contract relationship (Rodgers and Rodgers, 1989). Sargeant (2009) examines precarity and emphasises how workers are subordinate to organisational change. It is important to note that precarious work can also include standard employment contracts where workers are subject to organisational changes, such as restructuring and downsizing (Sargeant, 2009).

In this chapter, the focus is on the experience of once-insider workers who have been subjected to organisational change through a layoff and how they undergo a process of change in their working form, transitioning from insider to outsider status in the dual labour market structure while experiencing melting of the labour. The aim of this study is to examine not only the insider–outsider gap but also how the existing social protection systems fail to function sufficiently once the working form starts to melt down. The analysis focuses on the dismissed insiders who are now working in non-standard forms and how they experience exclusion from social protection such as employment insurance, active labour market policies, and other welfare systems. Specifically, this chapter presents a case study of the 2009 SsangYong Motor layoff, which exemplifies the changes in socioeconomic status and social security coverage and benefits for regular employees of large manufacturing companies during the six years following a mass layoff. The study highlights the limitations of the social protection system in the Korean dual labour market for those who were once considered insiders.

SsangYong Motor's 2009 mass layoffs and thereafter

SsangYong Motor is one of the five largest automobile manufacturers in Korea (Park J.Y. et al, 2016). The SsangYong Motor case started in the process of restructuring and mass layoffs when Shanghai Automotive Industry Corporation (SAIC) went bankrupt after four years of operation in Korea and filed for court protection in January 2009 (Gwak S.S. and Park M.J., 2013). SsangYong Motor, which used to be a large company with close to 23,000 employees in the early 2000s, was sold to SAIC in 2004 due to financial difficulties.

After the merger with SAIC, SsangYong Motor faced a decline in sales due to insufficient investment in new car development and the global economic downturn. Following four years of operation, SAIC withdrew from the Korean market and took SsangYong's production model technology to China, after filing for court protection with the Korean government. This move violated the agreement SAIC had made with SsangYong's union at the time of the merger, which involved large-scale investments in production facilities and employment succession to protect workers (Kwon J.Y., 2012).

In the face of a business crisis, SsangYong Motor announced in April 2009 a layoff-based restructuring plan. The layoff plan resulted in a workforce reduction from 7,130 to 2,646 (37 per cent), including 45 per cent of technical workers (Kim H. et al, 2009). Workers launched a general strike against the management on 21 May 2009, occupying SsangYong Motor's Pyeongtaek factory for 77 days from May to August 2009, which led to violent confrontations (Kwon J.Y., 2012; Gwak S.S. and Park M.J., 2013). This incident attracted great interest from the media and society at the time. The workers faced a situation of confrontation with the company's hired security guard for 24 hours, which led to clashes with the layoff survivors. As a result, 64 unionists, including the branch head, were arrested, and serious, even fatal, injuries were inflicted during the physical clashes (Kwon J.Y., 2012; Gwak S.S. and Park M.J., 2013).

The number of layoffs was adjusted through labour–management negotiations in August 2009. Of the 976 layoffs, 468 were converted to unpaid leave, and the remaining 508 layoffs were readjusted into 130 voluntarily retirements, 139 unpaid leave for three years, 83 disciplinary layoffs and 159 layoffs (Gwak S.S. and Park M.J., 2013).

In November 2010, SsangYong Motor was acquired by the Indian car manufacturer Mahindra & Mahindra, which was seen as a step towards normalisation. However, the conflict between the company and the union continued and, tragically, between January 2009 and May 2015, 28 unionists and their families lost their lives due to the stress and pressure of the ongoing dispute. This included 14 suicides and sudden deaths from myocardial infarction or cerebral haemorrhage (Gwak S.S. and Park M.J., 2013; Media Today, 2015). On 20 November 2012, three unionists, including a former branch leader, climbed to the top of a transmission tower to protest and demand a government investigation. On 10 January 2013, the union and the management agreed to reinstate 455 workers on unpaid leave. SsangYong Motor hired new workers in April 2012, with the normalisation of its business operation, but without prioritising the laid-off workers. As a result,

187 laid-off workers, including the temporary workers with terminated contracts, could not return to work by the end of 2015 (Kim N.G., 2012).

In June 2018, one unionist committed suicide, which became known as 'the 30th death'. This event led to the Blue House convening the Human Rights Violation Fact-Finding Committee and recognising SsangYong Motor's suppression of the union movement. In September of the same year, it was decided that all 119 laid-off workers would be reinstated. However, the victims of the 2009 SsangYong Motor layoffs were not protected through Korea's unemployment protection or the public job training system, but through media attention and the union's extreme protest methods. It is generally difficult for most labour market insiders, once dismissed and degraded, to regain their insider status in the internal labour market (Media Today, 2018). The victims of the 2009 SsangYong Motor layoffs were not protected through Korea's unemployment protection or the public job training system, but through the media attention and the union's extreme protest repertoire the laid-off workers could return to work. In general, however, most labour market insiders, once dismissed and degraded, cannot regain the insider status in the internal labour market (Hankyoreh, 2018).

Employment protection legislation and mass layoffs

This type of dismissal often occurs during economic downturns or when companies undergo restructuring or mergers. Layoffs can have a significant impact on the affected workers, not only causing financial hardship but also leading to social isolation and psychological distress. Moreover, the effectiveness of unemployment protection and active labour market policies for supporting laid-off workers to return to the stable labour market is often limited. The case of SsangYong Motor's 2009 layoffs highlights the difficulties that laid-off insiders face in re-entering the labour market and the limitations of the existing social protection system.

In general, layoff refers to dismissal due to an employer's circumstances, and its legal definition is dismissal for managerial reasons (Moon J.H., 2014). Layoffs, also known as 'managerial dismissals', have serious disadvantages, such as threatening employees' employment stability with no cause attributable to themselves, and have a great impact on society because they usually affect a large number of workers at the same time (Noh B.H., 2009; Shin S.J., 2013; Moon J.H., 2014). Since layoffs pose a serious threat to workers' employment security, the Korean Labour Standards Act stipulates strict standards for managerial dismissal, prohibiting dismissals without justifiable reasons. Article 24 of the Labour Standards Act stipulates strict restrictions on dismissal for managerial reasons, such as the presence of urgent managerial necessity, obligation to make efforts to avoid dismissal, application of reasonable and fair criteria for the selection of employees to be dismissed, notification to the labour union 50 days prior to the intended date and consultation with the labour union. In addition, if layoffs due to managerial difficulty are inevitable, it is a general practice that the laid-off workers are given priority, in compliance with legal provisions, court decisions and collective bargains, when the management is normalised (Kim N.G., 2012).

In Korea, employers are obligated to provide preferential re-employment for dismissed workers according to Article 25 of the Labour Standards Act. However, in the 2009 SsangYong Motor layoffs, the workers were dismissed without following the proper procedure stipulated in the Act and were not given preferential re-employment. As a result, 187 laid-off workers were still waiting for reinstatement by September 2015. Eventually, following media attention and the union's extreme protest repertoire, it was agreed that all remaining 119 laid-off workers would return to work by September 2018 (Hankyoreh, 2018). The re-employment of laid-off workers and voluntary retirees was carried out sequentially from 2015 to 2018, with 40 workers re-employed in 2016, 62 in 2017 and 87 in 2018 (*Chosun Ilbo*, 2020).

The Organisation for Economic Co-operation and Development (OECD)'s employment protection legislation (EPL) index is a measure of the strictness of a country's EPL. The EPL index is presented for regular and temporary contracts. In this OECD employment type classification, temporary contracts encompass all time-limited employment contracts such as fixed-term, temporary work agency, seasonal labour, on-call labour and daily supply contracts. On the other hand, defining non-regular employment is more complicated because a part-time worker can be either a regular or a non-regular worker because part-time or full-time does not depend on the employment duration, but on work hours per unit of service. In general, EPL-based studies use terms interchangeably among regular, permanent and unlimited term versus non-regular, temporary and fixed-term contracts.

The EPL index is calculated in four categories, including the EPL index of individual dismissals for regular contracts, EPL index for collective dismissals of regular contracts, EPL index for both individual and collective dismissals, and EPL index of dismissals for temporary contracts. The EPL index is calculated by assigning a score ranging from 0 to 6 to each indicator and multiplying its weight (in parentheses). The individual EPL indicators and their respective weights are listed in Table 3.2. Korea's EPL index of regular contracts is 2.18 (as of 2019), ranking 24th among 38 OECD countries, while the EPL index of temporary contracts is 2.54 (ranked 10th). However, when the EPL index of regular contracts is further broken down into individual and collective dismissals, a significant difference is observed. Korea's EPL scores have remained constant since 2008, with the EPL score for collective dismissals of regular workers, in particular, being measured since 2000. According to the EPL index, collective dismissals for regular contracts have a lower score than individual dismissals, indicating that collective dismissals

Table 3.2: Employment protection indicators: classification, definitions and weighting

Level 1	Level 2	Level 3	Level 4	
EPL indicators for regular workers	Individual EPL indicators (5/7)	Procedural inconvenience (1/3)	1. Notification procedure	(1/2)
			2. Delay to start a notice	(1/2)
		Notice and severance pay (1/3)	3. Period of notice	(3/7)
			4. Severance pay	(4/7)
		Difficulty of dismissal (1/3)	5. Definition of unfair dismissal	(1/5)
			6. Trial period	(1/5)
			7. Unfair dismissal compensation	(1/5)
			8. Extent of reinstatement	(1/5)
			9. Time limit for filing complaint	(1/5)
	Collective EPL indicators (2/7)		18. Definition of collective dismissal	(1/4)
			19. Additional notification requirements	(1/4)
			20. Additional delay to start a notice	(1/4)
			21. Additional costs to the employer	(1/4)
EPL indicators for temporary workers		Fixed-term contracts (FTC) (1/2)	10. Permissible scope of FTC	(1/2)
			11. Max. number of FTC renewals	(1/4)
			12. Max. total duration of FTC	(1/4)
		Temporary work agency contract (TWAC) (1/2)	13. Permissible scope of TWAC	(1/3)
			14. Max. number of TWAC renewals	(1/6)
			15. Max. total duration of TWAC	(1/6)
			16. TWAC report obligation	(1/6)
			17. Equal treatment for equal work	(1/6)

Note: The number in parentheses for each level is the weights applied when calculating the value of the upper level based on Version 3 (2008~) of the OECD EPL index. For example, if the scores of item 1 and item 2 of Level 4 are 4 and 5, respectively, the 'Level 3: Procedural Discomfort' index is (4*(1/2)) + (3*(1/2)) = becomes 3.5.

Source: OECD EPL index (OECD, 2019), reconstructed by the author

are easier in Korea. Specifically, Korea ranks 33rd out of 38 OECD countries in the EPL index for collective dismissals of regular contracts, with a score of 1.88 (as of 2019) (see Figure 3.1). This suggests that the legal regulations for collective dismissals are relatively lax in Korea, making it easier for companies to lay off a large number of regular workers at once.

Upon examining Korea's collective EPL index, it becomes evident that collective dismissals are relatively easy for employers to execute without incurring additional costs, such as re-employment, severance pay and training. This is because collective dismissals do not require a longer notice period compared to individual dismissals. Although Article 24 of the Labour Standards Act states that labour unions must be involved in setting the criteria for layoff decisions, it fails to provide specific criteria for selecting employees to be dismissed. Additionally, there are no regulations on severance pay related to layoffs, which places minimal burden on employers.

In the case of the 2009 SsangYong Motor layoffs, even if the company's 'urgent managerial necessity' was recognised under the Labour Standards Act, its legitimacy is called into question due to SsangYong Motor's failure to meet its legal obligation to 'make every effort to avoid dismissal' under Article 24(1). The company failed to take measures such as reducing work hours and reallocating personnel, as well as establishing a social support plan for those to be dismissed. Furthermore, after the business was normalised and new personnel were employed, SsangYong Motor neglected to preferentially re-employ dismissed workers, which is a normative duty based on the procedural duty of consideration under the labour contract, rather than a moral duty regarding compensation.

In the next section, the results of a questionnaire survey conducted with 187 victims of the 2009 SsangYong layoff case will be presented. A questionnaire survey was conducted to identify the characteristics of a population through sampling and explain the relationship between variables related to social situations or phenomena. This widely used data collection method in the social science field ensures objectivity and accuracy through standardised questions. The questionnaire items used in the study were composed through a review of existing research and interviews with laid-off workers of SsangYong Motor. The final questionnaire items were completed through pilot tests.

A questionnaire survey was conducted on 30 May 2015 for the dismissed workers who gathered at the union event at the psychological healing centre 'Warak' located in Pyeongtaek, Gyeonggi-do. The survey was conducted between 30 May 2015 and 2 June 2015. Of the total 187 subjects, 142 (60 in face-to-face, 82 in online surveys, 75.9 per cent response rate) responded. After excluding 14 workers who had not been looking for a job for six years, that is, had no work experience in the labour market after the dismissal, a total of 116 survey results were used in this study. Additionally, the questionnaire items used in the study were composed through a review of existing research and interviews with laid-off workers of SsangYong Motor, and the final questionnaire items were completed through pilot tests.

This section will examine how legislation and social protection systems have failed to protect those who were once considered 'insiders' in the labour market, and will track the living conditions of laid-off workers for six years after their dismissal. Of the 142 respondents to the survey, 116 were selected for analysis based on criteria such as being a regular worker before the layoff and having experience of employment over the six years after the layoff. All of the former SsangYong employees included in the analysis were male, with a mean age of 44.3 years (range: 34–58), and a mean tenure of 19.3 years in the same company (as of 2009) among the 115 respondents who indicated their career length (range: 11–35).[1]

Figure 3.1: International comparison of employment protection legislation score of individual dismissals and for collective dismissals (2019)

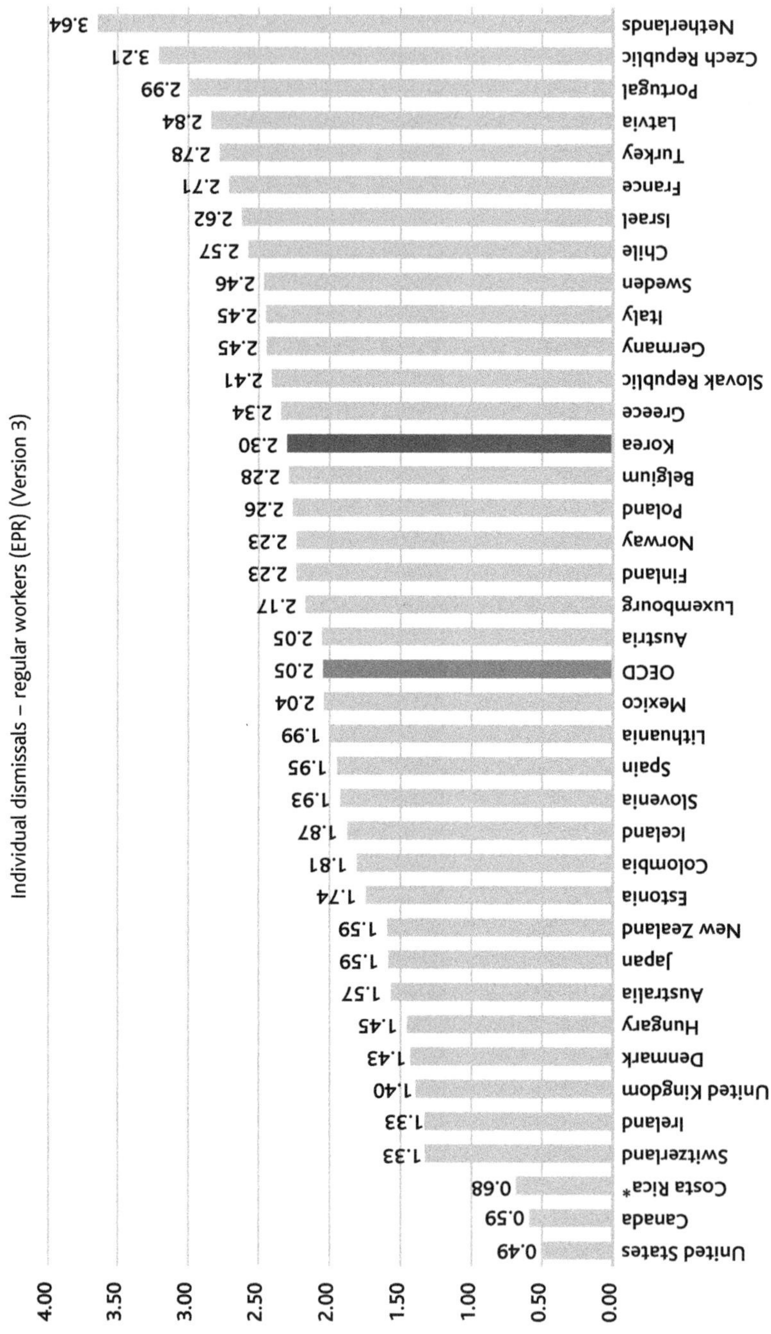

Individual dismissals – regular workers (EPR) (Version 3)
4.00
3.50
3.00
2.50
2.00
1.50
1.00
0.50
0.00
Netherlands 3.64
Czech Republic 3.21
Portugal 2.99
Latvia 2.84
Turkey 2.78
France 2.71
Israel 2.62
Chile 2.57
Sweden 2.46
Italy 2.45
Germany 2.45
Slovak Republic 2.41
Greece 2.34
Korea 2.30
Belgium 2.28
Poland 2.26
Norway 2.23
Finland 2.23
Luxembourg 2.17
Austria 2.05
OECD 2.05
Mexico 2.04
Lithuania 1.99
Spain 1.95
Slovenia 1.93
Iceland 1.87
Colombia 1.81
Estonia 1.74
New Zealand 1.59
Japan 1.59
Australia 1.57
Hungary 1.45
Denmark 1.43
United Kingdom 1.40
Ireland 1.33
Switzerland 1.33
Costa Rica* 0.68
Canada 0.59
United States 0.49

Figure 3.1: International comparison of employment protection legislation score of individual dismissals and for collective dismissals (2019) (continued)

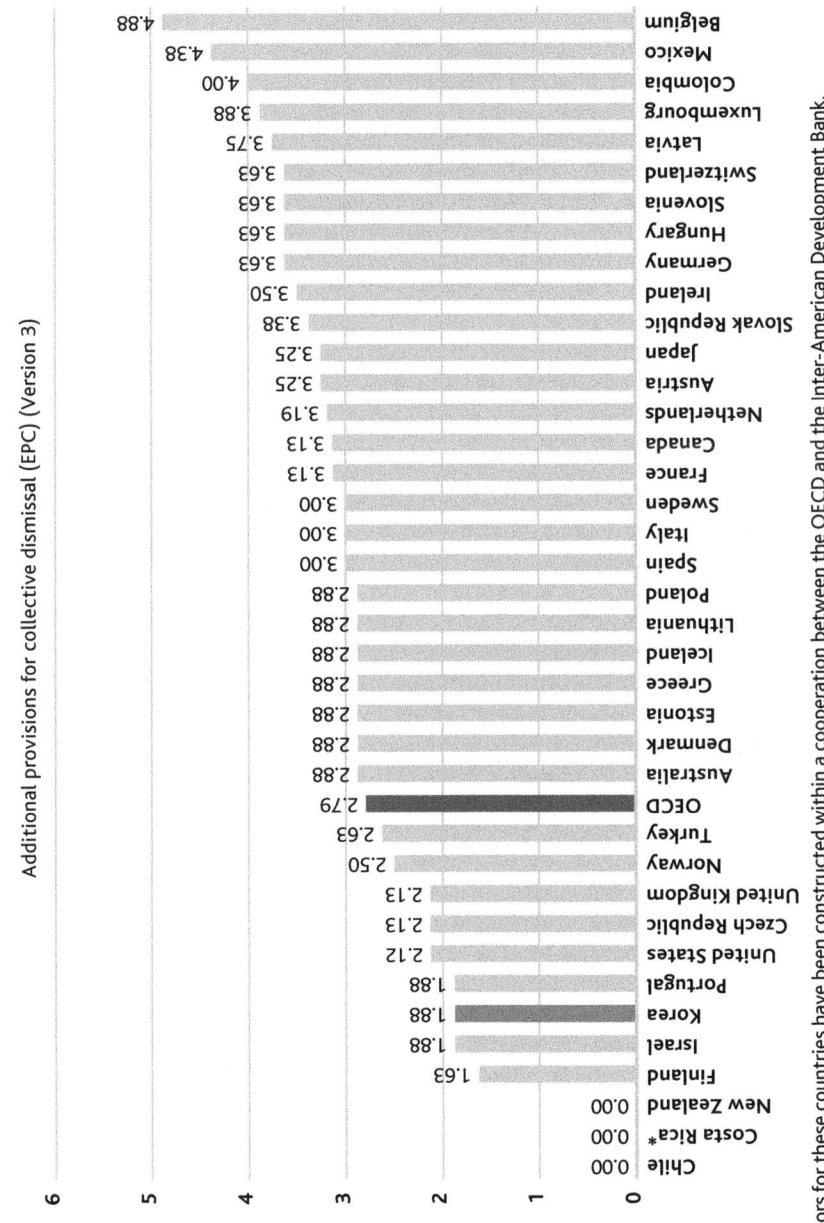

Belgium	4.88
Mexico	4.38
Colombia	4.00
Luxembourg	3.88
Latvia	3.75
Switzerland	3.63
Slovenia	3.63
Hungary	3.63
Germany	3.63
Ireland	3.50
Slovak Republic	3.38
Japan	3.25
Austria	3.25
Netherlands	3.19
Canada	3.13
France	3.13
Sweden	3.00
Italy	3.00
Spain	3.00
Poland	2.88
Lithuania	2.88
Iceland	2.88
Greece	2.88
Estonia	2.88
Denmark	2.88
Australia	2.88
OECD	2.79
Turkey	2.63
Norway	2.50
United Kingdom	2.13
Czech Republic	2.13
United States	2.12
Portugal	1.88
Korea	1.88
Israel	1.88
Finland	1.63
New Zealand	0.00
Costa Rica*	0.00
Chile	0.00

Additional provisions for collective dismissal (EPC) (Version 3)

Note: * Indicators for these countries have been constructed within a cooperation between the OECD and the Inter-American Development Bank.
Source: OECD (2020)

Regular employees in manufacturing entering the outside labour market

First of all, 3–4 million KRW (N=45, 41.7 per cent) was the most frequent mean monthly income (as of 2008) while working at SsangYong Motor among the 108 respondents who gave the answer, followed by 2–3 million KRW (N= 35, 32.4 per cent). With the former employees placed in 7–8 deciles (32.4 per cent) and 9–10 deciles (1.9 per cent), a significant proportion of them was found to have an above-average income compared to the Korean mean wage in 2008 (see Table 3.3). As explained, the survey respondents were regular employees in a manufacturing-oriented conglomerate called SsangYong Motor until just before the layout, and their monthly average income was relatively high enough to be classified as 'insiders of the dual labour market'.

To begin with, this study conducted an in-depth time-series analysis from 2009 to 2015 to examine the changes in occupation and income of the SsangYong workers laid off in 2009. The respondents were asked to indicate their primary source of income each year, and the analysis of 80 responses revealed that 'daily contract labour' was the most common occupation pursued, excluding 'unemployed', followed by 'self-employed'. The highest proportion of outsourced work was reported in 2011, reaching 21.3 per cent. This indicates that the laid-off regular employees of a big company were forced to work in the precarious outsider labour market.

Second, this study examined changes in the post-layoff income level by analysing the pre- and post-layoff income levels of 52 laid-off workers who reported their income as of 2008 and during the six years after the layoff (2009–2015). The analysis showed that only two respondents (3.8 per cent) earned less than 20 million KRW in 2008, which sharply increased to 49 respondents (94.2 per cent) in 2009, immediately after the layoff. The number

Table 3.3: Distribution of monthly average salary (as of 2008) of the laid-off employees while working in SsangYong Motor (N=108)

Pre-layoff wage level	2008 Korean monthly mean income deciles	Respondent fraction for each income decile (%)
1–2 million KRW	1–2 deciles	1.9
2–3 million KRW	3–4 deciles	32.4
3–4 million KRW	5–6 deciles	41.7
4–5 million KRW	7–8deciles	22.2
≥ 5 million KRW	9–10deciles	1.9
Mean income	3.81 million KRW (5–6 deciles)	

Source: Statistics Korea (2008) and Lee and Kim (2016)

Table 3.4: Ratio of laid-off workers with a pre- and post-2009 annual income lower than 20 million KRW per month (N=52)

Category	Year	N	%
Pre-layoff	2008	2	3.8
Post-layoff	2009	49	94.2
	2010	44	84.6
	2011	43	82.7
	2012	38	73.1
	2013	35	67.3
	2014	36	69.2
	2015	37	71.2

gradually decreased to 35 (67.3 per cent) in 2013 and stagnated, slightly increasing to 37 (71.2 per cent) in 2015. This suggests that the laid-off workers were unable to improve their income level and remained in the low–income group (< 20 million KRW) over six years after the layoff (see Table 3.4).

The survey found that daily contract labour was the most common source of income for laid-off workers, followed by self-employment and outsourcing. Only a small percentage of respondents earned less than 20 million KRW prior to the layoff, while the majority earned less than this amount during the six years after the layoff, indicating a decrease in income levels. The findings suggest that the laid-off regular employees of a big company remained in the precarious outsider labour market and were unable to move out of the low–income group over six years after the layoff.

Under the Labour Standards Act, SsangYong Motor has a legal obligation to 'make every effort to avoid dismissal' under Article 24(1), such as reduction of work hours and personnel reallocation, and to establish social support plan for those to be dismissed. However, as already explained, Korea's collective EPL index reveals that it is relatively easy for employers to lay off a mass number of workers as the layoff does not entail additional costs such as re-employment effort, severance pay and training.

Social protection becomes increasingly important when employers can dismiss workers at a low cost. Kim W.S. and Shi S.J. (2020) discuss two definitions of labour market policies: broad and narrow. Their study focuses on the broad definition, which is the relationship between active and passive labour market policies. The study aims to identify the factors that distinguish activation patterns in Korea and Taiwan (Kim W.S. and Shi S.J., 2020). The two countries took different paths to activation after the 1990s, with differences in direct job creation programmes compared to vocational training and employment services. Active labour market policies aim to promote re-employment through job placement, vocational training and wage subsidy systems. Active labour market policies have four subcategories: employment incentives; employment services; direct job creation; and job training. Bonoli (2012) classified different types of active labour market policies, such as direct job creation and job training, and found that a country's commitment to skill formation is most clearly revealed through expenditure on job training-type programmes among active labour market policies. The unemployment insurance system pays unemployment benefits and supports re-employment efforts during the period of unemployment of the insured. It is largely divided into job search benefits and employment promotion benefits. The former refers to the benefits paid for the livelihood of the unemployed, and it is what is generally meant by the mention of unemployment benefits.

According to a study by Lee S.Y. (2018), Korea's unemployment safety net is weak when compared to other OECD countries in terms of unemployment insurance, social assistance and active labour market policies. The country's unemployment insurance has a low safety net level because of the short duration of benefit payments and low income replacement rate. The benefits payment duration is only seven months, making it the third shortest after the US and the UK, while the income replacement rate of 50 per cent is the lowest among the countries analysed. The annual income replacement rate drops to 30 per cent when converted into the reference value of OECD data, 'the mean income replacement ratio during 12 months after the dismissal'. Although most regular workers are insured, the effectiveness of employment insurance decreases as unemployment is prolonged, and the benefit period is short. Consequently, the insufficient unemployment safety net is established due to the low-income replacement rate even during the benefit period, making Korea's social protection system for the unemployed weak (Lee S.Y., 2018).

Examining the spending on active labour market policies relative to the GDP in Korea, the level of spending was still the third lowest among the countries included in the analysis, following the US and Japan (Lee S.Y., 2018). Conclusively, Korea was found to have poor systems in both unemployment insurance and active labour market policies. This suggests that the benefits provided to workers during the unemployment period are far from sufficient, with a short benefit period and a low level of support for re-employment.

As part of the active labour market policy, job placement services are provided to support the re-employment efforts of the unemployed to find a position matching their capabilities and aptitude by comprehensively providing nationwide employment information, job guidance and in-depth counselling. Vocational training for competency development is provided to job seekers (all unemployed workers) in the form of a set amount of money as training fees and the 'Training Card for the Future', an integrated training record management system. Another important programme is the Workers' Vocational Skills Training Programme, a cash support up to 2 million KRW per year offered to fixed-term, dispatched, short-term, daily and 50+ (large company) workers, those subject to job change, those with no training records in the past three years, those on unpaid leave, temporary workers, self-employed, and so on.

However, Korea's active labour market policy mostly targets low-skilled workers, such as short-term, dispatched, part-time, daily or 50+ workers, or comprises welfare programmes accompanied by labour intended to induce the labour market participation of low-income groups. Unemployment benefits are paid in two strands of job search benefits and employment promotion benefits, which has a policy purpose of inducing stable livelihood and re-employment of the unemployed. Still, this approach has little effect on job search and employment promotion in the case of dismissal of insiders of the Korean dual labour market structure.

Looking at the income maintenance through unemployment benefits for the laid-off, 4.5 per cent (5/112) responded to the question of whether they had received unemployment benefits since 2009 with 'No' and 11 (9.8 per cent), 44 (39.3 per cent) and 34 (30.4 per cent) answered that they received unemployment benefits for the periods of 3–5, 6 and 7–8 months, respectively. Next, to examine whether these job search benefits have actually helped them find re-employment, the respondents were asked to answer the question 'Have you received or are you currently receiving education or vocational training intended to help you find a job, start a business or improve your job skills since 2009?' Of the 112 respondents, 42 (37.5 per cent) answered 'Yes' and 69 (62.0 per cent) answered 'No', which suggests that a large proportion of the laid-off workers were not exposed to the re-employment services of the Ministry of Employment and Labour. Asked why they did not receive education or vocational training after 2009, the most common reason was 'income loss during the period of training' (18.2 per cent), followed by 'no time' (15.2 per cent). Additionally, with answers such as 'no need for vocational training', 'financial burden of training fees' and 'lack of desired training courses', the practical effectiveness of the re-employment services was found to be very low (see Table 3.5).

Finally, asked whether or not they actually succeeded in re-employment through the programmes provided by job centres (such as the Hope Ribbon Project or the Employment Success Package Project), only 10 out of 110 respondents (9.1 per cent) answered with 'Yes', which allows the assumption that the contribution of job search support to re-employment is very low even after participating in vocational training programmes. Looking at the jobs the respondents found after the layoff, the level of the former employment was hardly maintained, with the majority of the laid-off workers moving from one job to another in the outsider labour market.

Table 3.5: Reasons for not participating in education or vocational training after 2009 (N=66)

	N	%
Income loss during the period of training	12	18.2
Lack of information about education/training programmes	12	18.2
No time	10	15.2
No need for vocational training	6	9.1
Financial burden of training fees	6	9.1
Lack of desired training courses	3	4.6
Schedule overlap with the training programmes	2	3.0
Others	15	22.7

When asked who helped them with finding the job, 88 out of 107 respondents, excluding those who answered 'N/A' (not applicable), indicated the persons from whom they actually received help in descending order of 'friends and acquaintances' (N=37; 42 per cent), 'others' (23; 26.1 per cent), fellow laid-off colleagues (17; 19.3 per cent) and family and relatives (16; 18.2 per cent). Only eight respondents (9.1 per cent) received help from government-run job centres. As shown in these statistics, most of the respondents relied on personal relationships in their job search process, and the use of job placement or employment services provided by the government-run job centres was very low.

In sum, active labour market policy in Korea is revealed to have poor systems in unemployment insurance and support for re-employment. Active labour market policies mostly target low-skilled workers, leaving those with higher skill levels without sufficient support. Despite job placement and vocational training programmes, they have little effect on the re-employment of insiders in the Korean dual labour market structure. Unemployment benefits are insufficient, with a short benefit period and a low level of support for re-employment. A large proportion of laid-off workers did not receive re-employment services, and the practical effectiveness of these services was found to be very low.

Following the analysis of the laid-off employees' experience of unemployment insurance and active labour market policy, we investigated the default rates on the premium payments for the national pension and health insurance, which are a basic part of social protection in Korea (see Table 3.6).

In the investigation of the initial default periods for the national pension and health insurance premiums, which constitute major compulsory social protection in Korea, the changes in income level resulted in the default on the national pension premium; 91 workers (81.3 per cent) had an experience

Table 3.6: Post-layoff (2009) experience of default on the national pension and health insurance

	National pension (N=112)		Health insurance (N=111)	
	N	%	N	%
Default after 2009				
No	20	18.0	36	32.4
Yes	91	82.0	75	67.6

of the default on the national pension premium, 55 of whom in 2009 immediately after the layoff, and 24 (26.4 per cent) in 2010; that is, 71.0 per cent of the respondents (79/112) experienced default on the national pension premium within two years of the layoff. For health insurance, 67.6 per cent (75/111) had experienced default on the health insurance premium and 53.2 per cent (59/111) within two years of the layoff (see Table 3.6). In other words, the majority of the layoff victims began to be excluded from the primary social protection immediately after the layoff because of the reduction in income.

The investigation of the initial default periods for the national pension and health insurance premiums in Korea found that the majority of workers experienced default on these compulsory social protections soon after being laid off, due to a reduction in income. These findings suggest that social protection is not functioning to protect workers who have been laid off, leaving them without adequate coverage for their basic needs.

Rethinking social protection and bridging the gap

Studies have mainly divided insiders and outsiders into belonging to the primary and secondary labour market, respectively, based on employment type (regular and non-regular workers) and company size (large companies and small- and medium-sized enterprises) (Jeong E.H., 2001, 2013; Lee B.H., 2004; Baek S.H. and Lee S.Y., 2014; Beck S.H., 2014). The dualisation thesis criticises existing discussions on polarisation, fragmentation and marginalisation; it only focuses on the outcome of labour market segmentation and overlooks the politics of change (Emmenegger et al, 2012). This theory starts with an understanding of the socioeconomic mechanisms in and processes by which non-regular workers are produced, and how employment protection (Rueda, 2005; Emmenegger, 2009) and labour market policies (Rueda, 2006) contribute to the formation of the dual labour market. Emmenegger et al (2012) focus on the dualisation process as the result of the differential application of social policies to insiders and outsiders, represented mainly by regular and non-regular workers. In other words, the dual labour market is deepened further by the existing dual institutional arrangement of the welfare system. Korea has been suggested as one of the typical countries experiencing dualisation of the labour market (Lee S.Y., 2016). The dualisation of the labour market proceeds without dismantling the internal labour market-related system while achieving partial deregulation that modifies existing regulations, resulting in the expansion of non-regular workers (Lee S.Y., 2018). Previous studies have focused on the gap between insiders and outsiders, but few examined how workers move between the two groups. This chapter discussed how insiders slide into the outside labour market and how once workers enter the category of irregular employment, they are likely to continue working in the outside labour market.

Victims of the 2009 SsangYong Motor layoff experienced a sharp decrease in their income immediately after the layoff. Even after six years, those with an annual income lower than 20 million KRW accounted for as much as 70 per cent. In addition, excluding the unemployed, they were drifting from one unstable job to another, such as outsourcing, daily labour and micro-scale self-employment. The proportion of those who worked hard for a bare livelihood or those whose spouses entered the labour market also increased.

Regarding social insurance premiums, a high percentage of national pension and health insurance defaults occurred immediately after the layoff. Additional defaults occurred the following year, showing their economic stability was continuously low or lowered. The reduction in income also immediately led the workers to be excluded from the social protection system. The active labour market policies, such as job search benefits and vocational training, were found to be of little help in aiding these high-skilled workers to re-enter the labour market. Instead, a significant number of respondents answered that they found a job through interpersonal relations with family or acquaintances or that participation in vocational training contributed only to income loss, demonstrating that the effectiveness of unemployment insurance and active labour market policies was very low. The effectiveness of income protection through unemployment insurance and active labour market policies was also low, suggesting that insider workers rapidly slid from their insider status to the level even below the outsider status. In other words, Korea's unemployment insurance and active labour market policies are insufficient to protect the insiders.

The regular workers of SsangYong Motor were initially placed in cell number 2 in Table 1.3, indicating a low level of job insecurity and high level of institutional consistency. However, after losing their jobs and transitioning to irregular employment, they faced inadequate social protection, which hindered their ability to return to stable employment. Many of these workers were forced to move between various forms of precarious work and some even became reliant on public assistance. This highlights the disparity between the current social security system and the reality for insiders who are forced into outsider status in the dual labour market structure in Korea, which is further exacerbated by the existing dual institutional arrangement of the welfare system.

The analysis of Korea's dual labour market has limitations in its focus on the insecurity of outsiders, as the difficulty of re-entering the outsider market for kicked-out insiders highlights the gap between insiders and outsiders. This emphasises the need to examine the role of unemployment insurance policies, including active labour market policies, in resolving dual labour market issues. However, Korea's active labour market policy, which primarily focuses on low and middle general skill training, makes it challenging for a worker to re-enter the insider labour market after being expelled from the high-skilled insider market.

If the gap between insider and outsider stability is significant in the Korean dual labour market and if layoffs mean an immediate slide down to the outsider labour market while the re-employment and income protection functions of the unemployment insurance are not working in this process, then the demand of the laid-off workers for reinstatement may be the only option for them to survive. The victims of the 2009 SsangYong Motor layoffs were not protected through Korea's social protection or the public job training system but by the union's extreme protest repertoire. In general, however, once dismissed and degraded, most labour market insiders cannot regain their insider status in the internal labour market.

Within the dual structure of the Korean labour market, the insecurity of the outsider labour market and the blind spot of the unemployment insurance are serious social issues, and related research is being actively undertaken. However, there are limitations to analysing the outside labour market and discussing the expansion of social protection with the current institutional inconsistency. When regular employees of large companies immediately slide down to the outside labour market, and when there is no active labour market policy to rescue them, the direction of labour market flexibilisation through deregulation on general dismissals will only result in expanding the outside labour market. The easily kicked-out insiders experience the melting forms of labour without adequate social protection, landing the 'former' insiders in a precarious state.

This chapter has emphasised the limitations of analysing only the outside labour market and expanding social protection while ignoring institutional inconsistency. It highlights the necessity for a comprehensive analysis of the intersection between melting labour and institutional protection to enhance our understanding of precarious work. The shift in worker status from traditional employment has led to the dismantling of solid boundaries that once defined standard employment relationships. This has resulted in a malfunction in social protection and an increase in precarity for workers.

4

Same boat, different destiny: subcontracted workers in the Korean shipbuilding industry

'An acquaintance of mine ... fell from a height of some 30 metres and died. But people just wiped the blood out and went back to work. Seeing things like that drives me nuts.' (In-house worker of a sub-subcontractor)

'Profits of employers of subcontracted workers vary depending on how much they save on the four major social insurance premiums and severance pay.' (Tax accountant)

Fissured workplaces and the expansion of subcontracting

This chapter delves into the employment structure of subcontracting within the shipbuilding sector, a practice that has become widespread among conglomerate-led manufacturing industries. The chapter primarily investigates the transformation of the prevalent employment structure involving contractor–subcontractor agreements in the shipbuilding industry, an area dominated by conglomerate manufacturing companies that are part of the so-called Korean insider labour market. It also explores the experiences of subcontracted workers within Korea's social safety net, examining elements such as the employment and wage structures, working patterns, and the relationship between subcontracted workers' labour market experiences and social security. The case study in this chapter aims to bring attention to the employment status of subcontracted workers who are excluded from institutional protections typically afforded to regular employees, thereby highlighting the plight of non-regular and subcontracted workers within the context of a fissured workplace and inconsistent institutional protection policies.

Since the 1970s, traditional Fordism, based on a rigid mass production labour process, has been replaced by flexible scaling of resource inputs. This shift enhances flexibility in terms of geographical change, labour markets, production processes, consumer markets and work process decentralisation, except for core competence areas (Kalleberg et al, 2021). Changes in capital accumulation methods through micro-adjustments have significantly increased workers' employment insecurity.

During the process of subcontracting or outsourcing all work processes, except for a few core competence areas, companies can exert pressure on subcontractors to reduce costs and increase efficiency. Developed countries have pursued capital accumulation by hiring subcontractors from developing countries for cost reduction. Similarly, at the national level, the subcontractor base has expanded, with large companies increasingly outsourcing their production processes, except for core competence areas. In their quest for higher flexibility and lower production costs, contractors outsource various competence areas and parts in the process of mass production of standardised goods. This creates asymmetric relationships between contractors and subcontractors, with the latter compelled to compete for contracts with the former (Kalleberg et al, 2021). Changes in the capital accumulation methods through micro-adjustments have considerably increased workers' employment insecurity. In the process of subcontracting or outsourcing all working processes except a few core competence areas, companies can exert pressure on subcontractors to lower costs and increase efficiency. Developed countries have sought to accumulate capital through cost reduction by hiring subcontractors from developing countries. At the national level as well, the subcontractor base has expanded, with large companies increasingly outsourcing their production processes except for core competence areas. Contractors, in their pursuit of higher flexibility and lower production costs by outsourcing diverse competence areas and parts in the process of mass production of standardised goods, enter into asymmetric relationships with the subcontractors who have to win the contracts with contractors.

Weil introduces the concept of a 'fissured workplace' to explain how changes in the organisational structure of large corporations have driven shifts in the overall employment structure (Weil, 2014). He identifies franchising, third-party management and supply chain systems as representative organisational forms of fissured workplaces. As discussed in Chapter 1, this management revolution refers to new management techniques introduced by companies, which can be summarised as labour market flexibility. Dispersion, geographical movement and scaling-up through labour market flexibility – characterised by outsourcing tasks other than core competencies – have begun to replace Fordism, which is based on mass production systems and standardised employment. The process of companies outsourcing all functions except core competencies exerts pressure to lower costs and increase efficiencies. As a result, all competencies, except for core competencies, are outsourced within the country, leading to an expansion in the number of subcontractors.

A prime contractor seeking flexibility and low unit prices outsources various tasks and projects to subcontractors. The pressure on subcontractors to lower unit prices often forces them to keep the wage level at the very minimum, and workers are exposed to workplace risks and safety threats. These fissured workplaces make it possible for companies to shift the obligations imposed on employers to sub-organisations, such as franchising contracts, third-party management, outsourcing and subcontracting. Shifting these obligations reduces labour costs, social insurance premiums, management costs and corporate welfare costs. The shift also allows companies to avoid the obligation to comply with consistent personnel policies and observe labour standards and the working environment. In a rapidly changing market, workers must work long hours to meet the order delivery deadline. Owners of subcontracting firms are less concerned about investing in facilities to ensure industrial safety in pursuit of capital accumulation. For workers, the marginal utility of market income earned by working an hour is greater than that of an hour invested in safety education. Flexibility in the production process supported by subcontracting and low-volume production requires the flexibility of human resources, which is accompanied by an increase in the number of precarious workers and the minimisation of the number of workers in the core competence areas, even in subcontractors.

Increased flexibility and the asymmetric relationship land workers in precarious conditions. Workers often must work long hours to keep up with contract times. The employer in the subcontracting company is passive in investing in equipment for occupational safety to profit from the fixed contract with the prime contractor. Flexibility in the production process required by the prime contractor also requires flexibility of the workforce in the subcontracting company, which is accompanied by an increase in the number of precarious workers while minimising the number of core workers (mostly standard workers) even in subcontractors. By leveraging atypical and ambiguous employment arrangements ranging from non-regular workers to special hires, freelancers and platform labour, employers can reduce human resources management costs, dismissal costs, skill investment and social insurance costs. In the end, the scope and limits of employment responsibilities become more ambiguous because of the fissured workplace.

This chapter investigates the working conditions and experiences of subcontracted workers within Korea's social protection system by examining the case of the Korean shipbuilding industry. It provides an in-depth analysis of the employment structure, wage structure, working patterns of subcontracted workers, and the relationship between their labour market experiences and social security. By conducting in-depth interviews with 12 individuals, including nine subcontracted shipbuilders, two industry experts and one tax accountant, the chapter exposes the disparities between the subcontracting labour market and institutional protection.

The expansion of subcontracted working in the Korean shipbuilding industry

Korea's shipbuilding labour market has undergone abrupt changes towards an increase in the number of subcontractors in the face of capitalist crises, such as the 1998 Asian financial crisis and the 2008 global financial crisis. This contractor–subcontractor relationship has continued to ramify with the trend of engaging 'supply teams' (*Mullyang* team in Korean; a workforce group consisting of skilled workers working on task orders to complete specific work processes within a narrow time window) that perform the same work under different contracts. Regular workers in a contractor are mostly responsible for various supporting tasks to be performed as the basis rather the actual production activities. In the shipbuilding industry, for example, 80 per cent of the workers engaged in the large-block assembly process are subcontracted workers, with a small number of workers directly hired by the contractor to supervise the assembly process.

In Korea, the size of contractors and subcontractors varies across different business sectors. In the manufacturing industry, contractors increasingly hire fewer workers while subcontractors employ more. According to a survey on the employment status at the contractor and subcontractor levels based on the contractor–subcontractor network and employment insurance administrative data (as of 2014), the industry with the highest subcontracting ratio relative to the total insurance subscribers was the shipbuilding industry (84.3 per cent), followed by the primary metal production industry (82.3 per cent), power plants (82.2 per cent), machinery (81.6 per cent) and the automobile industry (80.6 per cent). The manufacturing industry has the highest subcontracting levels. Even within the manufacturing industry, subcontracting varies among industrial sectors. For example, the survey results mentioned show that while the outsourcing ratio decreased in the electronic and electrical industries during the period from 2008 to 2014, it increased in the shipbuilding, automobile, electric power and telecommunications industries. Regarding changes in employment among the contractors and subcontractors of the automobile, shipbuilding and telecommunication industries due to economic fluctuations, the number of insured workers has decreased or stagnated among primary contractors since 2008, while that among subcontractors has rapidly increased (Lee S.G., 2015).

Currently, there is no direct statistical data available to estimate the extent of subcontracting. However, it can be indirectly estimated using the statistics regarding indirect employment from the results of the National Survey of the Economically Active Population conducted by Statistics Korea, which includes information on subcontracted workers. Indirect employment is a form of employment in which a company temporarily utilises necessary workers from other companies without entering into contracts with the workers themselves. Legal forms of indirect employment encompass workforce supply, dispatch, subcontracting and delegation. In workplace settings, indirect employment includes outsourcing, dispatch, private consignment, in-house subcontracting, sub-subcontracting and company spin-off (see Table 4.1).

Table 4.1: Frequency (n) and ratio (%) of indirect employment and other employments in time series (2001–2017)

Category	2001		2005		2010		2017	
	F	%	F	%	F	%	F	%
Regular employment	5,851	44.3	6,564	43.9	8,455	49.6	11,456	57.6
Temporary employment	7,366	55.7	8,404	56.1	8,592	50.4	8,427	42.4
Fixed-term employment	7,077	53.5	8,234	55.0	8,424	49.4	8,035	40.4
Long-term temp. employment	4,901	37.1	4,431	29.6	5,023	29.5	4,527	22.8
Fixed-time employment	2,176	16.5	3,802	25.4	3,401 (2,495)	20.0 (14.6)	3,509 (2,925)	17.6 (14.7)
Hourly wage employment	873	6.6	1,044	7.0	1,620	9.5	2,659	13.4
On-demand employment	305	2.3	717	4.8	870	5.1	792	4.0
Special employment	789	6.0	633	4.2	590	3.5	493	2.5
Dispatched employment	130	1.0	117	0.8	210	1.2	186	0.9
Temp. work agency empl.	319	2.4	430	2.9	608	3.6	688	3.5
Home-based employment	258	2.0	140	0.9	70	0.4	30	0.2

Note: * Dispatched employment and temporary work agency employment represent indirect employment.
Source: National Survey of the Economically Active Population (Statistics Korea, 2018)

The size of indirect employment can be estimated through the aforementioned National Survey of the Economically Active Population. According to the survey, the number of dispatched workers has been continuously increasing since 2001, the first year of the survey, from 450,000 in 2001 to 870,000 in 2017. This increase reflects the trend of cost reduction based on flexible production processes and workforce input (Cho D.M. et al, 2018).

The rapid propagation of indirect employment and subcontracting is attributable to the Act on the Protection of Dispatched Workers (hereafter the 'Dispatched Work Act') enacted in the wake of the 1997 Asian financial crisis. Before the enactment of the Dispatched Work Act, the Labour Standards Act prohibited indirect employment and made only direct employment legitimate. However, Article 22 of the Dispatched Work Act stipulated that worker dispatch is a system in which a dispatching company sends its employees to another company to work under the instructions and order of the latter, indirect employment in cases recognise knowledge and skills or temporary hiring.

The Act on the Protection of Fixed-term and Part-time Employees (hereafter 'Non-standard Worker Protection Act'), which came into effect in 2007, also contributed to the increasing proportion of dispatched and outsourced workers. The Non-standard Worker Protection Act is an overarching notion that includes the Act on the Protection of Fixed-term and Part-time Workers, the Act on the Protection of Dispatched Workers and the Labour Commission Act. Under this Act, the employment contract period was limited to two years for fixed-term workers, as was the dispatch period. An employer has the obligation to hire dispatched workers when the dispatch period of two years is exceeded (Eom E.H., 2007). Additionally, a new provision prohibiting discriminatory treatment of fixed-term, part-time and dispatched workers without reasonable grounds was introduced, and the government's regulations on non-standard workers were strengthened. In response to these legislative changes related to non-standard workers and the reinforcement of labour supervision, companies have increasingly utilised subcontracting to circumvent legal and institutional regulations such as the Non-standard Worker Protection Act.

Discussions about the expansion and precarity of subcontractors have spread across the country. Park J.S. (2014) conducted an in-depth analysis of the situation of in-house subcontractors who were paid less than the workers hired by the contractor while performing more labour-intensive and riskier work in the same workplace. This situation is attributable to the emergence of a peculiar employment arrangement called 'in-house subcontracting', which disproportionately exposes in-house subcontractors to job risks and lower pay. Park explained that the practice of in-house subcontracting expanded under the tacit collusion between regular workers who needed employment stability and companies that needed cheap labour after the financial crisis. Park also compared the difference in accident rates between workers with regular contracts and in-house subcontracting (Park J.S., 2014). Kim Y.J. (2004) examined industrial accidents in the top nine shipbuilders in Korea and revealed the increasing industrial accident death rate among in-house subcontractors, noting that they are increasingly exposed to job risks. Kim also found that the incidence of industrial injuries and diseases among subcontracted workers is much higher than among regular workers, but only a small percentage of affected subcontractors benefit from industrial insurance (Kim Y.J., 2004).

While existing research on the disparity between the situation of precarious workers and the social safety net has primarily focused on non-standard workers in the low-wage outsider labour market of the service industry (Olasunmbo Ayanfeoluwa, 2018; Prenovitz, 2021), this chapter concentrates on the changes in the predominant employment structure of contractor–subcontractor contractual arrangements in the shipbuilding industry. This industry, dominated by conglomerate manufacturing companies, is considered part of the so-called Korean insider labour market.

The shipbuilding industry is a labour-intensive, order-based manufacturing industry that typically relies on direct workforce input. It is difficult to automate the production process, and at the same time, the industry requires heavy-duty facilities and economies of scale. Korea's shipbuilding industry is the largest in the world. According to a report by Clarksons Research (as cited by the Ministry of Trade, Industry, and Energy), a British shipbuilding and shipping analysis institute, Korean shipbuilders won the most shipbuilding orders worldwide in 2020.

High value-added ships, such as large container ships, ships that transport liquefied natural gas (LNG) and offshore plants greatly contributed to this achievement of the Korean shipbuilding industry. In 2021, out of the global orders of high value-added ships totalling 11.89 million compensated gross tonnage. Korean shipbuilders received orders amounting to 7.23 million compensated gross tonnage (61 per cent): 21 out of 21 LNG carriers (100 per cent), 6 out of 6 Very Large Crude Carriers (100 per cent), and 10 out of 16 large container ships (62.5 per cent) (Ministry of Trade Industry and Energy, 2021). In tandem with receiving the largest share of the world's ship orders in recent years, Korean shipbuilders have increased employment, mostly through indirect employment (see Table 4.2).

Korean shipbuilders' increasing use of subcontracted workers since the 2000s has made subcontracting a general practice. As of the end of March 2016, the number of in-house subcontracted workers in the Big Three shipbuilders amounted to 95,000, that is, 3.5 subcontracted workers per production worker with a regular contract. In 2014, the wage level of second-year subcontracted workers was 73.8 per cent of that of their

Table 4.2: Order status in the first half (H1) from 2019 to 2021 (7.5 person-hours/day)

Category		H1 2019	H1 2020	H1 2021
Global	Number of orders	14.76	8.68	24.52
Global	Amount	3.74	1.84	5.49
Domestic (Korea/world)	Number of orders	3.85 (26%)	1.32 (15%)	1,88 (44%)
Domestic (Korea/world)	Amount	0.93 (25%)	0.34 (18%)	2.67 (49%)

Note: Unit: million compensated gross tonnage, billion KRW

Source: Ministry of Trade, Industry and Energy, Rep. Korea (2021)

counterparts with regular contracts (1,404,000 versus 1,180,000 KRW). In terms of employment duration, the mean number of service years is 16 years, one month for regular workers and 2.4 months for subcontracted workers (Heo H.J., 2016). In other words, subcontracted workers have unstable jobs with lower wages and shorter employment duration compared with regular workers. In-house subcontracting itself gradually expands to sub–subcontractors and even sub–sub-contractors (supply teams) in a pyramid structure. Supply team members are hired by in-house subcontractors to meet deadlines, reduce production cost and conduct specialised work processes.

In the Korean shipbuilding industry, while employment by contractors has increased by 4.5 per cent since 2010, employment by subcontractors has increased by 15.8 per cent, much higher in the latter compared with the former in a situation with high economic uncertainty. This suggests that they opted for enhancing the utility of subcontracting arrangements as an employment strategy to cope with the economic downturn (Lee S.G., 2015). As a result, 81 per cent of the sample population of workers in the shipbuilding industry are subcontracted workers (Ahn J.Y., 2015).

A qualitative analysis on the precarity of subcontracted workers

This section presents the results of an in-depth interview analysis focusing on subcontracted workers in the Korean shipbuilding industry, an area dominated by conglomerate-led manufacturing companies. By examining the employment structure of subcontracting and its impact on workers in the industry, we reveal the disparity between the subcontracting labour market and the social safety net. We analysed the experiences of subcontracted workers with the social safety net through interviews with 12 stakeholders: nine subcontracted shipbuilders; two experts familiar with the subcontracting employment structure in the shipbuilding industry; and one tax accountant responsible for the taxation of subcontractors in the shipbuilding industry in Ulsan (refer to Chapter 1 for details on the research method used). Our analysis also highlights the changes in the predominant contractor–subcontractor contractual arrangements and the increasing trend of indirect employment in the industry.[1]

The pyramidal employment structure and precarious working conditions

The employment arrangement in Korean shipbuilders is characterised by a pyramid subcontracting structure, typically composed of the contractor's shipyard → primary subcontractor → supply team leader → supply team members. According to the 2014 Hyundai Heavy Industries Comprehensive Safety and Health Diagnosis Report by the Korea Occupational Safety and Health Agency, all 296 primary subcontractors registered with Hyundai Heavy Industries operated supply teams (Korea Occupational Safety and Health Agency, 2017). In this arrangement, about 300 subcontractors (subcontracting companies) work under one contractor, and these in-house subcontractors hire supply teams through sub-subcontracting.

A supply team is a group of workers subcontracted by in-house subcontractors to perform a specific work process, focusing on quick delivery to the subcontractor. Work orders are given to supply team leaders, who each operate a supply team of 10 to 30 workers. In this employment structure, subcontractor workers and supply team members experience unstable employment, often becoming the first victims of restructuring-related layoffs. Subcontractors also establish short-term contracts with the contractor, which are subject to evaluation-based renewal, potentially jeopardised by any failure to deliver on orders received from the contractor.

Figure 4.1 illustrates the pyramid subcontracting and employment structure of Hyundai Heavy Industries and Hyundai Mipo Dockyard, large shipyards located in Ulsan. First, there are nearly 300 in-house subcontractors sharing the same building with Hyundai Heavy Industries. In-house subcontractors employ both regular and temporary workers directly, known as 'in-house workers', and supply team workers through sub-subcontracting, referred to as 'sub-subcontractors'. Various types of supply teams, comprising 10 to 30 members working on specific tasks, operate under formal subcontracting arrangements (see Figure 4.1).

> 'There are several hundred "leaders" of the supply teams at Hyundai Heavy Industries. It is no exaggeration to say that the entire company consists of supply teams. Only a small number of people, say, 10 to 15, are hired directed from the company. Inspecting team and managers are in-house workers.' (Subcontracted worker, male, age 45, shipping working experience 10+ years)

Figure 4.1: Pyramid subcontracting employment structure in the shipbuilding industry

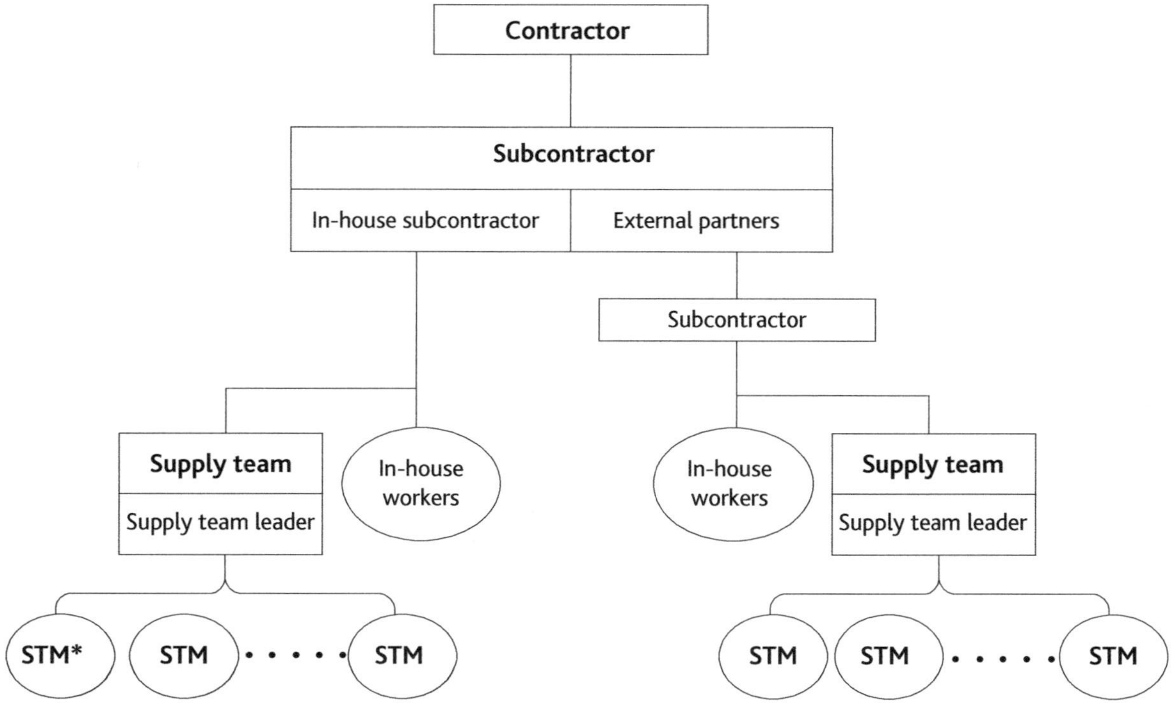

Note: * STM = supply team member

In addition to in-house subcontracting, there is also external subcontracting (see Figure 4.1). These external subcontractors are referred to as 'suppliers' to distinguish them from in-house subcontractors. They are companies responsible for producing small and large blocks in batches. Although labelled as 'partners' as external suppliers, they are effectively subcontractors since their operation relies on orders received from the contractor.

All regular employees of primary partners hold managerial positions, while most of the on-site workers are subcontracted workers. Consequently, under the external partners, another type of subcontractor operates their supply teams, employed for a wide range of production activities. This arrangement also forms a pyramid subcontracting structure, similar to that of in-house subcontractors.

In the shipbuilding industry's subcontracting labour market, the most prominent employment type is supply teams. A supply team mainly consists of members and a team leader who possesses high-level skills and familiarity with contract arrangements. Study participants described it as 'subcontracting of subcontracting'. Although supply teams initially emerged as 'working units formed ad hoc to work on urgent or large-quantity supply parts within an in-house subcontractor', this employment type is now used in diverse and widely branched forms. In other words, while some teams still work on short-term urgent supply orders received from different companies, a large proportion of supply teams work in one company for three to four years, continuously supplying ordered parts in the same manner as in-house workers.

Subcontracting is a non-standard employment pattern. Generally, subcontractors work through the night and the following day when there are many work processes with tight deadlines, but they must take unpaid breaks if their work parts are not scheduled. Consequently, they calculate their monthly pay in units of person-hours, applying one person-hour for work done during regular hours (8am to 6pm) and 1.5 person-hours for work done outside these hours. Interviewees reported working 20 to 25 person-hours per month. However, they generally agreed that estimating an average monthly wage is difficult, given the widely varying work hours and patterns among supply teams. The concept of weekends is also absent, as they 'work if there is work and do not work if there is no work'.

The labour intensity for supply teams (sub-subcontractors) is higher than that for in-house workers, as they are mainly assigned the more difficult initial tasks, while in-house workers complete the remaining work. This work allocation scheme contributes to the increased labour intensity experienced by supply teams. The current structure, characterised by escalating labour intensity and industrial accidents within the pyramid subcontracting system comprised of contractors, subcontractors and supply teams, can be described as 'risk outsourcing'.

In fact, numerous interviewees reported that they regularly visit hospitals to address various issues such as joint pain or resort to consuming alcohol before sleeping each night to manage the discomfort. Additionally, safety inspections are often overlooked due to the need for rapid completion of tasks under tight schedules. Consequently, the rights of subcontractors to work in healthy and safe conditions are not guaranteed in reality.

'[Referring to labour intensity] Supply teams do the hardest work. We have to be quick, too. Here, we don't need to hear "Hurry up" because we have no choice but to work fast. We don't have time to do a safety check. Work has to be done quickly, no matter what.' (Subcontracted worker, male, age 45, shipping working experience 10+ years)

'[On industrial accidents] Outsourcing of risk is worse for workers hired by subcontractors compared with those directly hired by the contractor. Subcontracted workers have to work faster. Even harder and more urgent work is done by supply teams. The structure itself is prone to accidents.' (Civic group activist, female, age 49)

The majority of in-house workers have employment contracts, with most reporting that their contracts are renewed annually. However, some are employed on a 2.5-month or six-month contract basis, revealing disparities among in-house workers. Furthermore, even if an employment contract is in place, the process typically does not involve discussions or negotiations between the employer and worker.

On the other hand, while the leader of a supply team usually enters into a subcontracting contract with a subcontractor, team members are mostly hired without contracts. Recently, there have been cases where the supply team leader registers as a business entity and enters into individual contracts with the team members. However, most of the supply team members reported that they had no employment contract. They explained that the current employment structure, in which supply team members can be jobless tomorrow if they don't receive any work order from a subcontractor today, makes the notion of contract duration or long service meaningless. In this employment structure, there are cases where the supply team leader disappears with the wages for the supplied person-hours of the team, leaving the team members unpaid.

The wage level differs according to the level of skills required for each work process. For jobs requiring highly skilled workers, such as welding, fitting and plumbing, wages are higher than for jobs that can be done by assistant workers or migrant workers with basic training, such as painting and grinding. By employment type, supply team members usually have a higher wage level for working faster and more intensively than in-house workers and wage differences exist even within a supply team depending on the skill level. For example, a highly skilled worker receives 150,000 KRW per hour, a moderately skilled worker 120,000 to 130,000 KRW and a less skilled worker 100,000 KRW. On the other hand, the pyramid top-down structure of contractor, subcontractor, supply team leader and supply team member carries an inherent risk of exploitation at different levels. For example, in the structure where it is difficult for the team members to know the details (amount of money received for the team) of the contract signed between team leader and subcontractor, the wages of the supply team members can be set arbitrarily by the team leader. In fact, unlike in-house workers, supply team members were found to receive no pay stub in many cases.

The pyramid structure of the shipbuilding labour market inherently leads to unstable employment for subcontracted workers. Contractors renew contracts with subcontractors on a monthly basis, allowing them to adjust the volume of orders according to the subcontractors' performance level. This employment structure enables a contractor to arbitrarily 'dispose of' a subcontractor or supply team workers by choosing not to renew the contract, which further contributes to the structural instability and the precarious nature of subcontractors' employment.

In this insecure employment environment created by the subcontracting structure, abrupt closures are a common occurrence in the shipbuilding labour market, negatively impacting the overall employment stability of subcontractors. All interviewees pointed out the routine closure of subcontractors as a pervasive issue. Although business downturns are cited as the reason for closures, many of these subcontractors often continue to operate under a new company name. Consequently, a significant proportion of workers experience wage arrears and severance pay issues.

'The problem of a subcontractors is that they don't know when they become insolvent. For example, we have worked today. Then, after a week of no work, a rumour goes that they would close down, and we have no jobs. Just like that. There is a rule on posting a notice within 15 days, but that never happens.' (In-house worker of a sub-subcontractor, male, age 53, shipping working experience 29 years)

'[Experience of overdue wages] Most of us have it. Our team was victimised once. We worked on blocks, and after delaying the pay for a while, it went bankrupt. There was no way to get paid.' (Supply team member, male, age 45, shipping working experience 8 years)

Supply teams are especially vulnerable to employment insecurity due to the intense competition to win subcontractor orders. Failure to gain recognition and demonstrate strong team performance can result in immediate replacement by another team. In this competitive environment, good teamwork is crucial for success, and underperforming team members can be quickly expelled.

Interviewees commonly stated that supply teams are most affected by employment insecurity since they are the first to lose jobs when a subcontractor considers personnel reduction. It was also noted that while in-house workers may appear to have higher employment stability, their employment insecurity is greater compared to regular workers of the contractor, as they too can be dismissed through contract termination.

'Supply teams are necessary for quick work for tight deadlines. Once such work is done, they are no longer needed. They are then fired without much ado.' (In-house worker of a sub-subcontractor, male, age 53, shipping working experience 29 years)

'In our company, there were some in-house workers. One day, out of the blue, the boss said that he would get rid of in-house workers and operate only supply teams. Then we had three less in-house workers and three more supply team members. Such things just happen depending on how the boss thinks.' (Supply team leader, male, 40s, shipping working experience 15 years)

Subcontracted workers' experiences of social protection and training

Regarding the four major social insurances – national pension, unemployment insurance, industrial accident compensation and national health insurance – interviewees were generally either not insured or unsure of their coverage. Even when insured, their trust in the system's effectiveness was low due to their 'repeatedly in and out of the insurance scheme' status and the low amount of social security benefits.

When faced with job loss, interviewees prioritised finding another subcontractor over claiming unemployment benefits, especially because they were 'pressed for money at that moment' or needed to continue earning income. Unemployment benefits were indeed low, and they had to keep working to support their families instead of going through a complicated application procedure and proving job-seeking activities to receive benefits.

In terms of preparing for retirement, they exhibited a high reliance on immediate market income by 'working throughout their lives' or at least 'making plans to work as long as possible'.

'I don't think I know any supply team workers who received unemployment benefits. We seldom come across such supply team workers. They try to join another supply team. It's a routine practice for 98 to 99 per cent of supply team workers.' (In-house worker of a subcontractor, male, age 42, shipping working experience 11 years)

'Unemployment benefits are not enough for living ... a fixed amount of 30,000 or 40,000 won per day. Apart from that, you have to prove that you are seeking a job twice or three times a week. ... But we are jobless just because the company has shut down. ... It's as if to say we should not receive unemployment benefits.' (In-house worker of a sub-subcontractor, male, age 53, shipping working experience 29 years)

As explained previously, the wage is calculated by dividing the work delivered by person-hours. The subcontractor pays what is left after deducting a certain amount for insurance premiums and income taxes. Subcontracted workers believe that their social insurance premiums are paid along with income taxes because they are deducted from their wages. Still, then they get a notice of default and find out that the subcontractor has not paid them. Since there is no pay stub, it is difficult to accurately check how much is paid as contributions and income taxes and whether the payees are insured or not.

'[Referring to the four major social insurance schemes] Supply team workers don't have them. Only the income tax on one million won is deducted, and the leader keeps his share and distributes the rest among the members according to their man-hours. Almost all supply team workers are not insured.' (Subcontracted worker, male, age 45, shipping working experience 10+ years)

'The boss just does it his way without any separate notice. It seemed that health insurance, industrial accident insurance and unemployment insurance were being paid. Then I got an NOD [notice of default] that seven months' national pension was not paid.' (Supply team leader, male, 40s, shipping working experience 15 years).

Regarding the four major insurances, most interviewees emphasised the necessity of industrial accident insurance and the system's low effectiveness. According to a fact-finding survey among 51 contractors in high-risk industries, where contractor–subcontractor employment arrangements are prevalent, a contractor's industrial accident fatality rate is four times higher when subcontractors are included (Korea Occupational Safety and Health Agency, 2017). Interestingly, however, the accident rate decreases when subcontractors are included. This suggests that the industrial accident fatality rate is disproportionately high among subcontractors, but the overall accident rate is lower. This could indicate that subcontracted workers are primarily responsible for high-risk, even life-threatening work, but non-fatal industrial accidents are handled quietly and informally without proper reporting.

During the interviews, it was evident that although industrial accident insurance is the most needed insurance, subcontracted workers had limited experience with the scheme. In most cases, incidents were privately resolved or compensated without reporting to the authorities.

'When I asked supply team workers, the need for industrial insurance coverage was mentioned most frequently. I think 94 per cent or so. … Supply team workers are prone to injury … because a healthy body is a critical asset of supply team workers, one injury is really fatal for the worker. And I could read in their answer their desperate need for industrial accident insurance to get paid and treated when injured.' (Civic group activist, female, age 49)

'When I was working in the supply team, I never had industrial accident insurance coverage. … During the ten years of working in the supply team, I was injured several times. Because of a dislocation, I stayed home for 20 days and was paid 70 per cent of the hourly wage of 9,000 won. So, I received 1.2 million won a month. [Interviewer: Where did that money come from?] From the company. With private health insurance. … Just saying that I fell down on the ground while walking, without disclosing the company. … It's like that in most cases.' (Supply team leader, male, 40s, shipping working experience 15 years)

The employment maintenance subsidy, intended to support workers, may not have the desired effect on employers. Additional costs are imposed on the employer, and such government support lacks incentive for employers who have no reason to maintain employment under these added expenses. This is because dismissing employees or not renewing contracts does not entail any significant costs for them.

Similarly, for subcontracted workers, their high dependence on market income influences their choices. They often prefer to move on to another subcontractor to enhance income stability rather than staying for 1–3 months in a company that may soon shut down. Consequently, the employment maintenance subsidy may not effectively serve its intended purpose for either employers or subcontracted workers in the current system.

Vocational training and job search services are not adequately tailored to the skill formation, job search methods and income levels of subcontracted workers in the shipbuilding industry. These workers possess specialised skills and have used them for an extended period, making it difficult for them to freely move between occupations. Consequently, job search services may not be effective without consultation from experts knowledgeable in shipbuilding and related industries. Furthermore, short-term vocational training by non-professionals is not suitable, as on-the-job training is the primary method of skill development in this industry, where industry-specific skills are crucial.

The interviewed workers received training informally in the workplace, emphasising that skill acquisition in the shipbuilding industry occurs on-site through learning from experienced colleagues over a relatively long period of two to three years or more. This informal path of learning takes place at subcontractors, regardless of the entry route. Workers typically begin as assistant workers, performing tasks that do not require specialised skills, and learn by observing experienced workers for one to three years. Only after mastering the necessary skills can they join a supply team, where the motto 'time is money' prevails.

Entry into a supply team primarily occurs through personal networking, and years of experience as an assistant and in-house worker are typically required before transitioning into a supply team. Current vocational training and job search services do not adequately address the unique aspects of skill formation and employment within the shipbuilding industry.

> 'In vocational training centres, skills are taught in a small-scale setting with the necessary tools. However, learning in such an environment is not helpful at all. The skills acquired in this manner cannot be effectively applied in the workplace. It is better to bypass this type of training and learn directly in real work settings. So people who go to subcontractors without attending vocational training can learn the fastest through hands-on experience.' (Supply team member, male, age 46, shipping work experience 21 years)

As analysed here, subcontractors are structurally unstable in a subcontracting relationship, and sudden closures are common occurrences in the shipbuilding industry. Frequent closures and employment insecurity also influence subcontracted workers' decision-making and preferences related to social insurance. In an employment environment where there is an underlying fear of wage arrears due to frequent closures, workers have little trust in receiving social insurance benefits for which premiums are deducted from their wages. Furthermore, they are not adequately informed about the procedure to apply for unemployment benefits when they lose their jobs due to unexpected closures. It is even more challenging to request cooperation from companies. In such consistently unstable employment relationships, workers prioritise securing as much income as possible over having insurance premiums deducted from their wages for future insurance benefits. Specifically, workers who have experienced a fraudulent subcontractor employer defaulting on social insurance contribution payments after deducting them from wages trust employers even less. They often say, 'I never believe it when they say I will benefit from welfare later if I pay premiums now.' Consequently, they tend not to prefer having their income reduced to pay social insurance premiums.

'As for me, it was really hard to find this job. ... Employers who close their businesses do not post a notice 15 days in advance. They just don't do that kind of thing. They suddenly go out of business and disappear within a day or two without paying their workers. Then the workers do not even know how to apply for unemployment benefits. ... They really don't know anything like that. More than 90 per cent have no information at all.' (In-house worker of a sub-subcontractor, male, age 53, shipping working experience 29 years)

In addition, it is difficult to actively apply for industrial accident benefits even after experiencing an industrial accident for fear that the company may be disadvantaged or that fellow team members, including the affected, may lose their jobs. Moreover, in the shipbuilding industry, manual labour is also as important as skills, and a record of industrial accident compensation can adversely affect employment.

'They didn't want it treated as an industrial accident, saying that it would hit the company badly. ... As for me, I almost died. Glass dust got into my eyes, and I groped my way down the stairs, smeared with blood all over. All I was told was that [at that time, 2001] a subcontractor involved in an industrial accident is shunned by contractors. I was even threatened that I would be no longer able to work in shipyard if I report an industrial accident.' (Supply team member, male, age 46, shipping working experience 21 years)

For subcontracted workers, receiving additional occupational safety education after recognising an industrial accident poses a significant burden in their work environment. Their survival is threatened if they cannot complete the assigned work on time. In situations where labour intensity is already high, the time required for taking safety education within working hours acts as a deterrent for subcontracted workers to actively claim industrial accident insurance benefits.

The primary cause of exclusion from social insurance for subcontracted workers can be traced to the asymmetric contractual relationship between contractors and subcontractors. As evidenced by statements like 'The contractor decides the survival of subcontractors' and 'If the contractor wants a subcontractor to leave, there is a long list of subcontractors to replace it', numerous subcontractors strive to maintain or secure contracts with the contractor. Subcontractors enter into contracts to supply the allocated work within a specified time frame. In other words, when a contractor and a subcontractor sign a contract for work worth 100 million KRW, the contractor pays 110 million KRW to the subcontractor, who then retains the remainder as profit after covering wages and management fees. In this contractual structure, profit is generated by reducing the share of wages and insurance costs from the contract amount established at the time of signing the contract.

> 'From the perspective of subcontractors, given the current practice, the big axis is the same as long as the excess profits can depend on how they manage the four social insurance systems. With other factors such as business operation, marketing and service quality not making great differences, because the quality of work delivered does not vary much among supply teams, the difference in profit can be made from HR management alone.' (Tax accountant, male, age 43)

As a result, if subcontracted workers are registered as part-time workers working less than 15 hours a week, which is the threshold for exemption from the obligation to enrol in the four major insurances, these workers are not insured in the national pension and health insurance schemes. Even when they are insured under the four major social insurances, insurance premiums may be in arrears. Subcontractors often close their businesses within a year of starting work to avoid the obligation to pay severance to workers and overdue social insurance premiums.

For employers and subcontracted workers, the total burden of the four major insurances accounts for 18 per cent of income, broken down into 9 per cent for pension, approximately 6 per cent for health insurance (6.10–6.12 per cent), and around 3 per cent for industrial accident insurance and unemployment insurance. Of the 18 per cent insurance premiums, the employer pays 10 per cent, calculated by adding half of the pension and health insurances, industrial accident insurance, and two-thirds of the unemployment insurance as the employer's contribution to the four major social insurances.

However, since the employer's profit is not made by expanding sales but by retaining the remaining amount of the total contract after paying wages and insurance premiums, subcontractor employers may be tempted to report work hours not exceeding 15 hours per week to avoid paying the insurance premiums. "Profits of employers of subcontracted workers vary depending on how much they save on the four major social insurance premiums and severance pay" (Tax accountant, male, age 43).

Another reason for this illegal practice is the absence of coercive and punitive clauses when employers fail to pay social insurance premiums. When a company closes down, subcontracted workers lose wages, severance pay and overdue social insurance premiums. However, in a structure where subcontractors can make profits by cutting labour costs and social insurance premiums, employers of subcontracted workers explore all possible methods to reduce costs as much as they can.

Inconsistencies in social protection and subcontracted workers' precarity

This chapter examines the inconsistencies between existing institutional protection policies and new forms of work that arise from fissured workplaces, which result in various precarious work situations. The focus is on wage workers excluded from institutional protection, such as non-regular and subcontracted workers.

Fissured workplaces, characterised by the expansion of subcontracting, enable companies to shift employer obligations to sub-organisations. This shift reduces labour costs and social insurance premiums, and allows companies to avoid investing in safe working environments. Subcontracted workers in the Ulsan shipbuilding industry experience lower labour standards and a lack of institutional consistency. The employment structure in Ulsan's shipbuilding industry is based on a pyramid subcontracting system consisting of contractors > in-house/external subcontractors > supply teams (sub-subcontractors). In addition to in-house workers directly employed by a subcontractor, there are supply teams, or sub-subcontractors, working under subcontracting arrangements with a subcontractor. Thus, the shipbuilding labour market has shifted towards increasing indirect employment during times of crisis, such as restructuring, with continuing ramifications evidenced by the prevalent subcontracting arrangements between contractors and subcontractors and the growth of supply teams.

The investigation of subcontractors' working conditions revealed several key findings. First, subcontractors experience irregular working patterns that range from working through the night to meet deadlines to not working for extended periods without any earnings. These working patterns and hours deviate from the traditional concept of work or job in each occupation. Regarding labour intensity, the lower the hierarchy in the pyramid subcontracting structure of contractor–subcontractor–supply team, the harder the work with the increasing rate and severity of industrial accidents. Institutional inadequacy results in health risks for workers in various ways.

Second, as regards employment contracts, since supply teams work on a subcontracting basis, no renewal of contract means out of work, and concepts such as the employment contract or continuous service were found to be meaningless. Third, regarding employment insecurity, the pyramid subcontracting structure fundamentally destabilises subcontractors' employment. Because of the short contract period between contractor and subcontractor, the employment of subcontracted workers is inherently unstable, and business closures are routine events.

Melting labour, which refers to the increasing ambiguity of the boundaries, is revealed in terms of working hours, employment relationship, workplace and income irregularity. These all contribute to the precarity of workers as the social protection and legal systems that ought to protect workers are found to be not functioning.

The experiences and perceptions of subcontracted workers regarding the social safety net reveal several issues. Most interviewees were not insured, and some were even unaware of their social insurance status. Their records related to social insurance were also irregular. With such uncertainty and low benefits, their trust in the effectiveness of the social insurance system was very low.

A key factor in the avoidance of social insurance by subcontracted workers is their preference for securing as much immediate pay as possible, rather than paying a portion of it as insurance premiums for future benefits. This preference stems from their low trust in receiving actual benefits, especially considering the high risk of wage arrears due to frequent closures of subcontractors.

The exclusion of subcontracted workers from social insurance due to employers avoiding their share of contributions can be traced back to the asymmetric subcontracting relationship between contractors and subcontractors. Subcontractor employers are more likely to avoid the burden of premiums for the four major social insurances, as their profits are primarily made by reducing labour costs and insurance premiums within the fixed contract price. Additionally, the absence of any penalty clause for employers defaulting on social insurance premiums encourages them to consider arrears through business closure.

Subcontractors inherently rely on the contractor in pyramid subcontracting structures. In this context, subcontracting companies can only make profits by reducing labour costs and social insurance premiums while supplying the agreed-upon quantity. There are no regulations on contract periods between contractors, subcontractors and sub-subcontractors (supply teams), nor are there any punitive measures for non-payment of social insurance premiums or severance pay. The pyramid structure of the shipbuilding labour market results in unstable employment for subcontracted workers, with contractors adjusting orders and potentially 'disposing of' subcontractors or supply team workers by not renewing contracts. This instability leads to frequent, sudden closures in the shipbuilding labour market, negatively impacting subcontractors' overall employment stability. Interviewees identified routine closures as a significant issue, with subcontractors often reopening under new names and workers facing wage arrears and severance pay problems.

The process of companies outsourcing all but core competencies has expanded the scope of the production process geographically to a global chain and also outsourced within Korea. The number of subcontractors increases, and in the competition for survival among them, the working environment and wage level of subcontracted workers are inevitably kept at the lowest level. These workers are excluded from social insurance, and the social safety net fails to protect them. Subcontracted workers are also highly dependent on immediate market income due to constant employment insecurity, which puts them in a weak position for negotiation regarding social insurances and improved employment arrangements. The investigation conducted in this chapter regarding subcontracted workers and their experiences with social insurance highlights the current discrepancy between the subcontracting arrangement between contractors and subcontractors, which is spreading throughout the shipbuilding industry and other manufacturing sectors, and the inconsistency of social protection, resulting in the precarity of subcontracted workers.

Young and old outsourced female workers in call centres and cleaning services

'I slipped and broke my bones while working on the stairs. I received medical expenses privately, but my subcontractor came and asked me to sign a statement agreeing that they could not give Industrial Accident Compensation Insurance benefits.' (Apartment cleaning worker, age 76)

The gender gap in the Korean female labour market

This chapter examines the rise of precarious jobs through outsourcing in the service economy, particularly affecting young and old female workers. The chapter sheds light on the inconsistencies between institutions for decommodification and melting labour, leading to an expansion of female precarious workers in the Korean labour market. The problems faced by these newly emerging forms of work overlap with those of non-regular workers, and it is necessary to comprehensively examine both types of issues. Through empirical data and interviews with 23 workers and union leaders, the chapter highlights the gender gap in the Korean labour market, focusing on young female call centre workers and examining the issues of institutional protection and job instability surrounding older and younger female subcontracted labour in call centres and cleaning services. The chapter underscores how outsourcing has become more accessible due to technological development and offers insights into the unique challenges faced by female workers in precarious forms of work.

The Korean female labour market is characterised by a high concentration of females in irregular employment and a wide wage gap. Despite the fact that more than 82.8 per cent of Korean women have tertiary education degrees as of 2020, the wage gap between genders in Korea is still high, at 33 per cent, which is significantly higher than in the US (19 per cent), the UK (13 per cent) and Germany (3 per cent) (Jung E.H., 2015). Lee S.Y. and Kim Y.H. (2020) also pointed out the barriers to gender pay equality presented by the South Korean gendered dual labour market structure, particularly the gendered division between regular and irregular work. While there has been some progress in recent years, with the ratio of female to total male earnings increasing from 58 per cent in 2006 to 64 per cent in 2018, this progress has been limited given the narrow and decreasing educational attainment gap between men and women and the introduction of legislative measures to address gender discrimination in the labour market. Additionally, the overall female employment rate remains relatively low at 57 per cent in 2018, with the steepest dip in female labour market engagement during family formation phases of the life course (Lee S.Y. and Kim Y.H., 2020). The participation of Korean women in economic activities began at 46.3 per cent in 1980 and has consistently increased since then, with a sharp decline during the economic crisis of the late 1990s and the stagnation of the economic crisis in 2008, reaching 52.8 per cent in 2020, which is still more than 20 per cent lower than that of men. The married female workforce emerged as a new workforce after the 1980s due to the lack of low-wage unmarried females (Kim M.S., 2006). The economic activity participation rate of married women during this period was higher than that of men or unmarried women, with the proportion of sales, service or production workers beginning to grow (Korea Women's Development Institute, 1992). However, female economic activity during marriage and childbirth was low (Kang H.A., 1996), and the growth of female workers was mainly comprised of temporary and daily work since the mid-1990s (Keum J.H., 2000).

A prominent feature related to Korea's female involvement in economic activity is the M-shaped curve of economic participation rate classified by age groups. The M-shaped curve indicates that young female workers engage in economic activity as males in their 20s and early 30s but pause during marriage and childbirth and return after the family formation phases of the life course. According to the Korean Economically Active Census Supplemental Census, the scale of irregular workers was 7,430,000 in August 2020, constituting 36.3 per cent of total wage workers, 29.4 per cent of male wage workers and 45.0 per cent of female wage workers (Statistics Korea, 2020). Meanwhile, the Korea Labour and Society Institute claimed that the standard of irregular workers of the Korean Economically Active Census Supplemental Census of Statistics Korea should cover permanent-temporary workers that work long-term in a temporary position without an contract and seasonal workers unaffiliated to a company, and reported that atypical temporary workers demonstrate low wage and poor working conditions (Kim Y.S., 2020b). Kim Y.S. (2020b) calculated the number of irregular workers composed of permanent, temporary, contingent, part-time and atypical workers using the same method (Kim Y.S., 2020b). In August 2020, the number of irregular wage workers in South Korea was 8,500,000, accounting for 41.6 per cent of all wage workers, which is more than 5 per cent higher than the figure reported by Statistics Korea. Of the total irregular workers, 34.5 per cent were male and 50.5 per cent were female, with the proportion of female irregular workers being significantly higher than that of males. Among male irregular workers, 43.2 per cent were permanent-temporary workers, 53.0 per cent were contingent workers, 23.5 per cent were part-time workers and 32.5 per cent were atypical workers, with daily workers accounting for 17.4 per cent of the total irregular workers (see Table 5.1). On the other hand, the proportion of female permanent-temporary and contingent workers was as high as that of males, while the proportion of part-time workers was 51.0 per cent, indicating a higher proportion of part-time workers among female irregular workers compared to males.

Despite the overall increase in employment and economic participation rates, the gender gap in irregular employment remains significant in South Korea. The proportion of irregular workers by gender has remained relatively stable over time, with female irregular workers accounting for a larger percentage compared to male irregular workers, even as aggregate employment grows. This highlights the persistent and significant disparity between male and female irregular workers in the Korean labour market.

The concentration of women in irregular employment is linked to the gender wage gap in South Korea. Even when working in the same status of regular or irregular, women are paid less than men on average. In 2020, the average hourly wage of female irregular workers was 10,562 KRW

Table 5.1: Irregular workers by gender and employment type, Korea (August 2020)

	Male	(%)	Female	(%)	Total	(%)
Total	11,362	100.0	9,085	100.0	20,446	100.0
Irregular workers total	3,921	34.5	4,584	50.5	8,504	41.6
Permanent temporary workers*	1,692	14.9	1,694	18.6	3,386	16.6
Contingent workers	2,079	18.3	2,558	28.2	4,637	22.7
Part-time workers	915	8.1	2,337	25.7	3,252	15.9
Daily workers	682	6.0	214	2.4	896	4.4
Workers of special forms	185	1.6	313	3.4	498	2.4
Dispatched or subcontract workers	400	3.5	316	3.5	716	3.5
Home-based workers	8	0.1	41	0.5	49	0.2

Note: Unit: 1,000 people. The sum of percentages in the different categories of irregular work does not match the total percentage in irregular employment because some of the workers fall into overlapping categories. * The category 'permanent temporary workers' includes long-term temporary workers without contracts, casual workers and seasonal workers.

Source: Reorganised data from Kim YS (2020) *Report on Irregular Employment*. Korea Labour and Society Institute

Figure 5.1: Hourly wage by gender and employment status (KRW)

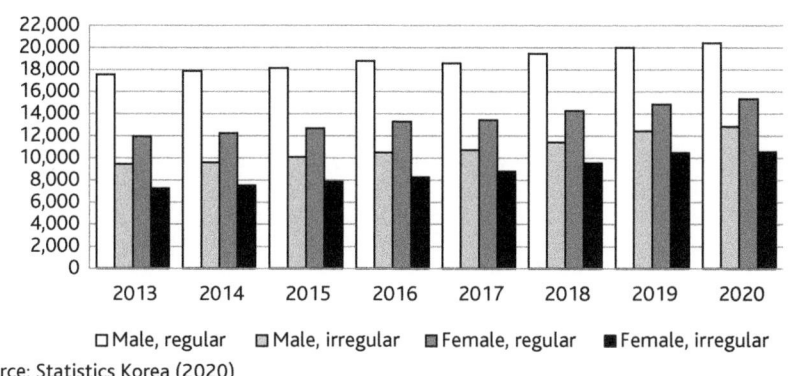

Source: Statistics Korea (2020)

(around US$10), which is almost half of male regular workers' average hourly wage. Additionally, the average hourly wage of female irregular workers is lower than that of male irregular workers. Although there is also a wage gap between regular and irregular workers among male workers, females in irregular status receive the most disadvantageous wage in all periods (see Figure 5.1). Another characteristic of the Korean female labour market is the M-shaped curve of labour market engagement rate by age group, with women leaving the labour market during childbirth and child-rearing periods. The percentage of regular workers is higher for young females, but the ratio of irregular workers starts to exceed the ratio of regular workers in the late 30s.

Upon examining the female labour market in Korea, it is evident that the proportion of irregular female workers is remarkably high between the ages of 40 and 50, in contrast to the proportion of irregular male workers, which is relatively low and steady across age groups. The number of female regular workers reaches its peak between ages 25 and 29 and rapidly declines thereafter. Meanwhile, the number of female irregular workers constantly increases from the 30s onwards, with the curves of regular and irregular workers intersecting at around age 50 (see Figure 5.2). This indicates that the number of female irregular workers significantly increases after marriage and childbirth, with the gap between the curves of regular and irregular workers lessening and becoming reversed after the 50s. This shows that not only do women exhibit lower economic participation rates than men, but the proportion of irregular workers among women steadily increases, comprising over half of all female wage workers.

Furthermore, when comparing the proportion of irregular workers by age group between men and women, it is clear that the percentage of irregular female workers between the ages of 40 and 50 in occupational activities after

Figure 5.2: Distribution of employment type by female age group (2020)

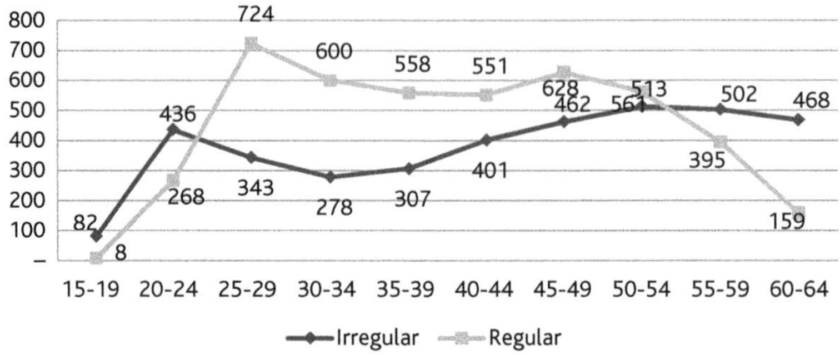

Source: Statistics Korea (2020)

marriage and childbirth is higher than that of regular workers. The point at which the curves of regular and irregular workers intersect indicates that most women stop their careers in regular jobs and switch to irregular jobs. In all types of the labour market in Korea, women tend to re-enter the labour market as irregular workers in their late 30s to 40s and 50s after taking time off for childbirth and child-rearing. This is in contrast to irregular male workers, whose participation rates remain relatively consistent across age groups.

Middle-aged and older women in South Korea face discrimination based on both age and gender, which limits their opportunities and choices for employment (Seo M.K., 2009; Kim S.H. et al, 2013). Despite their desire to participate in society, they often have to settle for precarious work with poor treatment, such as low wages and unstable employment (Seo M.K., 2009). They are also typically limited to low-skilled service jobs, including cleaning work, which is often devalued due to its association with women's work (Cho S.K., 2007). The situation is worsened for female subcontracted workers, who face even greater labour instability due to gender discrimination in the prime contract–subcontract structure (see Chapter 3). Women are often preferentially outsourced, and even within subcontracted work, there is a difference in wage levels based on gender. Moreover, female irregular workers, who are mainly concentrated after age 50, have limited social protection coverage (see Figure 5.3) and bargaining power.

Female employment policy in Korea

Korea's employment policies for women can be categorised into two types: those aimed at strengthening employment equality and those aimed at creating employment opportunities. The Labour Standards Act of 1953

Figure 5.3: Social protection coverage by employment type and sex (2020)

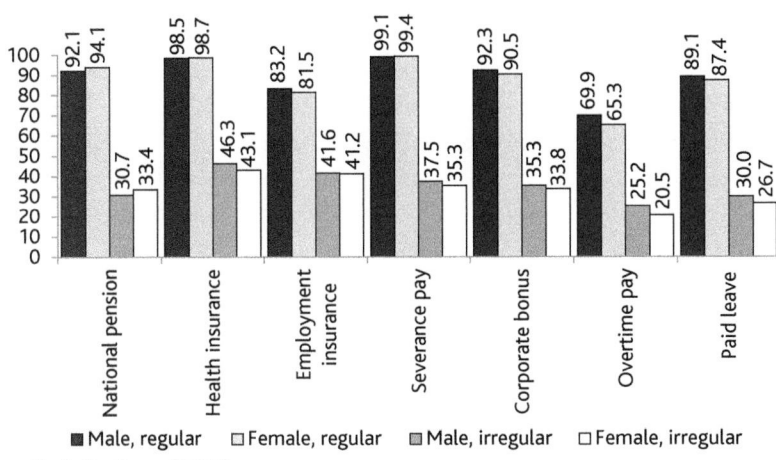

■ Male, regular   □ Female, regular   ■ Male, irregular   □ Female, irregular

Source: Statistics Korea (2020)

was the first policy to prohibit gender-based discrimination and ensure protection for pregnant and postpartum women. The Equal Employment Act of 1987 expanded on these protections and included affirmative action measures to combat gender discrimination and sexual harassment in the workplace. The third amendment to the Act in 1999 added provisions to address indirect discrimination. In 2007, the Act on Equal Employment and Support for Work-Family Reconciliation was amended to promote women's participation in the workforce and provide a better work–life balance. This legislation prohibits gender discrimination in all aspects of employment, including recruitment, hiring, wages, training, promotion, retirement and dismissal. The Act on Promotion of Economic Activities of Career-Interrupted Women was also enacted in 2008 to encourage women's economic independence.

In summary, Korea has implemented various policies to promote women's employment, particularly in the public sector, since the 1990s. These policies include affirmative action, vocational training, employment support programmes and part-time job opportunities for women. Two national plans for women's human resource development were established in 2006 and 2010, emphasising the importance of women's economic participation and work–family balance. In 2010, the Lee Myung-bak administration proposed the expansion of commercial-type part-time jobs, and in 2013, the Park Geun-hye administration implemented the high-quality part-time work policy, which aimed to provide basic working conditions for part-time workers and was primarily targeted towards married women. These policies were part of the government's roadmap to achieving a 70 per cent employment rate and aimed to create a total of 930,000 high-quality part-time jobs, including time-selective jobs in the public sector.

Korea has implemented female employment policies to address gender equality and the low birth rate problem. While there are laws in place to combat issues such as gender-based separation of duties and irregular employment of women, their effectiveness in practice is limited. Despite national emphasis on women's employment since the 2000s, the policy focus has been on increasing the rate of women's participation in economic activities rather than improving the quality of employment. The recent promotion of high-quality part-time jobs is a step in the right direction, but policies that provide subsidies without legal protections may lead to temporary job increases with long-term negative effects, such as unstable and low-paid labour. In order to create sustainable and quality employment opportunities for women, aggressive intervention and stronger legal protections are necessary (Kim Y.H. and Lee S.Y., 2014).

Outsourced female workers in call centres and cleaning services

Most cleaning service workers, typically known as 'female labour', are middle-aged and older women with relatively low education levels. Job insecurity in cleaning is related to the fact that most workers are indirectly employed by subcontractors. Cleaning jobs have expanded with a growing service economy and the trend of more flexible labour since the Asian financial crisis; most cleaning workers were transitioned from being directly employed by employers to being employed by subcontracted companies (National Human Rights Commission of The Republic of Korea, 2006). While cleaning workers in the public sector, buildings, apartments and universities were directly employed before the 1990s, almost all cleaning services transformed into indirect employment and subcontracting and, subsequently, cleaning workers have worked in very insecure conditions where employment renewal, working conditions and wages differ annually (Lee S.S., 2011).

For cleaning workers under the structure of indirect employment, responsibility by the employer disappears, and the client demands lower fees from the subcontractor in a contract, which worsens their working conditions (Lee S.S., 2011; Kwon H.Y. et al, 2016). Under the subcontractor structure, indirectly hired female workers have the lowest status, and their status in the labour market makes them fearful of dismissal and retribution in an insecure employment relationship; subcontracted workers generally cannot speak up even if they are treated unfairly (Kim S.Y. and Kim Y.M., 2015; Kwon H.Y. et al, 2016).

As a result, the employment relationship of subcontracted cleaning workers is very insecure (Kim S.Y. and Kim Y.M., 2015). Renewal of their employment is determined depending on a contract to be signed every one or two years between the subcontractor and employer (Ahn J.H., 2014; Kim S.Y. and Kim Y.M., 2015). Furthermore, the wage of subcontracted cleaning workers is generally at or slightly above the minimum wage and very low in the wage labour market (Kang S.B., 2011; Kwon H.Y. et al, 2016). Furthermore, they generally come to work earlier than the working hours stated in a contract to finish a given amount of work (Kang S.B., 2011; Park O.J., 2016) and have a very high workload and labour intensity (Yoon S.J. et al, 2012); workers also have substandard places to rest (Kang S.B., 2011). Furthermore, due to the nature of cleaning labour, most have poor joints and experience muscle pain and allergic rhinitis, and some are injured while working (Kim S.Y. and Kim Y.M., 2015; Lee Y.S., 2015; Park O.J., 2016).

Under these multifaceted discriminatory structures, they are humiliated because they do such work, are socially 'ashamed' of themselves, and engage in physical and highly intense emotional labour (Chae Y.J., 2015; Park O.J., 2016). Moreover, most female cleaning workers are breadwinners. They are more easily exposed to discrimination under a structure where it is difficult to speak up as their livelihood depends on keeping their jobs (Kang S.B., 2011; Kim S.Y. and Kim Y.M., 2015).

Most subcontracted cleaning workers are not guaranteed basic rights under labour laws and work without the minimum in-house employee benefits; it is difficult for them to demand statutory rights such as overtime pay or annual and monthly leave (Lee S.S., 2011). Furthermore, even if they are injured at work, filing for industrial accident compensation insurance benefits is perceived to lead to a layoff, and they consider it natural to take care of such injuries on their own (Lee S.S., 2011). Cho D.M. (2007) conducted a questionnaire survey on subcontracted cleaning workers and collected 759 cases. The cases where workers could not file for industrial accident compensation insurance benefits due to their fear of a potential layoff or disadvantage even though they were in a big or small accident or have physical abnormalities account for one-third of such cases (Cho D.M., 2007). In particular, it was reported that cleaning workers in universities and hospitals have a high incidence of industrial accidents and occupational diseases (Cho D.M., 2007).

The cleaning service industry tends to employ middle-aged to older female workers, while call centres attract relatively younger females. According to Statistics Korea, call centres and telemarketing service activities provide services via telephone, including receiving and handling customer complaints and requests, promoting and providing information about products and services, and receiving orders. These services have rapidly spread in Korea since the early and mid-1990s as a major business management means (Lee B.H. et al, 2006; National Human Rights Commission of The Republic of

Korea, 2008). While each agency has different estimates, surveys confirm that the number of businesses and workers in the call centre industry has increased over time, and young women constitute the majority of these workers (Kim J.J., 2013).

The expansion of outsourcing and subcontracting across Korea has contributed to the growth of the call centre industry. As companies seek to reduce labour costs for cost-effectiveness, most call centre workers are hired as contractors or outsourced service workers, with low job security (Kim J.J., 2013). While permanent workers account for the highest number of workers in the business, most workers are employed by subcontractors, and a permanent job status does not necessarily guarantee job security. It is widely perceived that call centre tasks are not highly skilled, which leads to low job security and wages and high turnover among call centre workers (Park S.E., 2015). Low-cost employment relationships based on control are dominant across call centres in Korea (Lee B.H. et al, 2006). While irregular employment was previously used to maintain such relationships, an increasing number of workers are now contracted as individual business operators, such as freelancers or work-from-home employees.

Based on this analysis, the characteristics of call centre and cleaning labour can be summarised as follows: first, most workers in call centres are relatively young females in their 30s, and although permanent workers account for a high percentage of workers, they are mostly indirectly employed subcontracted workers. Second, cost-lowering strategies have led to companies operating workers as contractors or outsourced service workers with a low level of job security. Furthermore, many businesses perceive phone call consultations and cleaning labour as low-skilled tasks, leading to the dominance of subcontracted workers. These outsourced female workers have complex employment characterised by insecurity and variation away from traditional employment relationships. In particular, subcontracted workers experience unemployment and job insecurity, and lack legal protection unless they are dispatched illegally. This is because subcontracted call centres are often located inside the original company's building, making it difficult to categorise them as dispatched workers and receive legal protection under the Act on the Protection and so forth of Temporary Agency Workers.

In this chapter, the focus is on the inconsistencies between institutions aimed at decommodification and the phenomenon of melting labour in the Korean labour market, which has led to an increase in precarious workers. The challenges faced by emerging forms of work, such as cleaning and call centre jobs, overlap with those of non-regular workers. A comprehensive analysis of both types of issues is necessary. The chapter examines the employment relationships and poor working conditions of cleaning and call centre workers, analysing how such relationships deviate from traditional standard employment and result in exclusion from legislation and social protection. It shows how the melting of labour and inconsistency of legislation and social protection reveals precarity, especially for female workers in the service industries where they are concentrated.

To explore the situation of cleaning workers in this sector, the study conducted a qualitative case study with in-depth interviews of cleaning workers who are indirectly employed by subcontractors through contracts in universities, companies and public institutions. For call centre workers, the study considered various types of call centres, including those in the public and private sectors, and conducted in-depth interviews with call centre workers employed in regular or irregular jobs as subcontractors. The study analysed how the outsourcing environment made the employment conditions of call centre workers insecure and how call centre workers experience social security schemes in Korea.

A qualitative analysis on the precarity of female cleaning workers

In this section, we present the findings of our in-depth interview analysis of female cleaning workers in Korea who are employed under subcontracting arrangements.[1] The study specifically examined the employment structure of subcontracting in the cleaning industry and the working conditions of cleaning workers who are indirectly employed. To understand the experience of social protection for these workers, we conducted in-depth interviews with 13 interviewees. These included nine cleaning subcontracted workers, three experts and activists who have been working with cleaning workers and researching subcontracting employment structures in the cleaning industry, and one outsourcing manager. Further information on the research methodology can be found in Chapter 1.

Outsourcing and cost-lowering strategies

The majority of cleaning workers, regardless of the sector they work in, the size of their workplace, or the type of building they clean, are indirectly employed by subcontractors. In the public sector, cleaning costs are not included as labour costs in the budget but are assigned to service costs in project expenses. This subcontracting through an outsourcing structure has become increasingly fragmented. Participants in the study noted that cleaning tasks, which were previously handled by a single subcontractor, are now divided among multiple subcontractors. Alternatively, the client may sign a contract with a subcontractor who manages outsourced services such as cleaning and security. The first subcontractor then subcontracts these services to multiple cleaning service providers.

The outsourcing structure through subcontracting has continued to expand due to incentives for both the original company (contractor) receiving cleaning services and the subcontractor. The original company benefits by taking no responsibility for worker employment or labour relations, reducing costs by assigning more buildings to the subcontractor who is more submissive through competitive bidding. While subcontractors can reduce management costs, they can still profit under the guise of management and operating expenses, making subcontracting through outsourcing structure beneficial for them. However, cleaning workers face job insecurity due to the contractor–subcontractor structure, which includes potential termination between the contractor and subcontractor and contract termination with their subcontractor or subsequent employment insecurity, including layoffs.

> 'It does not cost service providers much money to manage. Workers remain available, and only subcontractors change. So, a subcontractor does not need to hire many people. They only need some staff to manage contracts, and maintaining them does not cost much.' (Labour union expert, male)

Examining the process of subcontractor selection and profit-making within this structure sheds light on the insecure working conditions faced by subcontracted workers. In a structure where the cleaning service provider is chosen based on the lowest bid, the subcontractor determines the service fees based on the hourly rate and has a fixed number of workers for a contract, and cannot reduce labour costs due to the minimum wage law. Therefore, subcontractors often attempt to reduce costs by buying fewer cleaning tools and equipment or cutting down the number of workers. Large subcontractors typically provide cleaning tools, while small subcontractors may avoid spending money on such items. If the subcontractor wins the bid based on the total amount of subcontracting, they are incentivised to lower their bid or make a profit by reducing the number of workers, which can exacerbate labour intensity for workers due to a shortage of available labour.

In terms of job insecurity, most cleaning workers had a one-year employment contract, leaving them exposed to the risk of both the contractor terminating the contract with their subcontractor and their employer laying them off. Some subcontractors also attempt to reduce labour costs by cutting work hours, which intensifies the workload while reducing working hours. As there is often a lack of backup workers, employees are discouraged from using annual leave even when they are sick, as they worry about potential labour intensity for their colleagues, or they may be motivated to increase their income despite the small benefit.

'If you use the machine, it just sprays water and cannot clean up the edges. Humans must do it, and machines cannot do it. But the manager told me to clean up with the machine, and ordered me to come at 8:00 am and leave at noon. He told me to reduce hours and pay less. So, I told him honestly. You cannot clean up everything if you work only in the morning.' (Apartment cleaning worker, female, age 76)

There were discrepancies in wage levels based on the type of employment, with indirectly employed workers receiving lower wages than directly employed workers. In particular, those employed by sub-subcontractors had lower wages than those employed by subcontractors. One study participant, who was previously directly employed by a client and later worked for a subcontractor after outsourcing, reported that the subcontractor did not take into account the workers' years of service when determining wages. The participant's current monthly wage was lower than what she earned 17 years ago when the contractor directly employed her in 2000, before outsourcing. The study also found that the number of sub-subcontracts had increased, resulting in even lower wage levels as 'the subcontractor took fees, and then the sub-subcontractor took fees again'.

Cleaning workers' experience of social protection

Most female cleaning workers in Korea are elderly workers aged 60 and older who are not mandatory contributors but recipients of national pensions. While most are covered under the public pension scheme and not alienated outside of it, their post-retirement income level is low. Even though they receive both basic and national pensions, the amount is not enough to secure their post-retirement income, and their plan is to stay and work as long as possible in the labour market. They are already elderly and wish to continue working in their current job despite physical limitations until they are forced to quit due to 'disease or death'.

'(Public pensions) alone … I may need to work until 70. If I work until 70, I can earn 1 million won (around 1000 US$) a month. … So, I want to work as long as I am not sick and can move. (Ordinary building cleaning worker, female, age 63)

The national pension system in Korea is available to individuals aged 18–60. However, for those above the age of 60, there is an option to maintain membership as an 'optional continuous member' by paying all contributions themselves. In this study, the majority of interviewees were over 60 and no longer eligible to pay national pension contributions as waged workers, meaning that their employer did not pay contributions on their behalf. Many had been in the labour market for less than ten years, did not meet the minimum membership period for national pensions, or had a very low pension benefit level despite meeting the minimum membership period. Prior to working in the cleaning industry, many had worked in the informal labour market, such as household labour or small restaurants, and had received minimal contributions to the national pension system, resulting in limited benefits ranging between 300,000 and 520,000 KRW. Subcontractors were not required to join the national pension system for workers over the age of 60 who wished to join, so most female cleaning workers paid all contributions individually as local self-employed workers or local subscribers paying full contribution, despite their status as waged workers remaining unchanged.

'Pension premiums [contributions] are not withheld from my salary. I am 60 [years old]. [Instead of a company paying half of the national pension premiums] I am paying them as an individual, just self-employment. [Interviewer: Are many people doing it?] Yes. But you must pay for up to 120 months, and I have not reached 120 months. I need to receive pensions from then on.' (Private university cleaning worker, female, age 63)

The employment insurance system has two limitations in ensuring income for subcontracted cleaning workers. First, many cleaning workers continue to work until the age of 70. However, if they sign an employment contract with a new subcontractor after the age of 65, they are no longer eligible for employment insurance benefits, despite being previous members. This means that they are not entitled to employment insurance benefits due to age, despite being eligible workers. Second, frequent changes in subcontractors can increase insecurity for cleaning workers under the contractor–subcontractor outsourcing structure. Therefore, employment continuity is crucial for current cleaning workers to reduce income insecurity.

Workers employed by the same subcontractor after age 65 can receive employment insurance benefits when they lose their job, but the documentation for job-seeking activities or certain hours of job training they are required to complete were found to be unsuitable for middle-aged and older female cleaning workers. Given that they had long worked in household labour or small self-employed restaurants as unpaid family workers, job training in cooking or caregiving was seen as a mere formality.

'It is not easy to receive Employment Insurance benefits at this age. I need to prove that I am looking for a job somewhere constantly.

I should keep doing it. They call me, check, and come physically to ask whether I have been looking for a job. I need to give you a business card or something. It is tough. I also should receive training somewhere.' (Private university cleaning worker, female, age 60)

Due to the repetitive physical labour involved, cleaning workers are more susceptible to musculoskeletal problems compared to other occupations. However, receiving industrial accident compensation insurance benefits is rare for them, even if they are badly injured and recover. This is due to three limitations of the insurance system for cleaning workers under the subcontracting structure.

First, when an industrial accident occurs, the subcontractor often prefers to settle it privately with the worker as it may disadvantage the subcontractor or lead to contract renewal failure with the primary company. Second, identifying the specific subcontractor for which the worker is working can be challenging as subcontractors frequently change. While cleaning workers may continue to work in the same workplace through employment succession, the responsibility for industrial accidents becomes ambiguous due to the frequent changes of subcontractors.

Third, subcontracted cleaning work is often done with the minimum number of workers in a designated place, and it is not easy to find backup workers instantly. Therefore, if a worker makes themselves unavailable for work, it may increase the burden on their colleagues. Consequently, workers may feel that it is burdensome to file for industrial accident compensation insurance benefits.

'I have seen someone who slipped during room cleaning and took a month off. [Interviewer: Were they eligible for industrial accident compensation insurance benefits?] No. She does not get monthly pay and just takes time off. … As far as I know, the company gives some money for treatment, but not any wage. I have never heard that you can receive monthly payments if you just slip and strain your leg … I think you just take time off.' (Hotel cleaning worker, female, age 63)

'It is quite difficult to file for industrial accident compensation insurance benefits. It is difficult to prove it with documentation. Unless it is a severe accident, the subcontractor settles it privately in most cases, and to sign a service contract; they sometimes get a minus for their re-bid depending on the industrial accident or its incidence. So, if there is an accident, the subcontractor tries to hide it. As they try to hide it, most settle it privately.' (Labour union expert, male)

A qualitative analysis on the precarity of female call centre workers

This section presents the findings of an in-depth interview analysis of female call centre workers who are employed under subcontracting arrangements in Korea's service economy and labour market.[2] As companies continue to outsource their call centre services, subcontractors are also making contracts with sub-subcontractors, leading to a complex employment structure for call centre workers. The study analysed the working environment and social safety net experiences of call centre workers through in-depth interviews with eight subcontracted call centre workers, one expert on call centre employment structure, and one activist working with call centre workers.

Outsourcing structure and the competition mechanism

In the call centre industry in Korea, outsourcing typically takes the form of dispatching and subcontracting. When a primary company (the client) outsources call centre operations to a subcontractor, the subcontractor dispatches managers and hires new call centre representatives. Call centres in Korea tend to be small, with fewer than 50 employees, and some large primary companies outsource services to multiple call centres, resulting in several subcontracted call centres. The primary company uses this structure to encourage competition among subcontractors, which is passed on to frontline call centre representatives.

Call centre workers sign an open-ended contract with the subcontractor, making them not regular workers since the company they work for differs from the company they signed a contract with. These workers are indirectly employed, and their job security is dependent on employment succession. When a subcontract between the primary company and the outsourcing provider expires, most frontline call centre representatives have their employment continued with a new subcontractor. However, employment succession is also a corporate strategy to avoid employing regular workers, as some workers may change their affiliation every two years, even while doing the same job. For instance, a study participant worked as a call centre representative for six years at a financial institution. After her dispatch contract expired, she was hired again under another dispatcher. "After two years, you have to convert into a regular job. ... So, that is how they do it. ... These people ... I think they are taking advantage of a loophole in the system" (Public sector CSR,[3] female, age 41).

In the public sector, call centre outsourcing is divided into two categories: outsourcing to the private sector and outsourcing to subordinate public institutions. In the case of outsourcing to subordinate public institutions, local government entities establish a subcontract relationship with a private sector subcontractor, which then hires short-term, home-based workers to provide job consultation services. However, there is no central administration agency that hires call centre representatives as public servants and outsources call centre services to subordinate public institutions.

Call centre representatives' salaries are calculated based on a flat rate basic pay level plus performance pay, which is determined by performance evaluations. All representatives receive the same basic pay, and Grades S, A, B, C and D are set to provide different levels of performance pay. Grading is determined by both quantitative and qualitative evaluations. Quantitative evaluation factors include the number of calls taken per day and the duration of each call. Despite differences across call centres, inbound representatives are expected to take 150–170 calls daily, which puts a great deal of pressure on them to maintain a fast pace. Since representatives need to take the defined number of calls within a limited time, the number of calls and average call duration are critical. The company divides the average duration of a call into different stages and evaluates performance based on the stage. If a call takes longer than the average duration of a 'long call', representatives may risk not meeting the defined number of calls, which can be disadvantageous for their performance evaluation.

'They have the average call duration, which has the best score. They have four different stages. The best score is given for three minutes. ... It must not be too short or long. [Interviewer: What if you) have a long call?] It is disadvantageous.' (Public sector CSR, female, age 35)

In addition to quantitative evaluation factors, such as the number of calls and the duration of a call, call centre representatives are also evaluated qualitatively through quality assurance (QA) or quality control (QC). QA/QC representatives listen to recorded phone calls made by frontline representatives and evaluate the quality of their performance. The wage structure in call centres is characterised by a low level of basic pay and a high level of performance pay that is determined through competition among representatives. This structure can have implications for future national pension benefits, which are calculated based on the basic pay received.

'There is an evaluation checklist with items to tick off. If I misguided something, misguided is ticked off. If my call attitude is poor, it is ticked off. ... Every worker is evaluated once or twice a month, and the total score sums up work attitude or performance and is used to calculate pay.' (Contractor company CSR, female, age 41)

Most call centres disclose the performance of individual call centre representatives to other representatives and encourage competition for performance between the representatives to improve service productivity. Outsourced subcontractors view this competition as a way to increase the likelihood of the next re-subcontract. This competition among subcontractors leads to competition between workers within the subcontractors.

> 'There is a monthly performance evaluation. You get some score. Those with the best score ... get a few tens of thousands of Korean won more in monthly payments. [Interviewer: Do they disclose it to call centre representatives?] Yes. Everything. ... It creates some pressure. It makes you work hard.' (Public contracting CSR, female, age 48)

Call centre workers' experiences of social protection

The 2016 amendment of the Industrial Accident Compensation Act recognises mental diseases arising from emotional labour as occupational diseases, providing legal protection for the emotional labour experienced by call centre workers. However, none of the call centre workers in this study had their health issues caused by work recognised as an industrial accident. Workers must prove that their health issue is an industrial accident, and many were sceptical about filing for industrial accident compensation insurance benefits since they thought it would be difficult to prove that their disease stemmed from the stress experienced during call centre labour.

> 'I take calls all day long. My throat got so bad that I had a sore throat every two to three months. I could not speak. So, I could not work. In the end, my health got worse. ... I did not ask my company to cover it as an industrial accident.' (Banking industry CSR, female, age 35)

> 'We have many people taking neuropsychiatric drugs compared to other occupations. I have not surveyed them all, but I have been taking neuropsychiatric drugs for some years.' (Public sector CSR, female, age 41)

In addition, call centre workers are not provided with sufficient breaks, which can lead to health problems. However, it is unclear who should provide industrial accident prevention training between the client and subcontractor in the call centre subcontractor structure. Since working hours and instructions are regulated by the client, it is ambiguous who is responsible for an industrial accident if a health problem occurs due to a lack of break time. The competition mechanism structure discussed previously, which ensures an income level through competition between call centre workers, is related to the lack of break time. Performance pay accounts for a substantial portion of call centre workers' pay, and their basic pay is as low as the minimum wage. This creates an environment where 'voluntary' competition is encouraged during break time, and labour control practices further reinforce it.

'You just need to take a break … on your own. There is no guideline from the company. In the old days, [public sector call centre] 114 had a timetable of 50 minutes of work and 10 minutes of break time. Now, you sit and work for eight hours straight in 00 Card Company or 00 Capital.' (Banking industry CSR, female, age 35)

The call centre industry is characterised by poor job security and a high turnover rate, which makes it difficult for workers to rely on employment insurance benefits during their career breaks. While employment insurance benefits can provide some financial support during a break from work, call centre workers often prefer to move to another call centre rather than receive these benefits and job training. This is because the call centre labour market is insecure and there are always recruitment ads in the subcontractor labour market. It is easier to enter this market, and finding a job with another call centre subcontractor brings more immediate short-term income than receiving a low level of employment insurance benefits or job training. Therefore, employment insurance benefits were not seen as an effective means of guaranteeing income or an opportunity to find a better job in the call centre industry.

'[Interviewer: Have you received employment insurance benefits?] No. I was fired regardless of my intentions. I should have applied with the Employment Insurance Centre and received training. But I got a job (at another call centre) next month. Since then, my subcontractors have gone broke, or I quit voluntarily. So, I have not received the benefits.' (Outsourced public sector, regular worker, female, age 45)

In addition, there are issues with the national pension system for call centre workers under the subcontractor structure. National pension membership is limited to the period under the employment contract, and once the contract expires, call centre workers automatically become individual members instead of worker-members. This change results in an increase in premiums, as individual members pay higher premiums compared to worker-members. As mentioned earlier, call centre workers frequently move to another subcontractor upon the expiration of their employment contract or outsourcing period. Those who experience a career break of one to two months face a significant burden in paying national pension premiums as individual members. During this break, they do not pay national pension premiums and lose coverage for the period of the break. If the break is longer than the premiums payment period, call centre workers often choose to forgo paying national pension premiums instead of paying them during the break. Instead, they opt to save or put the money into a private savings account.

Another issue with national pensions is that they are linked to the basic payment system, excluding performance pay. Call centre workers' basic pay is close to the statutory minimum wage, with performance allowances accounting for approximately 40 per cent of their total salary. Therefore, while they may see some increase in total income if they continue to work, there is no increase in the basic pay level. Moreover, paying national pension contributions at the minimum wage level leads to receiving the minimum level of national pensions, which may not be sufficient to provide for their post-retirement needs.

Call centre workers are entitled to receive benefits during childbirth and childcare leave if they contribute to employment insurance for more than six months (180 days). Since most of them worked for more than one year on average and were a member of employment insurance, they are entitled to receive benefits during childbirth and childcare leave in principle. It was analysed, however, that the rights to use childcare leave were not a practical option for call centre workers who often changed subcontractors and felt that their work environment was insecure.

About 76 per cent of the call centre and telemarketing service workers are women, most of whom were in their late 30s and 40s after childbirth and during childrearing. Furthermore, they are entitled to receive benefits during childcare leave if they contribute to employment insurance for more than six months under the Employment Insurance Act. However, there was no call centre workers who applied for maternity or parental leave, and pregnancy led to them leaving the labour market amid insecure employment relationships. When childbirth and childcare became less burdensome, they re-entered the call centres. They find jobs in other call centres, trying to strike a work–family balance by exiting the labour market without parental or marital benefits and re-entering the call centre. In other words, family policy is ineffective even if the employment insurance covers them, and maternal leave is taken as exiting the labour market.

'Most just quit their jobs when pregnant and then get a job after childbirth. After you give birth and your kid has grown, you work at a call centre again. When they were pregnant, they were highly likely to quit voluntarily.' (Public sector CSR, female, age 45)

The inconsistency of social protection for outsourced female workers

According to the results of this study, many of the social protection programmes and related legal systems in place for subcontracted female workers are not effective in practice, and most workers are unable to use them.

First, two groups of outsourced female workers are poorly covered by public pension schemes such as national pensions, leaving them with inadequate post-retirement income security. Subcontracted cleaning workers, mostly middle-aged and older women, often worked in the informal labour market before cleaning and paid the minimum amount of national pension premiums or failed to meet the minimum membership period in many cases. As a result, public pension schemes could not contribute to alleviating their post-retirement income insecurity, and they had no other choice but to rely on low market wages. Similarly, the structure of call centre work, where basic pay is similar to the statutory minimum wage and performance pay accounts for up to 40 per cent of monthly pay, resulted in low national pension contributions linked to their basic pay. Therefore, call centre workers were also expected to receive a low level of pension benefits.

Second, there are limitations to employment insurance for cleaning workers and call centre workers. Cleaning workers are excluded from employment insurance benefits due to age limits and other requirements. If their subcontractor was changed after the age of 65, their eligibility for employment insurance benefits was taken away due to the current age requirement for employment insurance benefits, which is 65. Extreme job insecurity forced call centre workers to rely on market income rather than coverage by employment insurance. When they lost their jobs, they immediately found a job at another call centre instead of receiving employment insurance benefits. This was because call centre workers, who were mostly in their 30s and 40s, were unlikely to find another job by having their income covered by employment insurance benefits and receiving job training; it was easier for them to find a job at another call centre, which always had vacancies due to high turnover rates.

Third, both groups rarely received benefits from industrial accident compensation insurance, designed to resolve health problems arising from work. Due to the structural insecurity of subcontracted labour, both groups of workers were often excluded from industrial accident compensation insurance. For example, middle-aged and older cleaning workers were exposed to musculoskeletal problems due to repeated physical labour, yet it was rare for them to receive industrial accident compensation insurance benefits. Call centre workers had vague employment relationships under the client–subcontractor structure, making it difficult to determine which task under which subcontractor was responsible for an industrial accident. As a result, they were very sceptical about the possibility of filing for and receiving industrial accident compensation insurance benefits.

Finally, family policies targeting female workers during childbirth and childcare did not work sufficiently in the call centre subcontractor labour market. Although the majority of call centre and telemarketing service workers are women, family policies are ineffective due to the subcontractor structure. Female workers in this sector face extreme job insecurity, making it difficult to plan long-term across their life cycle related to marriage, pregnancy, childbirth and childrearing. Their rights to use childcare leave were not guaranteed in practice, and none of the study participants used maternity or parental leave. The lack of job security and low wages in call centre work make it difficult for female workers to take advantage of social security schemes related to work and family balance. Paradoxically, the low job security and wages also result in a high turnover rate among call centre workers, leading to a constant demand for workers in this sector.

In conclusion, the social safety nets and legal systems put in place for outsourced female workers were largely ineffective in providing sufficient protection. Both cleaning workers and call centre workers faced limitations and exclusions in terms of public pension schemes, employment insurance benefits, industrial accident compensation insurance and family policies. These findings highlight the need for policy interventions that address the challenges and vulnerabilities faced by outsourced female workers, particularly those in the cleaning and call centre industries. These workers are placed in cell 1 in the thesis matrix, which presents a high to middle level of melting labour and a low level of institutional consistency. Their workplace boundaries, wage system and employer–employee relationship are dismantled, resulting in high levels of precarity. The expanding subcontracted female service worker industry demands that Korean social security schemes be re-evaluated to ensure that they help these workers maintain the bare minimum in life, not just as workers, but as human beings.

Are freelancers really free? The Korean freelance labour market and the precarity of young freelancers

'If I tell my client that I caught a cold and need to take a break, I get no more work. When I am well again and tell the client that I can resume my work next month, the client may not need me because another freelancer has already replaced me. I live with this kind of anxiety. I think I shouldn't get sick, and I shouldn't take time off.' (Education freelancer, female, age 29)

The expansion of freelancing

The rise of freelancing has become a global trend, including in South Korea, where there is growing interest in this type of work arrangement. However, the term 'freelancer' is not clearly defined and is used interchangeably with other terms, such as independent workers, free agents, one-person entrepreneurs and portfolio workers. This lack of clarity has resulted in the notion of freelancers not yet reaching social and legal consensus. Despite the lack of official statistics, studies have identified the increasing demand for and importance of freelancers in society, particularly with the changes in entrepreneurial structures and technological development. This chapter aims to examine the characteristics of freelance work, the insecurity experienced by freelancers, and their experience with the social security system in South Korea, particularly focusing on the four major social insurances. This analysis is related to cell 3 of the thesis matrix, which represents melting labour excluded from institutional protection, such as platform workers and freelancers.

A freelancer is someone who performs professional work independently of an employer or builds a career by working in various organisations on a short-term basis (Lee S.R., 2013). Despite the growing interest in freelancing, there is no clear legal definition of the term, and various designations are used interchangeably, such as independent workers, free agents, one-person entrepreneurs and portfolio workers (Kwon K.W., 2007; Hwang J.W. et al, 2009). These designations explain that freelancers create value with their professionalism and generate economic results by working on free contracts without specific affiliations. The term 'independent workers' refers to people who work without employment contracts, while 'portfolio workers' are individuals who organise their career as solo entrepreneurs with portfolios of clients, tasks and roles, similar to professional freelancers. The emergence and interchangeable use of these terms indicate that the notion of freelancers has not yet reached social and legal consensus. Despite the lack of official statistics on the size and growth rate of the freelance market in Korea, various studies are underway to understand the increasing trend. Scholars explain that the rise of freelancing is a result of modern social change and that freelancers' demand and importance are growing as society modernises (Cho J.M., 2015). Kazi et al (2014) further argued that the number of freelancers would increase due to changes in entrepreneurial structures combined with technological development (Kazi et al, 2014). In Korea, studies on freelancers have been conducted with a focus on the market size and the insecurity experienced by freelancers, particularly among young people who show growing interest in freelancing (Kang S.T., 2014; Kim J.J., 2018).

It is important to differentiate between freelancers and other types of temporary workers, such as gig workers and fixed-term workers. Gig workers may enter into a contract with a company as independent entrepreneurs, but they work for one company for a fixed period, unlike freelancers who work on projects from multiple clients. Contingent workers, including fixed-time and temporary workers, are also different from freelancers as they work under a contract with a single employer within a set time frame.

Furthermore, freelancers can also be classified based on their independence and the presence or absence of an employer. While freelancers share similarities with the self-employed, there are significant differences. Freelancers are self-employed professionals without employees, and their work is fundamentally different from conventional self-employed businesses (Hwang J.W., 2009). Moreover, there is a distinction between entrepreneurial and non-entrepreneurial freelancers based on whether they possess a business registration certificate or not. Entrepreneurial freelancers are registered as self-employed professionals or operate a one-person business, whereas non-entrepreneurial freelancers privately receive work orders and earn fees without a business registration certificate. This distinction sets freelancers apart from self-employed individuals without employees.

Understanding these distinctions is important for policy makers to provide legal protection for freelancers and integrate them into the conventional social insurance system. It is important to recognise the growing importance of freelancers in the modern labour market and develop policies that reflect the changing nature of work.

This chapter explores the experiences of Korean freelancers, specifically those in the third cell of the theoretical framework, which includes melting labour but is excluded from institutional protection. As the trend of freelancing continues to expand in Korea, there are growing concerns about the insecurity experienced by young freelancers due to the ambiguous nature of their employment status. The chapter presents a case study that highlights the challenges faced by young freelancers in Korea and their experiences with the social protection system. Interviews were conducted with nine entrepreneurial and non-entrepreneurial freelancers to understand the precarious nature of their working conditions. The chapter also discusses the need for better social protection for this group of young workers, positioning their case within the theoretical framework's third cell. Overall, this chapter sheds light on the urgent need to address the challenges and vulnerabilities of freelancers in Korea and provides a valuable contribution to the broader discussion on precarious work and social protection.

Freelancers in Korea

Previous studies in Korea have used various definitions to infer the size and status of freelancers in the absence of an official definition and statistics. One such study estimated the number of freelancers to be 650,000 individuals by applying the definition of professional and managerial gig workers and self-employed without employees to the National Survey of the Economically Active Population (Lee S.R. et al, 2013). Another study (Jeong H.J. and Jang H.E., 2018) narrowed down the definition of solo self-employed business and freelance work to four cases, including possession of a shop, unspecified contract target, self-determination of services and fees, and no work instructions and work hour constraints. According to this definition, the number of self-employed businesses and freelancers in 2018 is estimated to be 2.48 million, accounting for 36.4 per cent of the total non-wage workers (6.81 million) and 61.7 per cent of the total solo self-employed (4.02 million). Solo self-employed is also referred as own-account workers.

The Office of Assemblywoman Hye-young Jang (2020) provided statistics on non-wage workers who are paid by performance as independent service providers without employees, based on the withholding tax on domestic source income released by the National Tax Service. Table 6.1 which is reorganised from the report reveals that the number of non-wage workers increased from 4.01 million in 2014 to 6.69 million in 2019, indicating an increase of about 2 million people compared to 2014. Interestingly, this growth occurred despite the ongoing debate over the wage gap between regular and non-regular workers. The number of non-wage workers in goods delivery and quick service has doubled over the past five years, reaching 63,000 and 13,000, respectively. The 'other self-employed' category also increased from 1.2 million in 2014 to 3.15 million in 2019, with an average annual income per capita of 10.55 million KRW (see Table 6.1). However, these 'ambiguous industries' are difficult to define by existing classifications and include computer programmers, electricians, gas meter inspectors, and

Table 6.1: Current status of withholding tax on business income by industry

Sector	2014		2015		2016		2017		2018	
	Number of workers	Income per person	Number of workers	Income per person	Number of workers	Income per person	Number of workers	Income per person	Number of workers	Income per person
Hospital doctor	86,797	259.11	87,610	272.79	86,615	296.84	88,335	318.43	89,579	345.59
Author	68,840	8.04	69,884	8.41	75,851	8.32	75,072	8.75	77,083	8.87
Painter	14,145	14.61	14,996	15.47	16,354	17.64	17,291	18.44	16,680	19.18
Composer	11,444	10.89	12,826	10.45	14,020	10.20	15,366	10.03	16,918	10.78
Actor	15,540	37.76	16,091	37.32	16,346	38.67	19,618	30.07	19,001	31.41
Model	7,733	9.23	8,561	9.12	8,454	9.93	8,285	9.64	8,495	10.47
Vocalist	4,946	55.86	4,619	63.97	4,799	76.73	6,322	53.48	6,437	60.64
Singer	8,465	6.00	8,774	6.10	8,550	6.99	8,806	6.71	9,303	7.04
Entertainment assistant	60,973	10.01	63,355	10.34	67,089	10.36	67,562	9.80	66,863	10.64
Adviser	77,255	11.85	84,118	11.71	87,534	12.35	90,898	12.19	97,250	12.26
Go player	347	23.50	353	25.93	393	27.51	419	27.73	420	26.35
Flower arrangement teacher	1,032	5.44	1,149	5.28	765	5.65	1,006	5.64	953	5.28
Academy instructor	362,971	12.76	367,184	13.09	384,063	13.29	400,529	13.26	409,603	13.40
Athlete	28,006	25.73	31,373	24.80	39,125	22.00	43,386	22.79	47,284	22.23
Service fee recipient	67,884	15.23	59,091	16.13	51,128	16.85	44,198	17.35	38,952	17.68
Insurance designer	82,743	49.31	90,620	48.35	92,375	50.83	101,226	50.71	102,316	54.51
Beverage courier	3,086	10.60	3,550	11.26	4,013	11.09	4,094	10.99	8,460	7.24

Table 6.1: Current status of withholding tax on business income by industry (continued)

Sector	2014 Number of workers	2014 Income per person	2015 Number of workers	2015 Income per person	2016 Number of workers	2016 Income per person	2017 Number of workers	2017 Income per person	2018 Number of workers	2018 Income per person
Door-to-door salesman	264,812	11.83	245,950	12.97	259,366	13.39	243,520	14.53	239,645	14.88
Other self-employment	1,019,449	10.08	1,322,665	10.36	1,734,651	10.45	2,192,801	10.70	2,647,339	10.61
Multi-level marketing salesperson	982,517	1.39	1,023,404	1.39	1,190,433	1.30	1,095,454	1.35	1,083,424	1.43
Other recruiters (stock, credit card, real estate)	589,237	12.52	838,126	11.13	741,842	14.41	776,327	14.16	771,334	13.83
Caregiver	36,631	8.00	37,883	9.18	41,380	10.41	45,210	11.25	51,706	11.79
Chauffeur	48,878	2.28	53,340	2.48	54,680	2.48	55,974	2.68	67,824	2.60
Golf caddy	1,793	2.57	1,962	3.21	2,515	2.48	3,109	2.36	3,379	2.27
Bath manager	864	16.33	1,054	15.39	1,027	16.97	1,051	17.10	1,036	18.03
Event assistant	110,346	3.37	130,410	3.11	141,285	3.33	156,853	3.28	156,630	3.36
Errand service	10,878	7.98	13,678	7.10	13,539	7.74	15,895	7.68	16,912	7.99
Quick service courier	6,796	8.87	9,184	7.93	11,705	7.93	11,705	9.12	13,198	8.63
Courier	31,317	11.73	38,382	11.02	41,444	11.02	41,444	12.66	63,843	9.49
Total	4,005,725		4,640,192		5,191,341		5,631,756		6,131,867	

Note: Unit: person, KRW million

Source: National Tax Service. data reprocessed by the Office of Assemblywoman Hye-young Jang (2020)

other self-employed people who receive commissions based on performance without fixed remuneration. This suggests that the expansion of new forms of work, not captured by existing industry classifications and belonging to low-income categories, is contributing to the growth of non-wage workers (Assemblywoman Hye-young Jang, 2020).

Although an official nationwide survey on freelancers in Korea has not yet been conducted, local governments in the Seoul Capital Area have carried out surveys to estimate the size and status of freelancers in the region. According to a survey on freelancers conducted by Seoul (2018), the number of young people engaging in freelancing is increasing rapidly, with those in their 20s and 30s accounting for 41 per cent and 28 per cent of the total, respectively (Seoul, 2018). The largest market size for freelancers was found in the education service industry, which accounted for 24.1 per cent, followed by the wholesale/retail industry at 11.8 per cent, and the arts/sports and leisure-related service industry at 10.6 per cent.

Freelancers in Korea are typically paid per project or task regardless of whether they run a business or not, and their remuneration is proportional to the input or output of the service, depending on factors such as professionalism, project structure and the non-repeatability of work. This project-oriented fee calculation is a defining characteristic of freelancing (Lee S.R. et al, 2013). In contrast, workers in special types of employment, as defined in Article 125, para 1, no 1 of the Industrial Accident Compensation Insurance Act, are routinely provided with work and remunerated accordingly, with their pay being performance-dependent income such as fees, service charges and allowances, along with basic pay and bonuses, varying slightly depending on the type of business. This is different from the calculation method used for the wages of non-regular part-time workers, which are based on the sum of working hours over daily, weekly and monthly time windows.

Second, freelancers typically secure jobs through various methods such as private-sector job portals and internet cafes, as well as acquaintances and public agencies' vacancy announcement portals. According to a survey conducted by the city of Seoul, private-sector job portals and internet cafes were the most common methods of securing orders (27.1 per cent), followed by the mediation of friends and acquaintances (21.9 per cent) and public agencies' vacancy announcement portals (12.4 per cent). Similarly, gig and contingent workers also use job advertisements or introductions from acquaintances to secure jobs.

Third, the relationship between freelancers and their employer is based on the task or project at hand and may involve entering into a standard or labour contract. Previous studies have found that freelancers working with contracts slightly outnumber those working without contracts. However, a significant proportion of freelancers are not given contracts, and the effectiveness of contracts in protecting their rights remains to be seen. In contrast, most gig workers enter into fixed–period labour contracts with employers without wage-related provisions, as they are typically paid per task or project. A survey conducted by Park C.I. (2018) found that while most gig workers had written contracts, some reported having no contracts or only verbal contracts, which differs from contingent workers whose contracts are based on hourly wages (Park C.I., 2018).

In terms of industry classification, entrepreneurial freelancers (one-person businesses) are mainly associated with the knowledge service and manufacturing industries, while non–entrepreneurial freelancers are found in industries such as publishing, advertising, design, interpretation and translation, marketing, research agencies, autobiography writing, rewriting, proofreading, revision, editing, lecturing, photography, broadcasting, reporting, MCing, broadcast composition writing, newsletter or magazine writing, architecture, IT and consulting. However, these industry boundaries are somewhat ambiguous (Lee Y.J., 2014).

While there is no official statistical definition for freelancers in Korea, previous discussions have referred to them as independent workers, one-person creative companies, workers in special employment types and own-account workers. Lee S.Y. et al (2019b) compared the main definitions and characteristics of freelance workers and workers in special employment types (for example, insurance solicitors, concrete mixer truck drivers, study guide teachers, golf course caddies, courier drivers, quick service drivers, loan solicitors, credit card member solicitors, and surrogate drivers) and found that while workers in special employment types can also sign contracts with companies as independent business operators, they differ from freelancers in that they sign contracts with a single company and work for a fixed period. Furthermore, workers in special employment types are often paid based on their performance, rather than under wage-work contracts (Lee S.Y. et al, 2019b).

Freelancers' precarity

In recent years, discussions have been focused on the precarity of freelancers and their association with the social security system. Gold and Mustafa (2013) compared freelancers who communicate and work using computer and telecommunication devices with traditional workers who work in fixed workplaces such as offices and noted that freelancers' blurred boundary between home and work could expose them to a new form of insecurity (Gold and Mustafa, 2013). The authors paid particular attention to the close association between freelancers' working methods and development in IT, such as digital platforms and social media. The study it is explained that their work routine is built to meeting clients' requirements and receive fees per project or per hour, describing them as 'connected freelancers'. It is vital for such connected freelancers to accumulate business experience through contacts with a wide variety of clients and maintain a long-term relationship with each client. In this respect, a qualitative study was conducted on their insecurity in relation to their dependency on and connection to information and communication technologies (ICTs) and mobile communication technologies (MCTs) for their livelihoods. Although most of the respondents preferred to keep their work and home activities apart, they had concerns about continuous workflow and were in a constant stand-by state by being connected to their clients on a 24/7 basis. Methods to secure work orders, evaluate their performance, and keep work and home separated were all closely associated with digital platforms, putting freelancers under the pressure of being connected to online platforms or workspaces. Such 'connected freelancers' were found to perform multitasking, blurring the boundary between income-generating activities and other activities, and increasing the use of ICTs and MCTs was analysed to increase the size of the polychronic system. In particular, freelancers' income volatility makes them rely on clients and makes it difficult for them to keep work and home apart under physical, temporal and emotional aspects. The authors emphasised the importance of establishing a new social safety net for freelancers.

Fersch (2012) defined freelancers as 'solo self-employed who pursued a profession without any long-term commitment to any particular employer' and pointed out that they are directly exposed to market risks with a very unsteady workload and income (Fersch, 2012). The author compared German and Danish freelancers' perceived insecurity based on their experience and trust in the social security programmes. She attributed the difference in the degree of insecurity between German and Danish freelancers to the difference in the national social security system. In particular, she analysed that being a freelancer in a conservative welfare state social security system based on the 'standard employment model' like Germany is associated with serious exclusion from the social security programmes such as health insurance and public pension. In this qualitative research, she raised doubt about whether a sustainable level of pensions could be expected under the low incomes and low contributions of German freelancers included in the German public social insurance system through the 'Artist Social Insurance' (*Künstlersozialkasse* [KSK]).

In contrast, the Danish participants perceived less insecurity than their German counterparts because they are all protected by the social security system, which is much more inclusive of freelancers. Unlike the German freelancers, they seldom mentioned insecurity and did not relate flexibility to employment insecurity. The latter mentioned that they were completely excluded from the social security system and considered insecurity the most serious problem in their lives. Thus, the level of insecurity perceived by freelancers was analysed to vary depending on the structural social security framework.

Fachinger and Frankus (2015) examined the social security system and the insecurity of freelancers and self-employed people in Europe. They revealed that while freelancers are provided with minimal security as part of the general social protection scheme, they are not or only partially covered by statutory social security systems (Fachinger and Frankus, 2015). If ever, the coverage of social security for self-employed persons varies greatly across countries. The authors also analysed that the extent to which the social protection scheme protects freelancers from social risks varies from country to country, although freelancing is a transnational phenomenon.

In Korea, the freelancing status survey and the qualitative study of young freelancers of the city of Seoul convey the characteristics of freelancers, and the current labour environment can give a clue as to their insecurity (Kim J.J., 2018; Seoul, 2018). According to the survey results released by the city of Seoul (2018), respondents gave personal reasons such as studying at university (22.3 per cent) as the most frequent motive for entry into the freelance marketplaces, followed by the pursuit of a free and flexible lifestyle (21.3 per cent) and the inherent nature of profession (12.6 per cent), which suggests that they entered the freelance marketplaces for both voluntary and involuntary reasons. On a different note, Kim J.J. (2018) attributed the increasing trend of freelancing to the work–life balance highly valued by young people, despite being in the blind spot of the social safety net (Kim J.J., 2018).

The precarity of freelancers refers to their unstable work conditions and the lack of social safety nets that protect them from risks such as income volatility and exclusion from social security programmes. This precarity is further complicated by the fact that freelancers often rely on digital platforms for securing work orders, which can blur the boundary between their work and personal lives. This issue has been the focus of recent discussions, and comparisons between countries have shown that the level of insecurity perceived by freelancers varies depending on the social security framework in place. Despite the lack of institutional protection, surveys and studies in Korea have shown that freelancers are entering the marketplaces for both voluntary and involuntary reasons, with work–life balance being a significant factor.

A qualitative analysis of the precarity of young Korean freelancers

This section introduces the results of an in-depth interview analysis of young freelancers in Korea.[1] This study conducted in-depth interviews with nine individuals who were classified as either entrepreneurial or non-entrepreneurial freelancers. Separate interviews were also conducted with experts for further information. The final number of participants was determined when it was deemed that all necessary information had been collected, as the content of the statements became repetitive. The study subjects were young workers aged from their mid-20s to around 40 years old. The selection of study subjects involved the introduction of freelancers through an expert in the relevant industry or related labour unions, followed by recruitment using the snowball sampling method, based on identified freelance labour patterns. The selection criteria included being classified as a freelancer according to Table 6.2, and providing labour as a freelancer for more than one year.

Irregularity in income, plural employers and fierce competition

The individuals interviewed for the study entered the freelance marketplaces in various fields and worked in ways specific to their respective sectors. However, they were typically paid on a per-project basis, with the fee calculation based on either a per-hour rate or per-case remuneration. While the wage-setting mechanism and payment modality were generally similar among the freelancers, the wage level varied somewhat depending on the type of business and length of experience. As a result, their income was usually irregular, and the interviewees rarely felt that their income level was stable: "Usually, if I set the cost of living at 1 million won per month, sometimes I get less (monthly wage), and sometimes much more. Then I save some" (Illustrator, male, age 41).

The remuneration level for each business field may have some established standards, but freelancers still need to work hard to fully appreciate the value of their labour. Industrial sectors where external evaluation is critical often use human capital variables like experience, qualifications, education level, age and recognition value as important evaluation criteria. In addition to human capital, portfolios, which are the results of past work, are key evaluation criteria for freelancers. The freelance marketplaces have a structure where freelancers have to keep proving the value of their labour as the negotiation basis while building a career.

> 'There were items checking whether you have more than seven years of experience, whether you have a master's degree or higher, and what types of certificates you have. If three or more conditions are satisfied, the lecture fee is over 300,000 won, and otherwise, further adjustments are made.' (Education freelancer, female, age 29)

The majority of freelancers enter the freelance market through acquaintances or companies, which often leads to informal contractual arrangements that are insufficiently drafted or made verbally. As they gain more experience, they start to receive orders through online platforms, but contracts are still

Table 6.2: Definitions and main features of Korean freelancers and workers in special employment types

	Freelancers		Workers in special employment types
	Not-officially self-employed workers	Self-employed workers	
Definition	A person who enters into a contract at that time for specific matters, provides labour independently according to his or her own judgement without being bound by a group or organisation, and does not have a business registration certificate	A person who enters into a contract for specific matters at that time, provides labour independently according to his or her own judgement without being bound by a group or organisation, and holds a business registration certificate (single-person company)	A person who is subordinate to the contracted business owner, but seeks or greets customers by himself, provides goods or services directly, earns income according to his or her performance, and works in a form whereby he or she decides on how to provide labour and working hours
Wage calculation method	Work system (according to the characteristics of work, annual salary system, fixed-term system, part-time system)	Work (Contract system for job completion)	Operating allowance or operating allowance on base salary
Work order method	Announcement, introduction of acquaintances, bidding		Recruitment announcement
Contract type	(Long- and short-term) contract relations according to work		Contract relationship with a fixed period, but not an employment contract
Major industry	Publication, advertisement, design, interpretation and translation, marketing, coverage agency, proofreading/provisioning, editing, various lecturers, photography, broadcasting, reporter or MC, broadcast composition writer, writing of company newsletter, magazine, architect, IT consultant	Knowledge service industry, manufacturing, and so on	Insurance agent, concrete mixer truck driver, workbook teacher, golf caddy, delivery driver, quick service driver, loan recruiter, credit card recruiter, chauffeur

Source: Lee S.R. (2013); Lee S.Y. et al (2019b); Lee Y.J. (2014); Statistical Office employment award classification (Statistics Korea, 2019)

commonly made verbally or via email and focus on the project rather than long-term relationships. Unfortunately, this informal approach to contracting can lead to unreasonable outcomes, such as wage arrears, delays or loss of copyright, due to unclear contract terms. These experiences contribute to the insecurity of freelancing: "There are no special contracts or anything like that, verbal contracts are common practice. Sometimes there are email exchanges. … But they don't explicitly make documents. They do mention this and that, but nothing was documented" (Videographer, male, age 37).

The difficulties in the freelancing contract form and method can be roughly divided into the negotiation and implementation stages of the contract. First, it was found that both entrepreneurial and non-entrepreneurial freelancers have difficulties due to the project-based system in which an agreement on an appropriate wage level is hard to reach in the contract negotiation stage. There were also cases where an attempt at raising the remuneration during the consultation process was frustrated for fear of losing the next contract, in a situation of pay per work, when work could not be completed due to unexpected circumstances such as illness, no payment was made for the work done.

'I didn't know how to get a quote, sign a contract, and get a task evaluated. … The desired result didn't come out, so even though I finished my work, I was put in a position to be apologetic. … After we broke up, the balance was not credited, but I didn't claim it.' (Marketing field worker, female, age 32)

Freelancers place a significant emphasis on evaluating their work, tasks and final products as it is crucial for securing future work opportunities. Unlike traditional employees, freelancers receive evaluations from diverse entities such as project managers, clients and agencies rather than a single company superior or customer. Additionally, freelancers prioritise self-development and ongoing learning related to their area of expertise, which is essential for building a strong portfolio and securing future work. This emphasis on continuous improvement and skill formation blurs the boundary between work and personal life, as freelancers must always be working to improve and develop their skills. Also, freelancers recognise the importance of adapting to the development of ICTs and MCTs in their work. They acknowledge that the expansion of social media and online platforms can provide opportunities for marketing and publicity, which they actively try to utilise. Those who successfully adapt to technological changes found that it expanded their business opportunities.

'For example, people can contact an artist if their pictures appeal to them by sending a DM [direct message] or leaving a message on Facebook. Compared to mobile phone numbers or email addresses available for contact in earlier years, it has become much easier and more convenient with many channels for direct and personal contact for suppliers and consumers.' (Photographer, male, age 32)

'I think technological development has made a difference. I could promote things and got lots of work. … For example, I advertise myself if I sing and upload my songs on YouTube. It's a way of telling people "Get to know me, I want to be famous." It's a kind of publicity. … When I post "I'm looking for people interested in learning how to sing" on Instagram, there are people who see it and contact me.' (Arts education worker, female, age 28)

The increasing accessibility of freelance marketplaces through platforms and social media has led to a rise in competition, blurring the line between experts and non-experts. The interviewees noted the difficulty in competing with the increasing number of freelancers in the market. However, those who were able to adapt to the expanding IT-based industries and diversified platforms mentioned that they could secure jobs more easily due to the diversity of sales channels. Nonetheless, they also expressed concerns about the increasingly fierce competition resulting from the growth of these platforms.

'It seems that the boundaries between professionals and amateurs are gradually disappearing. … With the advent of the era where anyone can come in and do business, anyone can talk about their pay rate, and there will be more and more people in the very low and very high quotes. Then there are things that are gradually eroding. … Consumers cannot really see the differences.' (Photographer, male, age 32)

Irregular working hours and an ambiguous boundary between work and life

Freelancers have to be available on a 24/7 basis to ensure that they can communicate with clients and work on urgent projects. The flexibility of their working time and location also creates a challenge in separating work and personal life, leading to a constant feeling of being on-call. Moreover, since freelancers are paid per task or project, there is no clear distinction between work and leisure time. This situation can result in burnout and physical and mental health problems. Therefore, it is essential to establish a work–life balance that considers both personal life and work demands. The working hours of freelancers can extend beyond the traditional eight-hour workday, with many working non-stop to complete tasks and even sacrificing sleep. Even when not actively working, freelancers often feel preoccupied with work-related concerns, leading to a feeling of being on-call or always connected to their work. This pressure to be constantly available can contribute to a sense of precarity and blurs the line between work and personal time.

'While working, I am a bit impatient and feel like being chased. … Too many things are changed and cancelled and come back again.

Yesterday, too, three items shifted back and forth.' (Education freelancer, female, age 29)

'The contract time was four hours, but I continued to work even after coming home. If I was supposed to post the result at 10pm, of course I turned on the computer back home. And even when I'm not in the company, they can tell if I'm working or not, because we are networked.' (Marketing field worker, female, age 32)

'When I'm busy, I am busy around the clock, especially three days before the deadline. Then again, I am not busy at all when I don't have a backlog of orders. If I am asked to make ten songs within, say, one month, I have to work without doing anything else. … So, daily workload varies widely depending on the work type and time window.' (Musician, male, age 32)

Additionally, the interviewed freelancers expressed concerns about the sustainability of their freelance work and the uncertainty of their future in the market. Many of them reported not knowing how long they could continue working as freelancers, which made them reflect on ways to ensure competitiveness and mitigate future uncertainty. They were aware of the increasing competition in the market and the need to adapt to technological changes to remain relevant.

The institutional inconsistency of social protection

In Korea, freelancers face institutional exclusion from social insurance, as the current social insurance system is geared towards employees defined in the Labour Standards Act based on contractual employment arrangements (Jang J.Y. et al, 2017; Lee Y.J., 2017). While the national pension plan, national health insurance and industrial accident compensation insurance are designed to cover all known forms of employment by law, the higher insurance cost burden among non-standard workers creates a practical vulnerable spot for freelancers. Although the scope of unemployment insurance was recently expanded to include self-employed individuals with a business registration certificate, artists and special types of employment, freelancers are still mostly excluded. This institutional exclusion is due to a combination of problems, including the misclassification of workers who require protection under labour law and the narrow interpretation of the term 'employee' in the Labour Standards Act, which is only applied limitedly to the Social Insurance Act (Lee Y.J., 2017).

There are several challenges that freelancers face when it comes to social insurance in Korea. First, the premium burden for joining the national pension plan as self-employed is higher for freelancers (9 per cent of income) than for regular employees (4.5 per cent of income). This can lead to non-subscription or exemption from premiums. Second, freelancers are often excluded from the national health insurance due to difficulties in determining their income levels, as their insurance premiums are calculated based on not only income but also assets, resulting in high premiums for those with unstable income. Additionally, the calculation and imposition of annual insurance premiums designed for wage workers do not reflect the changing income situation of freelancers. Finally, freelancers are subject to institutional exclusion in the industrial accident compensation insurance system, with gig workers sharing the burden of insurance premiums with the employer, and solo self-employed workers paying the full cost. While progress has been made in reducing this exclusion, there is still much work to be done to provide social insurance coverage for freelancers in Korea (Industrial Accident Compensation Policy Division of the Ministry of Employment and Labour, 2019; Assemblywoman Hye-young Jang, 2020).

The Ministry of Employment and Labour submitted data to the Environment and Labour Committee of the National Assembly indicating that only 16.84 per cent of the 503,306 special employment type workers who were legally required to subscribe to workers' compensation insurance had done so as of May 2020. The remaining 83.16 per cent (418,546 people) voluntarily applied for exclusion, despite being eligible for coverage through the special case system (Assemblyman wung rae Noh, 2020) (see Table 6.3). The Industrial Accident Compensation Protection Act allows for exclusion from coverage in certain cases, as stated in Article 125, paragraphs 2 and 4.

Table 6.3: Subscription rate for industrial accident compensation insurance among selected special employment-type workers

Year	2019	2020
All	15.25	16.84
Insurance designer	11.83	12.21
Construction machine operator	21.19	11.70
Workbook teacher	14.64	15.48
Golf caddy	4.02	4.70
Courier	37.26	39.76
Quick service courier	77.69	81.13
Loan recruiter	18.20	18.66
Credit card recruiter	14.82	15.38
Chauffeur	22.22	23.08

Source: Assemblyman Wung rae Noh (2020)

However, this exclusion does not apply to special employment workers whose employers pay full insurance premiums. The introduction of the exclusion system was intended to allow workers to choose, but it has the unintended consequence of reducing the effectiveness of expanding industrial accident insurance coverage to workers with special employment status (Yonhap News, 2020).

In other words, although there have been some institutional efforts to include workers as freelancers through the special case system for special type workers, both self-employed individuals and freelancers are excluded due to the fundamental limitations of the system, which primarily focuses on wage work. According to the National Statistical Office's Economically Active Population Survey from 2019, only 55.5 per cent of self-employed workers subscribed to industrial accident insurance (Statistics Korea, 2019). Given that self-employed individuals without employees make up around 75 per cent of all self-employed persons, it can be assumed that there is a significant blind spot for industrial accident insurance related to these new forms of non-standard work. The low enrolment rate of self-employed workers is similar to that of national pension and employment insurance.

Additionally, freelancers are excluded from unemployment insurance, although registered self-employed businesses with 50 or more regular workers, artists and gig workers can subscribe voluntarily. However, the burden of premium payment is higher than that for wage workers, as the self-employed must pay the entire amount without the assistance of an employer.

The preceding analysis reveals that freelancers, who have moderate and unpredictable incomes, are more susceptible to social insurance exclusion compared to regular wage workers. To mitigate this practical vulnerability, various central and local government social insurance premium support programmes are implemented, such as 40–80 per cent support for the national pension insurance premium and refund support for the industrial accident insurance premium through the Korea Artists Welfare Foundation for artist freelancers, and 20–50 per cent of unemployment insurance premiums for solo self-employed persons from the Small Business Corporation, in addition to social insurance premium support projects offered by many local governments. Although entrepreneurial freelancers can enrol as local subscribers in the national pension scheme, almost all of the freelancers interviewed in this analysis were not enrolled in the scheme, as they found it difficult to pay a set amount from their irregular incomes as contributions to the fund. They also had low expectations of receiving a sufficient amount of pension in their old age and lacked trust in the system. Instead, they relied more on personal investments or private pension plans. For the freelancers interviewed, securing the next job was essential, and they used any surplus income to purchase further education and equipment for the next freelance activity. When asked about their retirement income, they expressed anxiety but considered contributions to the pension fund a burden, given the unpredictability of their income and the immediate need to focus on the next job: "To be honest, I'm in my early 30s. ... Right now, I would rather expand the scope of my freelance activities by upgrading my equipment and raising my pay. I can not be so worried about the distant future of 30–40 years ahead" (Photographer, male, age 32).

Freelancers' income is irregular because they work according to when they receive work orders. Even if they receive no orders or have no source of income, it does not fit the state of unemployment as defined by the unemployment insurance system. Freelancers are excluded from the unemployment insurance system because unemployment benefits do not apply to their state of no income, which is different from the state of 'unemployment' after working a certain length of time, as is the case with typical wage workers: "If we don't work to do, we just starve to death. To be honest, it is something that freelancers and self-employed persons can never experience to be dismissed, live on unemployment benefits and find another job" (Photographer, male, age 32).

The interviewees expressed their need for a social protection system that includes freelancers for basic income security in case of irregular income levels and low regularity of income flow. They shared their concern about the lack of a safety net for freelancers, citing cases of scriptwriters and actors who committed suicide. They believed that having even an elementary form of social security could help decrease such cases. However, because freelancers do not have a fixed workplace or working hours, the current industrial accident compensation insurance system cannot fully protect them. Injuries or damages to freelancers often fall outside the category of accidents incurred while doing fixed work at a workplace. Even if freelancers get hurt or fall ill while working, they often deal with the situation on their own, thinking that it is an individual event or relying on help from someone close to them.

'It has never happened to me, but many other actors. If injured while rehearsing for a performance, they are replaced by other actors. Then they have to stop without being paid for all the hours of practice and rehearsal.' (Actor, male, age 29)

'I don't care much about my injury while I'm working. I'm focused on working when I am at the location [working as a freelancer] ... I don't expect anybody to do anything for me if I'm hurt.' (Marketing field worker, female, age 32)

Freelancers' income is directly tied to the amount of work they do, so finding the next job as soon as the current one is completed is crucial. Falling ill or being injured can mean no income at all because there is no paid time off or sick leave, and there are no other sources of income or social security schemes to fall back on. As a result, freelancers often feel pressured to continue working even when they are sick or injured, out of fear that they will lose their clients or be replaced by other freelancers. When low-income freelancers do become ill or injured while working, they often rely on the help of family or acquaintances to make ends meet.

'If freelancers fall sick, they no longer have earnings. If freelancers cannot work for disease or other circumstances, they are left with nothing. ... If they are hospitalised after a car crashes for a week or a month, there is no work when they are discharged. If I tell my client that I caught a cold and need to take a break, I get no more work. When I am well again and tell the client that I can resume my work next month, the client may not need me because another freelancer has already replaced me. I live with this kind of anxiety. I think I shouldn't get sick, and I shouldn't take time off.' (Education freelancer, female, age 29)

Are freelancers really free?

The interviews conducted for this study revealed several ways in which the insecurity of freelance work manifests. First, freelancers experienced employment insecurity due to non-transparent contractual arrangements and a lack of bargaining power. They often relied on verbal contracts that put them in a weak position to demand fair remuneration and claim their basic rights as workers. Second, they faced constant income insecurity, as they had to constantly compete for work orders and worry about the uncertainty of future contracts. Third, freelancers struggled with work–life balance, often working long hours and sacrificing sleep to meet deadlines, and feeling pressure to be constantly connected to social media and online platforms. This ambiguous boundary between work and rest contributed to their internalisation of responsibility for injury and illness, exclusion from the unemployment benefits system, and the psychological burden of paying social insurance premiums from irregular income. In summary, freelancers face a challenging structure that makes it difficult for them to safeguard their basic rights as workers and maintain a healthy work–life balance.

The position of freelancers and disguised self-employed workers in the thesis matrix is cell 3, which is characterised by a high level of melting labour and a low level of institutional consistency (Kim Y.S., 2017). The increasing prevalence of non-regular work and the externalisation of costs and risks have altered the temporal and spatial organisation of work and jobs and resulted in the individualisation of risks. Many freelancers and disguised self-employed workers are excluded from the protection provided by labour-related laws such as the Labour Standards Act and the Trade Union Act, as well as social insurance laws, as they are not recognised as workers due to their status as freelancers, independent contractors or disguised self-employed workers. The dissolution of boundaries regarding working time, solo employers (clients), workplace, working period, and evaluators has led to uncertainty, insecurity and instability for freelancers and dependent self-employed workers. As their income is based on the amount of work they complete, freelancers often work for multiple clients simultaneously rather than signing a contract with a single entity. Moreover, their performance is evaluated by multiple entities. Additionally, freelancers and dependent self-employed face challenges due to institutional exclusion from social protection schemes, such as social insurance and unemployment benefits, which are designed mainly for regular employees. The high premium burden for social insurance is a significant barrier for freelancers with irregular and moderate incomes to participate in social insurance schemes. The exclusion from social protection schemes increases the economic insecurity of freelancers and dependent self-employed, leaving them vulnerable to income shocks and poverty.

Despite the challenges, freelancers have been actively utilising the expanding ICTs and online platforms, which provide them with diverse sales channels and marketing opportunities. The growth of short-term projects and work-centred service industries has contributed to the expansion of the freelance labour market. However, the growth is not without its challenges, and the increasing number of freelancers has intensified competition, leading to concerns about the sustainability of freelance activities.

In conclusion, the expansion of non-regular work and externalisation of costs and risks have transformed the traditional employment landscape, leading to the rise of freelancers and dependent self-employed. The flexible nature of freelance work has attracted young people who value self-realisation and work–life balance, but institutional exclusion from social protection schemes remains a significant challenge. The growth of ICTs and online platforms has expanded the freelance labour market but also intensified competition, leading to concerns about the sustainability of freelance activities.

As we have seen in this chapter, the working conditions of freelancers in Korea reveal a high level of precarity. The insecurity of freelance work is manifested in many ways, such as unclear contractual relationships, unstable income guarantee and work–life imbalance. Furthermore, the Korean social security system seems to be inconsistent in providing coverage for freelancers in both institutional and practical terms.

For instance, unemployment and industrial accident benefits were found to be difficult to apply to income loss caused by the risks of industrial accidents, injury/illness and lack of work. Unemployment benefits could not be applied because the state of no job due to no work orders is different from the state of unemployment defined by the unemployment insurance. Similarly, the freelancers' desire for continuous education and vocational training could not be fulfilled because their state of no work was not recognised as the state of unemployment as defined by the vocational training or employment success package provided by the unemployment insurance, and also because of a lack of business registration.

Moreover, the industrial accident compensation insurance also showed institutional and practical limitations in providing freelancer coverage. Characterised by the absence of a fixed workplace and flexible work time, freelancers encounter institutional limitations in applying for industrial accident insurance benefits, for which only accidents incurred while doing fixed work at the workplace are eligible. On the practical aspect, freelancers have internalised injury and illness incurred while working as personal responsibility.

Finally, regular payment of the contribution to the national pension fund for old-age income security is also a great burden for freelancers with irregular monthly income and fluctuating income levels. In summary, the inconsistency of social protection and working of the freelancers reveal precarity which raises the question: are freelancers really free?

The digital precariat: various Korean platform workers and the new work logic

'Artificial intelligence [AI] calculates the quantity and route together. It means that the AI sets up for whom, how much volume, and which route to allocate. But there, now called the baseline, there is accumulated data for this route. Here, the hourly workers delivered to several households, the difficulty of the route, and all these data are collected and set again as the baseline.' (Delivery platform worker, male, age 30)

Insecurity of platform work

This chapter examines the labour status of platform workers in the Korean digital labour market, situated in cell 3 of the theoretical framework, which is characterised by a high level of melting labour but a low level of institutional protection consistency. Melting labour emphasises the ambiguity in determining a worker's identity or employer, resulting in a legal blind spot for workers in new forms of work. The inconsistency of existing institutional protection policies and new forms of work brought about by the digital economy results in various forms of precarious work. Official data and legal definitions of platform work in Korea are presented, and the expansion of the platform labour market into diverse sectors with the advancement of technology and high internet usage rates in Korea is explained. The chapter categorises platform companies and workers and conducts interviews with workers in delivery, housekeeping services and high-skilled freelance platforms, examining their working conditions and experiences with social protection. The aim of this chapter is to shed light on the precariousness and lack of institutional protection experienced by platform workers in Korea. Specifically, it highlights the inconsistency of the social security system in providing coverage and mitigating insecurity for those situated in cell 3 of the theoretical framework.

Platform workers differ from traditional workers in that they typically have mediated employment arrangements rather than direct employment contracts, performing fragmentary and intermittent work while bearing costs for safety accidents and various expenses, such as computer or vehicle purchases, fuel, insurance premiums and repairs. As the digital division of labour expands, the insecurity of platform labour is exacerbated by the following characteristics of the labour process. The first characteristic is the three-sidedness and power asymmetry in data exchange (Schmidt, 2017). A platform comprises three sides: supply, demand and platform provider. The platform provider not only facilitates the exchange between the other two stakeholders but also controls the interaction between them. In this structure, platform workers, as contractually independent contractors on the supply side, are effectively platform–dependent employees. Consequently, the platform's control arises from information and power asymmetries. Although suppliers and users have limited access to their respective information, the platform company has unlimited access to all information. It can influence the interaction between the other two parties by accessing their information, creating a power imbalance in the platform marketplace. This three-sidedness allows platform companies to transfer risks, legal liabilities, labour costs and means of production to the other two parties.

However, this flexibility comes at a cost. Platform workers are required to work at all hours and accept any job that is offered to them to maintain a steady income. This can lead to a work–life imbalance and mental and physical health issues. The atomisation of platform labour means that workers are isolated from each other, making it difficult to form unions or negotiate better working conditions. Moreover, as platform workers are not considered employees, they are excluded from labour protections and social security benefits such as health insurance, pensions and workers' compensation. This highlights the inconsistency of the social security system in providing coverage for workers in the digital economy, resulting in precarious work.

The insecurity of atomised platform labour offsets the advantages of flexibility and gives rise to problems related to income insecurity. Platform labour is characterised by the atomisation of work into smaller units and the distribution of those units to a crowd. This means that working hours and wages are also divided into smaller units, which increases the potential for risk related to platform workers' wages. If the outcome of microtasks is unsatisfactory from the client's perspective, they can easily replace platform workers with another round of labour. However, getting compensation for the labour input in the process is difficult for platform workers. Even in legal disputes over unpaid wages, platform workers are at a disadvantage. The atomisation of labour not only raises issues related to labour law, such as the definition of 'work' or 'labour', and the application of standards like wage levels and working hours, but also issues related to qualification standards specified in the Social Security Act.

Platform work is characterised by melting labour, which creates ambiguity in determining a worker's identity or employer, leaving them in a legal blind spot. This situation is compounded by income instability since platform workers are contracted in units of tasks rather than jobs and are excluded from social security protection. The work is subdivided into tasks and distributed to many platform workers through a competitive system, meaning they only participate in the production process fragmentarily and intermittently to perform work in units of work. Atomisation makes it difficult for platform workers to act collectively to negotiate power to deal with the labour control of platform companies. Furthermore, power imbalance arises due to an information asymmetry between the platform providers, suppliers (independent contractors) and users (clients), allowing platform companies to control the labour process. This lack of bargaining power and exclusion from existing labour-related laws and social protection systems creates a vicious cycle of income instability, leading to precariousness for platform workers.

This chapter analyses the precariousness of platform work in the Korean digital labour market, which is characterised by melting labour and low institutional protection consistency. Platform workers have mediated employment arrangements, and the expansion of the platform labour market intensifies their insecurity. They are excluded from labour protections and social security benefits, leading to income instability. Atomisation of platform labour means that work is divided into smaller units, increasing the risk of wage instability. Power imbalance arises due to information asymmetry, enabling platform companies to control the labour process, leading to a vicious cycle of precariousness for platform workers. The chapter's findings are based on in-depth interviews with platform workers, managers and experts.

Types of platform labour in Korea

The rise of platform capitalism is causing fundamental changes in the labour market ecosystem, beyond the changes in companies themselves, as goods and services are now traded via online platforms. This suggests that the organisation and operation mechanism of labour are changing. While work organisation and operation mechanism have been changing since the transition to a service economy, with companies downsizing and using various production methods such as outsourcing, dispatch and service supply (Weil, 2014), the emergence of the platform economy is leading to a new type of evolution in the organisation and operation mechanism of labour. Studies show that the number of workers with atypical work arrangements, such as freelancers and independent contractors, is increasing in the platform economy (Katz and Krueger, 2016; Manyika et al, 2016a).

Platform labour in Korea refers to jobs where individuals or unspecified organisations provide services and earn income through online platforms.

Platform workers generally experience weakened employment relations as they perform tasks and projects through ambiguous contractual relationships, rather than adhering to traditional working hours. This form of labour highlights the complexity and diversity of work arrangements in the modern digital economy, which often leads to challenges in defining and regulating employment relationships and worker rights. According to Nam J.W. (2021), platform labour is characterised by 'labor mediated through a digital platform', encompassing various types of labour with only 'task' and 'intermediary through the digital platform' in common (Nam J.W., 2021). The Korean Jobs Committee (2020) proposes four conditions for platform labour in Korea: service provision through a digital platform, seeking temporary jobs, digital platform-mediated payment, and open access to the majority (Korean Jobs Committee, 2020).

As of 2022, the number of platform workers in Korea is estimated to be around 800,000 people or 0.92 per cent of the total employed (Ministry of Employment and Labour, 2022). The survey differentiates between 'platform worker(s) in a narrow sense' and 'platform worker(s) in a broad sense', with the former being defined as someone who provides labour through platforms that affect the allocation of work and remuneration, and the latter being a person who provides labour through any platform. The number of platform workers has increased due to the spread of the digital economy after COVID-19, particularly in fields such as housework, cleaning, care, art and professional services. However, despite the increase, 63.4 per cent of the respondents did not sign contracts or were unsure of their terms.

In Korea, the survey of the Jobs Committee (2020) defines digital platforms as structured spaces where labour is exchanged and platform labour as a service traded through a digital platform (Korean Jobs Committee, 2020). However, Jang J.Y. (2020b) questions the adequacy of classifying all labour providers using online job matching as platform workers, particularly those matched for short-term, part-time work, and argues that the platform should have a coordinating role in the process (Jang J.Y., 2020b). Furthermore, the case of e-commerce or leasing business is excluded from the definition of platform labour, as workers who earn income by selling goods or leasing assets through the platform are considered part of the broader platform economy.

In summary, in Korea, various non-standard forms of work exist, such as regular, temporary and daily workers. Non-regular workers can be categorised as non-permanent, part-time or non-typical workers. Special employment types consist of workers who are excluded from the social security system due to factors like low wage levels, employment instability and irregular income activities. Disguised self-employed workers represent a group of individuals that include freelancers, dependent self-employed people, and those with ambiguous employment relationships. These workers occupy a grey area between employees and self-employed individuals in the informal sector.

Schmidt's (2017) typology of platform work distinguishes between two main categories: gig work and cloud work. Gig work involves online platform labour done at a specific location by a specific person, while cloud work can be done from any location. Crowd work, a subclass of platform labour, is further divided into two categories: microtasking crowd work and contest-based crowd work (Schmidt, 2017). In Korea, the dominant type of platform labour is location-based app labour, classified as gig work, and typical examples include food delivery, domestic work and surrogate driving (a driver employed to drive for the owner of a car).

The labour market in Korea has a more diversified location-based platform than a web-based platform. Hybrid companies that mix cloud and location-based platforms mediate services such as translation, private classes, cleaning and interior decoration online, and labour is performed in physical places. Some labour takes place in freelance marketplaces within web-based cloud work. These companies mostly trade in intangible services and knowledge, and examples of talent brokers include Kmong and Withmon. Microtasking crowd work in Korea is usually done by brokers of specialised tasks, verifying the competence of platform workers in addition to the intermediary role. For instance, Talent Bank matches executives of small and medium-sized enterprises or managers of large companies to form an ad hoc team of proven experts in all industrial sectors to implement a project according to the client's requirements. Companies in Korea that operate contest-based crowd work allocate a creative task to the crowd and ultimately pay for the results of one creator (contest winner). There are several contest-based crowd work platform companies in the field of arts and culture marketing in Korea.

In location-based gig work for accommodation-related labour, companies mainly generate profits from commissions earned through a brokerage. Physical labour, such as managing and cleaning the accommodation, is performed by the accommodation provider. Airbnb is a prime example, charging guests a 6–12 per cent service fee. In the transportation sector, companies can be divided into transportation and delivery services. Transportation services include surrogate driving and ride-sharing rental car use, such as Kakao Driver and Tada. However, Tada was accused of offering illegal taxi services and indicted in 2019, sparking controversy. Delivery services are the most active platform of labour in Korea. Delivery brokerage platforms take commissions from platform workers and member food delivery shops. Baedal Minjok and Yogiyo are prime examples of food delivery platform companies, offering telephone ordering, immediate payment, meet-and-pay services, and membership points proportional to grades.[1]

In recent years, there has been an increase in the number of users for domestic and caregiver work platforms in Korea. Domestic service is usually provided on an hourly basis and at a desired time slot. Childcare platforms have also gained popularity, with brokerage service platforms matching dual-income couples with childcare providers. These interpersonal service platforms not only act as intermediaries but also take over personnel management such as identity verification and interviews. Moving and transportation service platforms are also available, providing a service that compares moving estimates and matches moving companies with clients. Location-based microtasking platforms include those that mediate part-time jobs, recruit entertainers and performance teams, exchange interior information and mediate construction services. These platform companies take brokerage fees for their services. Some platforms have only improved the efficiency of supply–demand matching for conventional brokerage services, while others have pioneered new brokerage business areas. However, they all have in common that they act as intermediaries between service providers and users, generating profits through commissions. Their emergence and expansion are closely linked to the development of information and communications technologies (ICTs). Unlike Schmidt's (2017) classification, Korea has hybrid platforms with both web-based and location-based characteristics, as well as cases where member companies and platform workers use multiple platforms. For instance, freelancers utilise multiple platform accounts to offer their services.

However, the diversity of platform companies and labour types creates varying employment relationships and worker dependencies. For instance, online-based crowd work and local-based gig work have different criteria for determining worker dependence. Depending on the number and type of platforms used, workers may have different levels of an employment relationship, exclusivity and dependence. Nonetheless, all platform workers typically have weakened employment relations, performing tasks and projects through ambiguous contractual relationships instead of working traditional hours. These features are likely to create blind spots in the Labour Standards Act and the Social Security Act, which were enacted and developed based on traditional employment arrangements.

The empirical landscape of the Korean platform labour market

Statistics Korea categorises the working population into wage workers and non-wage workers, so the dependent self-employed are not counted separately in the Economically Active Population Survey. The closest equivalent to the status of 'dependent self-employed' in Korea is 'workers in special employment type' as explained previously. Workers in special employment type are classified as a subtype of non-regular workers in the

Economically Active Population Survey every year. However, the subtype of 'non-wage workers' is only divided into self-employed without employees, self-employed with employees and unpaid family workers, rather than the actual number of dependent self-employed in the labour market. As a result, it is limited to identify the exact size and characteristics of dependent self-employed or platform workers through official Statistics Korea data.

First, the increasing share of own-account workers within the non-wage workers also deserves special mention. Table 7.1 shows the share of own-account workers as a percentage of total non-wage workers by gender and age. We see that the share of own-account workers in total non-wage workers increased from 60.2 per cent in 2008 to 64.9 per cent in 2022. By gender, own-account workers are more likely to be male. In 2022, 73.1 per cent of male non-wage workers are own-account workers and 51.4 per cent of female non-wage workers are own-account workers. In addition, nearly 70 per cent of non-wage workers aged 60 or older are own-account workers.

Among the different types of non-regular workers surveyed by Statistics Korea, 'workers in special employment types' are the closest to the statistical concept of 'dependent self-employed workers'. From 2008 to 2022, the proportion of workers in special employment types has been around 10 per cent of the total non-regular workers. Among female non-regular workers, 7.9 per cent are workers in special employment types, while among male non-regular workers, 5.6 per cent are workers in special employment types (see Table 7.2).

However, it is important to note that the share of 'workers in special employment types' published by Statistics Korea does not accurately represent the actual share of dependent self-employed workers. This is because when conducting the Economically Active Population Survey, Statistics Korea divides the total employed population into wage workers and non-wage workers, and then only surveys 'workers in special employment types' within the wage workers category. Dependent self-employed workers are in a grey area between wage workers and self-employed workers, so it is possible that the number of 'workers in special employment types' is underestimated (see also Chapter 2 for related explanation).

To estimate the size of the dependent self-employed, it is necessary to refer to other surveys and studies, such as focusing on specific occupations where dependent self-employment contracts are common or removing 'true wage workers' and 'true own-account workers' within wage workers and own-account workers (for example, Jung H.J., 2019). Although data is only available for 2017 and 2020, the number of dependent self-employed in South Korea is estimated to be between 4 per cent and 5 per cent of all employed people. On the other hand, the proportion of dependent self-employed within the total non-wage workforce is lower, ranging from 20 per cent to 24 per cent (see also Chapter 2).

Table 7.1: Percentage of own-account workers in total non-wage workers, by gender and age group in Korea

		2008	2009	2010	2011	2012	2013	2014	2015	2016	2017	2018	2019	2020	2021	2022
Total		60.2	59.6	59.6	59.9	59.7	60.1	59.2	58.8	59.3	60.2	58.7	60.7	63.2	64.4	64.9
Gender	Male	69.8	68.5	68.2	68.2	68.3	69.1	–	67.1	–	68.7	67.2	69.0	71.6	73.0	73.1
	Female	46.6	46.4	46.3	47.1	46.2	46.2	–	45.8	–	46.7	45.3	47.6	49.5	49.5	51.4
Age group	15–29	60.1	56.2	54.7	51.2	55.0	51.9	–	49.0	–	52.1	56.1	56.8	61.4	55.6	66.5
	30–39	55.1	54.8	52.2	51.3	52.4	53.5	–	53.9	–	56.6	52.8	56.8	61.0	60.7	61.2
	40–49	54.5	52.0	53.0	53.9	52.7	52.2	–	52.2	–	55.1	54.0	56.7	58.8	62.3	61.2
	50–59	60.3	61.0	60.0	60.5	60.9	60.4	–	57.5	–	58.0	56.7	58.4	59.6	60.8	61.5
	60–	71.9	72.1	72.9	72.3	70.8	72.3	–	70.5	–	69.5	67.1	67.5	69.7	70.1	70.1

Note: Ratio of own-account workers = (number of own-account workers ÷ number of total non-wage workers) × 100

Source: Statistics Korea, Economically Active Population Survey, 1 November 2022. Own calculation

Table 7.2: Percentage of workers in special employment types in total non-regular workers, by gender

		2008	2009	2010	2011	2012	2013	2014	2015	2016	2017	2018	2019	2020	2021	2022
Total		11.0	11.7	10.9	11.4	10.1	10.1	9.7	9.1	9.1	9.1	9.2	9.6	9.1	10.2	10.2
Gender	Male	6.8	7.7	7.3	7.1	6.9	6.8	6.8	4.9	5.3	5.4	5.3	5.4	5.5	5.8	5.6
	Female	15.1	14.2	13.2	13.1	11.4	11.4	10.4	10.6	9.8	9.3	9.5	8.4	7.7	7.9	7.9

Note: Ratio of workers in special employment types = (number of workers in special employment types ÷ number of non-regular workers) × 100.

Source: Statistics Korea (2022)

Meanwhile, shifting the focus to platform workers makes the problem more complicated. This is because the number of platform workers cannot be estimated with official data that cannot distinguish dependent self-employed workers. Therefore, it is possible to consider how to utilise the results of other studies, which are largely divided into two types: combining with other statistical items and conducting a social survey.

In the case of the first methodology, it is the work of adding new standards by reflecting the labour market characteristics that appear in dependent self-employed workers. For example, Kim J.J. et al (2021a) attempted to estimate the size of dependent self-employed workers (freelancer) by combining the level of work autonomy and occupation types (management or professional) with existing data from the National Statistical Office (Kim J.J. et al, 2021a). In addition, it was attempted to estimate the size of dependent self-employed workers based on the size of workers in these industries by deriving industries in which dependent self-employed type of work is frequently observed. However, this type of work has limitations in that the estimate is indirect or the selection of criteria is somewhat subjective.

The second methodology is a method of calculating the size of dependent self-employed workers by designing their own social survey. For example, a study by Jung H.J. (2019) suggests a 'new approach to estimating the size of special type workers' through additional questions such as work dependency, economic dependency and presence of a fixed workplace, noting that the worker nature of special type workers exists between wage workers and single-person self-employed (Jung H.J., 2019). However, there is a limitation in that this is also not a survey that can directly identify platform workers. Therefore, this section will present the size and characteristics of platform workers in Korea based on the survey data and results designed for the purpose of 'estimating the size of platform workers'.

Among the definitions of platform workers discussed earlier, we would like to compare the current status of platform workers nationwide and in Seoul, focusing on Jang J.Y. (2020a, 2020b)'s definition of 'platform workers in the narrow sense' (see Table 7.3). According to the existing survey, the metropolitan area accounts for two-thirds of platform economy workers (people seeking work through platforms) in Korea, and we want to grasp the status of platform workers around the nation and Seoul at the regional level (Kim J.J. et al, 2021a). In December 2020, platform economy workers accounted for 7.6 per cent (1.79 million) of the total employment in Korea and 9.3 per cent (461,000) of the total employment in Seoul. In addition, 25.7 per cent of the Korean platform economy workers were confirmed to be in Seoul. Further, in the case of 'platform workers in the narrow sense', which is being discussed as a policy target in Korea, they accounted for 0.92 per cent (220,000 people) nationwide and 1.16 per cent (58,000) in Seoul, and 26.4 per cent of platform workers in Korea were found to be in Seoul.

Table 7.3: Comparison of rates and estimated size of platform workers: nationwide and Seoul (2020)

Division		Employed people aged 15–64	Platform economy workers (people who seek work through the platform)		
			E-commerce app users	Platform workers in the broad sense	Platform worker in the narrow sense
				Simple job search app users	
Nationwide	Rates (%)	100	7.61	0.16	6.54	0.92
	Estimated size (thousands)		1,827	38	1,569	220
Seoul	Rates (%)	100	9.38	0.17	8.05	1.16
	Estimated size (thousands)		469	8	402	58

Note: Period of Surveys: Both surveys in Seoul and nationwide were conducted for two months from October to November 2020. Method of Surveys: The landline and mobile telephone random digit dialling (RDD) method (sample error 2.71% ± [95% confidence level], gender, age, Seoul population proportional assignment extraction population 17,343).

Source: Jang J.Y. (2020b); Kim J.J. et al (2021a)

Table 7.4: Percentage of platform workers by platform types and industry: nationwide and Seoul

Online platform			Offline platform		
Industry	Nationwide	Seoul	Industry	Nationwide	Seoul
1. IT	19.7	23.3	1. Delivery	67.8	48.8
2. Professional service	15.2	20.6	2. Domestic work	5.0	5.4
3. Creative/art service	26.2	22.9	3. Professional service	11.8	21.7
4. Simple tasks	34.4	23.6	4. Made to order	2.5	4.4
5. Other	4.5	9.8	5. Other	13.0	19.7
Total	100.0	100.0	Total	100.0	100.0

Source: Jang J.Y. (2020b); Kim J.J. et al (2021a)

Estimating the proportion of platform workers by sector (see Table 7.4), delivery service (67.8 per cent nationwide and 48.8 per cent in Seoul) has a high proportion of location-based platform workers in Korea. In addition, Seoul has more than double (21.7 per cent) the number of professional services nationwide (11.8 per cent). In the case of web-based platform workers, the proportion of simple tasks (34.4 per cent) is high nationwide, but Seoul has a similar distribution of IT, professional service and creative services overall.

Table 7.5 shows that the monthly working days, daily working hours and income-related working conditions of platform workers in Korea differ from those in Seoul, according to primary or secondary jobs and web-based or location-based platforms (Kim J.J. et al, 2021a). First, there was an average gap of about nine working days per month of platform workers, between the primary job (19.4 days nationwide and 19.3 days in Seoul) and the secondary job (10.3 days nationwide and 10.1 days in Seoul). Meanwhile, the average working hours of platform workers are 6 hours (6.5 hours nationwide and 6.3 hours in Seoul), with longer working hours of location-based platform workers (6.9 hours nationwide and 6.4 hours in Seoul). In the case of monthly income, the difference between Seoul and nationwide was greater depending on whether they were primary or secondary jobs, and the monthly income of web-based platform workers, which had a relatively high proportion of secondary jobs, was generally lower than that of location-based platform workers.

Finally, it is necessary to compare the survey data that estimated the size of platform workers based on the four criteria for platform workers presented by the Korean Jobs Committee (2020). In this survey, a standard similar to that of the Korean Jobs Committee (2020) was used, and the survey period corresponds to 2021 and 2022, respectively.

Table 7.5: Working conditions of platform workers: nationwide and Seoul (2020)

| | Platform types | | | | Primary or secondary job | | | | | |
| | Online | | Offline | | Primary job | | Secondary job | | Total | |
	Nationwide	Seoul	Nationwide	Seoul	Nationwide	Seoul	Nationwide	Seoul	Nationwide	Seoul
Monthly working days	14.1	14.9	15.1	15.4	19.4	19.3	10.3	10.1	14.8	15.3
Daily working hours	5.3	5.6	6.9	6.4	8.7	7.7	4.3	4.3	6.5	6.3
Monthly income (KRW 10,000)	116.1	129.3	154.9	149.3	238.4	207.9	54.8	63.0	145.9	145.3
Proportion of earned income to total income (%)	56.0	53.0	60.3	64.9	90.9	89.9	21.7	26.5	56.0	62.5

Source: Jang J.Y. (2020b); Kim J.J. et al (2021a)

Table 7.6: Estimated people and percentage of platform workers in total employed people

		2020	2021	2022
Platform worker (broad sense)	N (thousand)	1,790	2,197	2,920
	(%)	(7.46)	(8.5)	(10.95)
Platform worker (narrow sense)	N (thousand)	220	661	800
	(%)	(0.92)	(2.6)	(3.0)

Note: Ratio of platform workers = (number of employed people ÷ number of estimated platform workers) × 100. Each value includes all those who have worked for income in the past three months who have earned income using the online platform.

Source: 2020 = Jang J.Y. (2020b); 2021 and 2022 = Ministry of Employment and Labour (2021, 2022)

As previously explained, the Korean Jobs Committee (2020) has proposed four conditions for platform labour in Korea:

1. service provision through a digital platform;
2. the work was sought through a digital platform;
3. digital platform-mediated payment; and
4. open access to the majority (Korean Jobs Committee, 2020).

The Ministry of Employment and Labour has defined workers who meet Standards 1 and 2 as 'platform workers with a broad definition', and those who meet all Standards from 1 to 4 as 'platform workers with a narrow definition' (Ministry of Employment and Labour, 2022). Platform workers in a broad sense refer to workers who trade 'service or virtual goods' through digital platforms and seek 'work' through these platforms. Platform workers in a narrow sense are defined as cases where 'compensation and work provision must be mediated by a digital platform' and 'when the work to be mediated is open to the majority, not the individual'. These definitions are consistent with the platform workers in the broad and narrow senses as defined by Jang J.Y. (2020b). Table 7.6 presents three-year time-series data that includes the results of the Ministry of Employment and Labour survey and the survey data of Jang J.Y. (2020b).

A qualitative analysis of platform workers in Korea

This section presents the findings of an in-depth interview analysis of platform workers in Korea.[2] The study involved interviews with platform workers, platform managers and owners, and related experts to investigate the labour process of platform work and its inconsistency with the social security system. To gain a comprehensive understanding of how platform labour functions, policy managers of platform companies-related associations and managers of platform companies were also included as field experts.

The platform workers were selected based on the advice of trade unions and academic experts, taking into account their industry and age. The interviewees included platform workers in the delivery, housekeeping service and media industries, and their skill level was also taken into consideration. The selection process involved first determining the industry to be analysed through interviews with platform economy experts, and then platform workers were introduced through experts in the relevant industry and related labour unions. Participants were recruited using a 'snowball sampling' method that considered age and gender according to the identified platform labour patterns in the relevant industry.

The selection criteria for study participants were those who (1) work as freelancers or are self-employed, and (2) provide labour through the mediation of online platforms, including online agencies, apps or programming companies. After interviewing managers of platform companies and platform worker union leaders, six platform workers were selected for the in-depth interviews, which lasted for approximately one to two hours. Before the interviews, the research and participation methods were explained, and all procedures for obtaining the participant's voluntary consent were followed.

The primary role of platform companies is to mediate between service consumers and providers, resulting in the creation of value. This mediation function helps to address information asymmetry and improve the efficiency of service provision. The effectiveness of a platform company can be attributed to three factors:

1. efficient matching of service demand and supply;
2. enabling service providers to focus on their core competencies, without wasting time on non-essential tasks such as customer service and delivery; and
3. facilitating the flexible supply of workforce, especially in the delivery labour market, by addressing issues of excess and shortage of delivery workforce.

Although online intermediary platforms have not entirely replaced direct employment and location-based agencies, they continue to compete for market share using various operating methods. However, the increased efficiency of current platform marketplaces is primarily due to the use of ICT tools. This allows platform companies to provide increasingly efficient services compared to their offline counterparts, through better information management, evaluation and workforce management. Consequently, the key competitive advantage of platform companies is related to their ICT-related human resources.

'If you go to a startup office, more than half of the employees have green computers. They are all developers. Developers are everywhere. Once developed, half done. Development is the key ... uh, development is the key. ... Then, a bit more advanced, if there are more than two or three hundred people, they move over to CR [cooperation resource] one by one, the external cooperation team. That's why developers and external cooperation (outsourcing) are two categories that are the most difficult to obtain in this industry. They are not affordable.' (Platform specialist, female)

The core competitive edge of platform companies is in their use of ICT, and this is also where their employment centre lies. So what role do platform workers play in this context? Managers of platform companies often argue that their relationship with platform workers is not that of employer–employee, but rather a type of company–client relationship.

'The quality of delivery is ensured only when the driver quality is good, and the really important client of ours is not the small business owners who use us [platform] or the consumers who buy fried chicken, but rather the riders. So, we [platform companies] have incentives in getting high-quality riders and then the rest.' (Platform specialist, female)

Platform workers are not just employees, but also users or customers of platform companies who subscribe as members. Initially, users of platform companies believed that the user status was a voluntary choice made by platform workers. However, as platform companies increasingly take on management and control functions for platform workers, it is limited to view platform workers solely as users or clients of platform companies. The main differences between platform companies and traditional production-based companies are their workforce supply and demand mechanisms and their process for improving skills. In the traditional working environment, companies lead the recruitment process by selecting workers. However, the workforce supply and demand mechanism in the platform labour market is completely different. Coordination of workforce supply and demand is automated in a virtual space known as a platform.

'For graphic designers and illustrators, there were indeed agencies. ... In general, such agencies dispatch a dealer to negotiate agreement when they spot appealing articles on Instagram or self-presentation websites where artists post their work, or artist directly contact the agency to present their portfolios. ... Suppose such conventional business operation methods centred on agencies looking for talents and selecting their artists or partners. In that case, the artists register themselves and post their works in Kmong, demonstrating their skills and capabilities and quoting their prices. They form their own markets.' (Platform worker graphic designer, male, age 26)

'It runs as a reverse auction; a customer requests a job, and the potential suppliers look at it and quote their prices. On the customer side, they decide after comparing the profiles, reviews, ratings and prices.' (Vice president of platform enterprise, male)

In traditional industrial societies, companies motivated workers to acquire firm/industry-specific or general skills. However, platform companies do not have much incentive to provide skills training for platform workers. Nonetheless, the service quality of platform workers affects the reputation of the platform company, so some basic service education, such as how to maintain high ratings, is being provided. The responsibility for skill formation beyond basic service education largely falls on platform workers. While platform companies do provide some basic service education (such as how to get a good rating), they have little incentive to form skills for platform workers beyond that. The skill level of platform workers is typically disclosed through portfolios or customer rating systems, which are directly linked to income. Therefore, platform workers have a strong incentive to accumulate skills at the individual/private level in order to improve their portfolio and ratings.

'In the past (agency method), when the number of cleaning service workers was small, we called them all and offered offline education. Now that the number of workers easily surpasses 10,000, the standard itself needs to be changed. It is safe to consider that ratings, reviews and client evaluations do the job. Rating is the most important element; rating is money. So, we tell our cleaning service workers to prove good services to get good ratings and politely request the clients to give good ratings, for rating is money.' (Vice president of platform enterprise, male)

The remuneration system for platform workers differs from conventional workers who sign an employment contract and receive a set salary or wage. In the platform economy, the remuneration for platform workers is determined and paid in various ways, without negotiation between platform companies and workers. The platform companies simply disclose the consideration for the work, mainly in the form of a commission rate. The commission rate is posted for their standard service and is subject to change by the platform company. To clarify, in platform labour, there is no concept of a fixed minimum wage as the price is typically set per hour or per task. While there may be a predetermined hourly rate, the actual pay for the work performed by the platform worker can vary depending on the amount of work completed.

> 'When business was good, in winter, for example, I earned close to five million won. In the off-season, like now, I make about three million won. The difference is huge. So these days, after the hard winter, I think it's time to take a break, I think positively.' (Delivery driver, platform worker, male, age 31)

The absence of a minimum wage concept and the remuneration for platform work being set by the platform company rather than the legal user may result in a power imbalance in the pricing of platform labour. This is especially concerning given the high risk of monopoly due to the network effect inherent in the platform. Payment for work is typically handled through the platform company, which acts as an intermediary between the consumer who requests the work and the platform worker. The platform company receives payment for the work and then forwards payment to the platform worker, while retaining a certain portion as commission.

> 'How do I get paid? The amount displayed on my phone through the app goes straight into my virtual account. Then I can withdraw it to the bank account I registered. I can do it after every payment, but I accumulate money and withdraw when needed. So, I cannot tell the exact amount of the fee. I just know that I received the amount displayed.' (Delivery driver, platform worker, male, age 31)

In the platform economy, the concept of standard working hours has been replaced by a more flexible working arrangement. Platform workers have the autonomy to decide when they want to work, but it does not necessarily mean they work fewer hours. Since the amount of work received is directly linked to income, many platform workers strive to maximise their work hours. It is important to note that the time spent waiting for an order does not count as working hours. While some platform companies provide waiting spaces for platform workers, the majority do not offer a physical workspace for their workers: "Usually, orders for single item don't usually come with plenty of time. In that case, it is not work to be done just day and night, but just a long race against time. I may say I just do it till it's done" (Platform worker graphic designer, male, age 26).

Most platform workers did not have an employment contract, but rather an agreement or code of conduct outlining their responsibilities when providing services to clients. As there is no formal control over the labour contract or workplace, achieving systematic control over work is difficult, unlike earlier employer–employee relationships. Platform users often claim that they do not control platform workers: "We are just a platform operator; they have only to come over and register to the system, just like an Uber driver registers to Uber. We can't force them to go to work or hit a certain number of cases" (Manager of platform companies).

However, as described previously, platform companies exercise a certain degree of control over platform workers in order to manage service quality. This control takes place through an ICT-based rating system as well as through direct and indirect intervention. As such, it is difficult to consider platform workers as truly independent workers who simply use the platform, as platform users often claim.

> 'I am now a delivery rider, but I receive a separate allowance from the company for "managing" other riders. The same goes for general branch offices. To senior riders who are experienced and older than others, the company pays additional 500,000 won, or one million won extra and asks them to manage the riders. … So, I earn some extra pay and manage the riders.' (Delivery driver, platform worker, male, age 31)

The institutional inconsistency of social protection

As the nature of work changes with the rise of platform labour, the definition of industrial accidents must also be reconsidered. Location-based platform labour is currently the dominant form of platform labour in Korea and carries a greater risk of accidents compared to web-based platform labour. While platform workers are at risk of accidents during work, the absence of an established employment relationship often results in ambiguous liability in case of accidents. In many cases, platform workers are held individually responsible for accidents. Therefore, the need for industrial accident compensation insurance has become a significant concern among platform workers. However, due to the absence of an employment relationship, neither the platform operator nor the platform worker has subscribed to industrial accident compensation insurance, and the idea of seeking compensation for injuries through insurance has not occurred to them.

> 'Once an accident occurs, even if the insurance company is ready to set up a product, they ask for extremely high premiums, given the sheer number of motorcycle accidents and rent-seeking cases for Quick and two-wheelers. … So, big companies now negotiate with individual insurance companies. Because of too high premiums, riders refuse to subscribe to existing insurance companies. Taking out insurance is not incumbent on the company, either.' (Platform specialist, female)

Platform companies tend to rely on separate private insurance policies instead of providing platform workers with insurance coverage for work-related accidents through public social insurance. In some cases, they were willing to support industrial accident compensation insurance but did not implement it for fear of it being interpreted as a work agreement, which could lead to the occurrence of responsibilities equivalent to an employment relationship. Therefore, most platform companies were found to be subscribed to private insurers. While the liability in the event of an accident is often ambiguous since the employment relationship is not established, platform workers are held responsible individually. Therefore, the need for industrial accident compensation insurance was high among platform workers, but the absence of an employment relationship made it difficult for them to subscribe to such insurance. In addition, there is no statistical accident-risk assessment of platform labour available, and domestic private insurance companies have no experience in dealing with similar products. Thus, accident risk coverage through private insurers for platform workers may result in excessive cost burden or insufficient risk coverage.

Furthermore, the social security system in Korea presents a blind spot for platform workers. Most platform workers interviewed did not have industrial accident compensation or unemployment insurance coverage. They were also exempt from contributing to the national pension fund, which could affect their eligibility for old-age benefits. Despite their economic activities, some of them were considered dependents to their colleagues who subscribed to health insurance. This is due to the fact that the social insurance system in Korea is based on the premise of employment relationships, and since platform workers make contracts as independent contractors to provide labour, they are classified in the same category as self-employed in the social insurance system, resulting in no or insufficient coverage.

> 'It would be, of course, good to have the four major insurances as a full-time regular employee with job security. But most of my fellow workers, just like me, do not feel the merits of the four major insurances. Apart from this, many have poor credit ratings. ... They work somewhere and refuse to subscribe to the four major insurances for fear of being revealed. They deliberately choose work that is not covered by the four major insurances. ... Also, most workers here prefer taking the entire amount of their earnings to pay the insurance premiums.' (Delivery driver, platform worker, male, age 31)

The classification of platform workers as independent contractors rather than employees results in many of them being excluded from the social insurance system, which can be the only option for low-income workers who cannot afford to pay insurance premiums. This lack of coverage creates a sense of insecurity among platform workers, and it was found that they have a complex desire for social insurance. Despite this desire, many platform workers do not have industrial accident compensation or unemployment insurance coverage, and it is uncertain if they will be eligible for old-age benefits as they are exempt from contributing to the national pension fund. This exclusion from the social insurance system is a result of Korea's social insurance system, which is based on the premise of employment relationships. As platform workers provide labour as independent contractors, they are classified as self-employed and do not receive adequate coverage or no coverage at all.

> 'Bank loans or something like that is not in the four major insurances. I'm in my 30s now, and I would need some bank loans. Now I know the value of the four major insurances in proving my earnings.' (Delivery driver, platform worker, male, age 31)

The study found that platform users view the lack of legal and institutional regulations as a major issue in the platform economy, highlighting the need to recognise the unique nature of platform labour and provide legal protections and social insurance coverage. However, platform entrepreneurs and managers have a mixed perspective on this issue, recognising the need for social protection while also considering the unique characteristics of platform-based work when developing regulations.

Despite differences in the types of platform work (delivery, domestic service and high-skilled freelance), they share commonalities, such as platform companies acting as intermediaries, platform work not being performed under traditional labour contracts, skill formation being largely achieved by workers themselves, and working hours being autonomously determined by workers. Furthermore, all platform workers desire income security, and the need for industrial accident compensation insurance varies across the different types of work. The delivery platform has the highest degree of intervention from the platform company, while the freelance platform has the least.

The precarity of platform workers

This chapter focused on Korean platform workers who are in a labour status with a high level of flexibility but a low level of institutional protection (cell 3). The chapter described how the Korean platform labour market has expanded to various fields, such as transportation, delivery, domestic work and caregiving, due to advancements in technology and high internet usage rates in Korea. The labour process in platform-based delivery, domestic service and freelance activities has four common features:

1. the platform company acts as an intermediary between consumers and producers;
2. platform work is not performed under a labour contract but under a consignment contract or membership subscription;
3. platform workers are responsible for their own skill formation beyond basic service education; and
4. working hours are determined autonomously by platform workers.

However, the autonomy in skill formation and working hours is not necessarily positive since it places the responsibility on platform workers to maintain a high skill level and secure working hours to increase their income. Therefore, platform workers may work more and put in extra effort to achieve higher qualifications, leading to a semi-coercive autonomy situation. The chapter also highlights the need to recognise the distinct nature of platform labour and to protect platform workers under labour or social insurance law, as well as the ambivalent stance of platform entrepreneurs and managers on platform worker protection. Second, platform workers expressed a strong desire for income security. However, the application of the current unemployment concept, as defined by unemployment insurance, was unclear because payment was based on an hourly rate or pay-per-work. Moreover, in the case of delivery platforms, there was a four-party relationship involving the consumer, rider, restaurant and platform, while domestic service and freelance platforms had a three-party relationship involving the consumer, manager/expert and platform. As more parties are involved, the scope of regulations and interventions on platform workers tends to expand. The multi-party mediation system of platform companies makes it difficult to identify who the user is (Jang J.Y. and Lee H.G., 2019).

Regarding the three types of platform work, the delivery platform had the highest degree of intervention in receiving work orders, compensation and control, while the domestic service and freelance platforms relied more on the client's choice for work allocation. The platform company tended to have a stronger role in the delivery platform, with predetermined remuneration. Meanwhile, freelance platform fees were generally determined by negotiation between consumers and experts, with consumer ratings playing a bigger role in controlling the work.

In terms of industrial accident compensation insurance, there was variation among the three platforms. Delivery platforms, which have a high risk of industrial accidents, had a strong desire for insurance coverage, as did the platform workers and companies. Private insurers attempted to meet this need, but the high-risk rate assessment and excessive premiums made it difficult for most platform workers and companies to take out private insurance. Domestic service platform workers had a lower demand for industrial accident compensation insurance than delivery platform workers but had a higher demand for property insurance for damage to home appliances. However, the risk of musculoskeletal disorders was expected to be high due to the manual labour required in domestic services. Despite this, domestic service platform workers did not feel an urgent need for industrial accident compensation insurance. Freelancers online did not express any desire for compensation insurance, and the risk of industrial accidents was invisible to them.

In addition to the need for industrial accident compensation insurance, there are also differences between platforms in terms of the occurrence and identification of industrial accidents. While accidents in the delivery platform are explicit, this is not the case for domestic service and freelance online platforms. Identifying the cause of accidents is also difficult for these platforms under current regulations. Freelance platform workers face issues such as stress and irregular working hours, which may not be recognised as the cause of industrial accidents under current laws. While discussions about recognising delivery platform workers as statutory workers have received attention, this is not the only concern. The cause of industrial accidents is also an important topic for discussion. Overall, platform work represents the dismantling of traditional boundaries surrounding work and workplace, and represents a high level of melting labour. Platform work is characterised by the subdivision of tasks and their distribution to many platform workers through a competitive system, resulting in the atomisation of labour. Platform workers do not participate in the production process and only perform microtasks, and even their labour hours and wages are divided into smaller units and distributed to the majority. The current Labour Standards Act and Trade Union Act, which protect workers with contractual relationships in waged work, do not adequately address the ambiguity of melting labour in determining a worker's or employer's identity. Furthermore, the melting labour faces weakened bargaining power and income instability as contracts are made in units of tasks rather than jobs. Additionally, platform workers are excluded from social protection systems due to the existing social insurance's design mainly to protect waged workers. This exclusion, coupled with the atomisation of labour and deepening of the digital division of microtasks, leads to a vicious cycle of income instability and low bargaining power.

Based on the previous responses, it is clear that platform workers in Korea face a number of challenges related to social protection. One of the biggest issues is the fact that platform workers are often not covered by the social insurance system, which leaves them feeling insecure and vulnerable. This is due to the fact that platform workers typically work as independent contractors rather than having a traditional employment relationship with a company.

In addition to the lack of social insurance coverage, platform workers also face issues related to industrial accident compensation insurance. While some delivery platform workers have expressed a strong desire for this type of coverage due to the high risk of accidents in their work, it is difficult to find suitable insurance products for platform workers. The lack of clear regulations and guidelines around industrial accidents also makes it difficult for platform workers to identify the cause of accidents and receive compensation.

The lack of social protection for platform workers, including the absence of social insurance coverage and legal protections, has resulted in income instability and low bargaining power. The atomisation of platform work, in which tasks are subdivided and distributed to many platform workers through a competitive system, has weakened the bargaining power of workers and exacerbated the need for social protection. The current labour laws and social protection systems are not designed to address the unique nature of platform work, leading to a blind spot in the laws that leaves platform workers vulnerable. Overall, the implications for social protection are clear – there is a need for greater recognition and support for platform workers in Korea. By developing new policies and programmes that are tailored to the unique needs of platform workers, it is possible to create a more just and equitable system that provides greater security and stability for all workers.

8

Conclusion: Towards universal institutional protection for precarious workers in the era of melting labour

Melting labour and the variety of precarious workers

The concept of melting labour served as the analytical prism throughout the book to establish the contours of emerging precarious workers and their variety. The book focused on melting labour as companies and capital evolved the capital accumulation mode alongside technological development. The issues observed in newly expanding forms of work overlapped with the Korean labour market, such as platform work, freelancers and other long-standing issues related to non-regular workers and precarious self-employed workers. The new non-standard forms of work went beyond the departure from the standard 'employment relationship', and the forms of work were changing in ways that differed from existing standards. However, the precariousness issues associated with these types of work were consistent with those discussed thus far for non-regular workers. The long-standing problems of non-regular workers and those brought about by the emerging 'form' of work needed to be explored from a comprehensive and integrated perspective.

In this book I presented a comprehensive analysis of the intersections between institutional protection and melting labour in the Korean context, utilising a theoretical framework that categorises precarious workers based on their level of institutional protection and melting labour. The specific case studies in this book illustrate the experiences of precarious workers in Korea, including the process by which regular workers can fall into precarious work, the disparities between the subcontracting labour market and social safety net, the concentration of female workers in precarious forms of work, and the challenges faced by freelancers and platform workers. The studies utilised qualitative research methods, including in-depth interviews and case study analyses, to provide a detailed account of the implications of institutional protection and melting labour for precarious work in Korea.

Precarity is closely tied to workers' experience of uncertainty, as they are unable to predict the future and lack control over it. Unlike risk, which can be measured and addressed through public and private management programmes, uncertainty poses a sunk cost to human capital and income irregularity can complicate future planning and diminish workers' control over their lives. Melting labour is a concept that describes the diverse types of work and workplaces that blur the boundaries of traditional 'standard' work, particularly formed during times of industrialisation. This shift in the capitalist system has led to fissured workplaces and ambiguity in defining standard employment. By conceptualising melting labour as a cross-cutting change in the nature of work and the workplace, we can move beyond the current understanding of precarious work and establish reform principles that address fundamental issues of social security. These principles should be solutions to the problems faced by each type of work that deviates from traditional forms of work and the workplace. However, melting labour is particularly vulnerable to the lack of institutional protection and often leads to a precarious working environment.

The concept of melting labour describes the evolution of forms of work and the workplace after the industrialisation period, from the manufacturing economy to the service economy, and now to the platform economy. It refers to the dismantling of boundaries surrounding traditional work and workplace forms after the construction of standard employment relations during the Fordist period in advanced economies. As platform work has gained attention among scholars, discussions on work have focused on this new type of work. However, the long-standing problems of the precarity of non-regular workers, subcontracted work, fissured workplaces and the precariousness of new self-employment remain unsolved. The concept of melting labour includes the increase in new forms of work that deviate from standard employment, such as non-regular and atypical work, subcontracted and outsourced work, dependent/disguised self-employment, freelancers and increased platform work. Melting labour can help us understand precarious work by moving beyond the binary of regular and irregular work focusing on employment relationships.

During Korea's industrialisation period, social protections for workers were institutionalised primarily to focus on the standard employment relationship. These institutional protections included labour law, social security law, working environment protection, union law, regulation of the minimum wage and working hours, and education and skill systems. While management innovation and technological progress have increased productivity and social advancement, the features of melting labour have caused inconsistencies with the existing social protection designed based on standard employment relationships. This has resulted in various forms of precarity for workers.

As discussed in Chapters 3 to 7 of this book, the Korean social protection system fails to adequately protect and include workers, leading to precarious work situations. Through specific case studies, each chapter illustrates how workers can become vulnerable when the intersection of melting labour and institutional protection is inconsistent. This study provides a comprehensive examination of the features of melting labour in Korea and highlights the inconsistencies between existing institutions and new forms of work, resulting in various forms of precarity for workers.

The dualisation literature tends to focus on the distinction between regular and non-regular workers, but very few studies have examined how workers move between these categories. Chapter 3 of this book delves into the process by which insiders enter the outside labour market and how, once they become non-regular workers, they are more likely to remain in that category. In the six years following the 2009 mass layoffs at SsangYong Motor, the social security coverage and benefit levels of the employees changed as their employment status changed. Those who were once insiders were now on the periphery, working as non-standard and atypical workers, and were excluded from social protection such as employment insurance, active labour market policies and other welfare systems. These employees were initially regular male workers in the standard employment relationship in the manufacturing sector, which is a typical case of low melting labour and high consistency of social protection with the work form. However, when the work form begins to disintegrate, and workers in the internal labour market move to the external labour market, the existing social protection system fails to function adequately.

Chapter 4 of the book explores the situation of subcontracted workers in the Ulsan shipbuilding industry, while Chapter 5 focuses on outsourced female workers in cleaning services and call centres. It is important to note that even standard employment contracts can become precarious when workers are subjected to organisational changes such as restructuring, downsizing, privatisation or outsourcing. In the case of subcontracting or outsourcing, companies can pressure subcontractors to reduce costs and increase efficiency by outsourcing all working processes except for a few core competence areas. This leads to the expansion of subcontractors in the country. While subcontracted workers in the Ulsan shipbuilding industry experience a comparatively lower level of melting labour, their workplace is still dismantled, and the labour market's employment structure is based on a pyramid subcontracting structure consisting of contractors, in-house/external subcontractors and supply teams (sub-subcontractors). Dismantled workplaces allow companies to shift their obligations to sub-organisations, such as franchising contracts, third-party management, outsourcing and subcontracting, thereby reducing labour costs, social insurance premiums, management costs and corporate welfare costs. This shift also enables companies to avoid complying with consistent personnel policies and labour standards, including working environment regulations.

The gender gap in the Korean female labour market is linked to a high proportion of females in non-regular jobs, as well as females working in outsourced and subcontracted jobs. A notable proportion of non-regular female workers are in their 40s and 50s. After taking time off from the labour market for childbirth and child-rearing, Korean females in their late 30s, 40s and 50s re-enter the labour market as non-regular workers, subcontracted workers, and outsourced workers. The desire to participate in society is present throughout the life cycle of middle-aged women; however, they often experience gender and age discrimination when re-entering the labour market, resulting in limited options and opportunities. Middle-aged female workers are often concentrated in occupations considered 'women's work', such as cleaning or care services. As discussed in Chapter 5, middle-aged and older females have fewer options for regular jobs, leading them to accept low-wage employment with precarious working conditions.

Female workers are particularly vulnerable to outsourcing. In the structure of indirect employment, the employer's responsibility for cleaning workers disappears, and clients demand lower fees from subcontractors, exacerbating their working conditions. While middle-aged to older female workers are employed in cleaning service jobs, relatively younger females are employed in call centres. The rise in the number of call centres is attributed to the expansion of outsourcing and subcontracting relationships. Chapter 5 explains how females employed by subcontractors as permanent employees are not necessarily guaranteed job security. Their working status has been dismantled since the relationship of outsourced call centre workers' employment was further blurred, as call centre workers also work as freelancers and self-employed, performing outsourced call tasks.

While women in their 30s and 40s dominate the call centre subcontractor labour market, family policies aimed at female employees during childbirth and childcare have been inadequate. Dispatching and subcontracting jobs are rampant in the insecure call centre labour market under the subcontractor structure. Chapter 5 reveals how female workers struggle to set up a long-term plan throughout their life cycle in terms of marriage, pregnancy, childbirth, child-rearing and parental leave benefits, despite being institutionally covered by employment insurance. The outsourced female workers analysed in Chapter 5 represent a middle level of melting labour and a low level of institutional consistency. Their workplace boundaries, working time and employer–employee relationships were dismantled, and Korean social protections revealed many limitations in protecting Korean female workers.

The service sector's expansion and the high rate of self-employment in Korea have led to an increase in the number of freelancers. Freelancers often perform professional work independently of an employer or build a career by working in a series of short-term employment. Self-employed businesses and freelancers constitute a significant portion of non-wage workers in Korea. As described in Chapter 6, freelancers' employment status is ambiguous, which contributes to their labour market precarity. Their wage calculation method, methods of securing orders and relationships with employers or contractors differ from waged workers with standard employment relationships and traditional self-employment.

Freelancers are workers between employees and self-employed workers, and their working methods are closely associated with digital and social media platforms. Their insecurity regarding their dependency on and connection to information and communication technology (ICT) and mobile communication technology (MCT) for livelihood is critical. Chapter 6 reveals that freelancers tend to multitask, blurring the boundary between income-generating activities and other activities, and increasing the use of ICT and MCT expands the polychronic system. Mainly, freelancers' income volatility forces them to rely on clients and makes it difficult to separate work and home from the physical, temporal and emotional aspects.

Despite the various elements verifying the insecurity of freelance work, such as unclear contractual relationships, unstable income guarantees and work–life imbalance, Korea's social security system struggles to cover freelance work in institutional and practical terms. As a result, freelancers are positioned precariously with a high level of melting labour and a low level of institutional consistency.

As the economy continues to shift towards digital capitalism, traditional offline economic activities have moved to online platforms. This has led to the emergence of various platform companies and platform work. Platform work involves providing specific services or connecting service consumers and providers using online platforms such as the internet and social networks to carry out projects or provide specific services. This new form of work is characterised by its fluidity and liquidity, making it difficult to categorise into traditional dichotomous divisions such as regular and non-regular workers. The labour process in platform work is entirely different from traditional labour, from contract relationships to receiving work orders, skill formation, compensation and labour control. Furthermore, platform work is characterised by ambiguity in the employment relationship, sophisticated evaluation systems and control of invisible labour through algorithms. In Chapter 7, platform work is described as the most melted form of labour, characterised by a high level of melting labour and low institutional consistency. One notable feature is the use of artificial intelligence to determine work volume, routes and assign tasks based on management and human resource data. Platform work in Korea has expanded to various sectors, including transportation, delivery, domestic work and caregiver work, due to technology development and high internet usage rates. Platform companies act as intermediaries between service consumers and providers, and platform work is often carried out under a consignment or membership subscription contract, shifting the responsibility for risk from the platform company to the platform workers.

The working hours and portfolio of platform workers are directly linked to their income, which leads to semi-coercive autonomy. This means that platform workers have to work more to maintain their income, which puts them in a precarious situation. The current Labour Standards Act and Trade Union Act are designed to protect workers with contractual relationships, but they do not cover most platform workers in legal or practical terms. As a result, platform workers are excluded from social protection systems, which exacerbates their atomisation in the labour process and creates a digital division of microtasks. This vicious cycle leads to income instability and low bargaining power, making them increasingly precarious.

At the start of the book, I presented the puzzle of the complex relationship between the Korean welfare state and its labour market. Despite achieving economic affluence and rapid institutional development in welfare institutions, a distinctively high rate of new forms of precarious work has prevailed in Korea since the 2000s. This raises the question of why the compressed institutional development of the welfare state fails to protect precarious workers in South Korea. Each chapter of this book examines and explains how the mismatch between social protection and work-related legislation enacted during the compressed welfare state development and the melting labour results in various forms of precarity. In the next section, I will explain how this mismatch between institutions and melting labour gradually renders old institutions obsolete, employing the concept of policy 'drift' (Hacker, 2004).

Welfare state 'drift'

The Korean social insurance system that exists today has its roots in social security laws that were introduced in the 1960s (see Chapter 1). Acts such as the Civil Service Pension Act of 1960, the Industrial Accident Compensation Insurance Act (enforced in 1964) and the Medical Insurance Act (implemented in 1977) were initially applied only to employees in standard employment relationships. Similarly, the National Pension Act enacted in 1973 was first applied to employees in the formal sector in 1988. The Employment Insurance Act was enforced in 1995 and initially covered employees of large firms, but it has expanded continuously and now covers employees of small workplaces as well (see Table 1.1 in Chapter 1). Despite the rapid institutional development of the welfare state, Korean welfare spending has stagnated, and actual coverage and benefit levels have decreased. There is also a significant disparity in subscription rates for social insurance between regular, non-regular and self-employed workers. The book's chapters demonstrate how social protection institutions and other legal protections for workers fail to function adequately in both legal and practical aspects.

The Korean welfare state was developed with the assumption of standard employment and an unfissured workplace, but the rise of melting labour and other societal changes have created a blind spot where the levels of melting labour and institutional inconsistency are high. As a result, the existing welfare state model is under increasing pressure. Life course trajectories and welfare needs are less predictable, and the class structure of the working class is also being challenged as more workers are engaged in non-standard employment relationships. However, policy makers have failed to adapt the existing institutions to the new labour market context, resulting in a form of 'welfare state drift'. This drift has led to a mismatch between social protection and work-related legislation, leaving precarious workers without adequate protection. It is important to note that social investment policies were implemented to address new risks in Korea in the late 2000s (Lee and Baek, 2014). However, these policies were primarily focused on family policy and did not fully consider the changing forms of work. This highlights the need for policy makers to adopt a comprehensive and integrated perspective when addressing the challenges faced by precarious workers in the new labour market context. The book's analysis demonstrates that adapting existing institutions to the changing nature of work and institutional protection is crucial for the protection of workers' welfare needs and social protection. The book's chapters provide evidence of this mismatch and demonstrate the need for policy makers to adapt the existing welfare state to better protect workers in the changing labour market.

To understand how existing institutions and policies persist despite changes in the environment, the concept of path dependency is often used, although it has limitations in terms of institutional determinism. Punctuated equilibrium theory suggests that sustainable and stable systems change at critical junctures due to external events such as war or economic crises. However, this theory may not adequately explain gradual institutional changes. An institutional approach, such as Hacker's policy 'drift' argument, may be more appropriate in explaining the institutional inconsistency analysed in this study (Hacker, 2004). The argument of policy drift suggests that policies or institutions may not be updated to reflect changing external circumstances. This can help to explain how social protection frameworks remain in place, but their ability to achieve their goals has weakened due to changes in the nature of work and the dismantling of traditional workplaces. The institutional approach of welfare state 'drift' can explain the institutional inconsistency with melting labour in the Korean welfare state and labour market. The welfare state was built on the assumption of protecting workers in standard employment relationships, but the compressed top-down welfare state structure created a blind spot where the level of melting labour and institutional inconsistency was high. Therefore, the institutional combination designed for the industrial period and the advanced social democratic welfare state still govern a 21st-century digital economy, but their ability to protect workers in precarious employment has been limited.

Drift occurs when policies or institutions are not updated to reflect changing external circumstances. This is particularly problematic when a policy designed to protect against a specific socioeconomic risk remains unaltered, but the nature of the risk has evolved. In the case of Korea's welfare state and social policy, a range of social protections were introduced between the 1970s and 2000s, based on the underlying assumption of standard employment and an unfissured workplace. However, the emergence of new forms of work and a melting labour market, as well as changes to family structures and life course trajectories, have challenged these assumptions. For example, the male breadwinner model of family life is no longer the norm, and assumptions about childcare responsibilities have become less credible as women have entered the labour force. Despite these changes, policy makers have failed to adapt the existing welfare state model to new social contexts, resulting in a form of policy drift. This drift is particularly problematic as institutional arrangements have reached a state of equilibrium, making change difficult.

Policy drift, that policies or institutions fail to adapt to changing external circumstances, often the result of maintaining the status quo of existing policies, which can be a more easier option than attempting to revise and reform them. As a consequence, policy drift can lead to a substantial change in outcomes without necessarily changing the formal rules or their interpretation. The melting labour, with its increase in precarious workers not covered by social protection, is a transformation of an external context that highlights the institutional inconsistency of existing policies. Failing to update institutions that no longer function as intended can, in a sense, be a powerful way of altering their impact.

Recognising the limitations of the logic of path dependency and institutional determinism in explaining institutional changes, the theory of gradual change of institutions focuses on the gradual transformation that evolves through internal factors. This argument is explained by gradual internal change, as institutional change is the 'reconfiguration' of the components of the existing system rather than the 'replacement' of the existing system with the new system. The theory of discontinuous institutional change distinguishes the 'formation' mechanism through contingency and the 'reproduction' mechanism through self-reinforcement, while the gradual institutional change theory emphasises that the system's 'reproduction' mechanism is not consistently the same, suggesting various agents of gradual change other than self-reinforcement.

When changes in the environment, participants and power relations create gaps between formal rules and actual implementation of institutions, gradual institutional changes occur through strategic actions, such as reinterpreting institutional rules or introducing new elements. Layering refers to the partial renegotiation of certain institutional elements, leaving others in place. However, path dependence due to interests in existing systems makes layering a complex strategy for promoting radical change. Conversion describes how existing institutions are redirected to serve a new purpose. Understanding how policy drift affects political dynamics in Korea is crucial. Policy drift can create new political debates and result in winners and losers. It is essential to examine who the losers are and what that means.

Policy drift in the Korean welfare state and labour market also creates winners and losers. The first group consists of the original supporters of the old social protection institution who become disadvantaged when it no longer functions as intended. The second group includes new actors who emerge in response to new problems, constituencies and opportunities created by drift. The mobilising and constraining effects of drift increase the demand for new arrangements and new groups to represent those affected. This can channel actors' responses in particular directions, delimiting a range of possible paths and leaving disadvantaged groups to develop second-best solutions. Meanwhile, the problems created by drift encourage political actors to focus on alternative venues and develop new institutions, organisations and strategies. The silver lining is that institutional drift can encourage policy changes by adapting old groups and emerging new groups in response to new problems. In this way, drifting policies can create new politics.

The two-by-two matrix provides insight into drift dynamics, showcasing the range of variation across different cases (see Table 8.1). The effects of drift create new political spheres, with winners and losers emerging as a consequence. Winners may include experts with high levels of ICT and knowledge-based skills, who have high mobility and can utilise their skills as assets in the melting labour market. Additionally, individuals with significant wealth generated from property rather than work income also emerge as new winners, as institutional inconsistency provides leeway to those who do not need public welfare provisions or work income.

Another group of winners are platform companies, who are less obligated to pay for social protection contributions or invest in job training since their workers are now considered clients rather than employees (see Chapter 7).

Table 8.1: New and old precarious workers and possible alliance for institutional reform

	Low level of melting labour	High level of melting labour
Low level of institutional consistency	(1) New loser group	(3) Emerging loser group
High level of institutional consistency	(2) Old loser group	(4) Winner group

These groups are new winners who do not actively seek to win but benefit from institutional inconsistency. On the other hand, old loser groups also emerge (those who moved from cell 2 to cell 1) (see Table 8.1). Standard workers who experience melting labour are the original backers of the policy or institution, known as 'old groups'. Once institutions no longer suit traditional forms of work, employees of standard employment relations and the direct employment relationship, these workers are subtracted and outsourced as 'standard waged workers' and non-standard workers. Trade unions represent workers of the standard form, and these old groups must effectively push back, adapt or be exposed to the risk of perishing.

Another group of losers includes workers experiencing a higher level of melting labour and institutional inconsistency (those in cells 1 and 3). These 'new groups' are exposed to risk due to the lack of institutional protection, political representation and power. Workers in this group include freelancers, platform workers and other atypical forms of work. As the process of melting labour progresses from the post-industrial to the digital economy, institutions to protect workers become rigid, primarily designed to protect the risk of standard workers in the Fordist industrial period. This has led to the malfunctioning of institutions, resulting in drift.

Various types of precarious work are emerging in the gap between melting labour and institutions built with the assumption of the standard employment relation. However, identifying the instigator of welfare state drift or the opponent of reform is difficult. Melting labour occurs gradually, and little visibility exists when institutional drift occurs due to the absence of reform. The cause of drift is mainly due to inaction, not action, which makes identifying the opponent of reform challenging.

The creation of new winners and old and new loser groups can create new politics of institutional change, and drift can be a pervasive way for institutions to change in the melting labour era. Failure to update policies or institutions when they cease to function as intended is a powerful way to alter their impact (Hacker, 2004). The emerging new players can have a political effect, and drifting policies can create new politics. Some new politics can be expected to bring about positive changes. For instance, the Rider Union, a platform delivery union, conducted collective bargaining with the delivery agency Baedaleun Brothers, and reached an agreement that raised the issue of poor working conditions for riders and demanded a new heat wave allowance. Moreover, the Rider Union has also been instrumental in the revision of the Industrial Accident Insurance Act and the Collection Act, which includes the abolition of the industrial accident-exclusive standard. The Broadcasting Staff Union is another new union that was formed in response to the tragic death of two independent producers during filming. This union launched the 'Independent Producer Union Promotion Committee', holding the EBS accountable for the accident.

Part-time Workers' Solidarity is a union that campaigns for the 'minimum wage of 10,000 won' and conducts labour law consultations to solve the problems of workers who have been unfairly treated. They have urged the compulsory issuance of wage statements, and collective bargaining and protests were held for employers and companies exploiting part-time workers. These unions and advocacy groups are a response to institutional drift, highlighting the need for policies and institutions to be updated to reflect the changing nature of work. As the process of melting labour progresses from post-industrial to a digital economy, institutions to protect workers present their rigidity, mainly designed to protect the risk of standard workers in the Fordist industrial period. The emergence of new winners and losers and the changing nature of work make it necessary to reassess and update existing policies and institutions.

Next avenue of research

Is the group of precarious workers in the melting labour and institutional inconsistency zone a new working class? The traditional manufacturing-based working class had welfare benefits and services tailored to their life cycle, with guaranteed work rights. However, melting labour workers face an uncertain future regarding their careers, income, (un)employment trajectories, care services, and so on. Moreover, they are fragmented into various forms throughout their life cycles. While this book confirms the 'positions' of the various precarious workers in slots, this is a static approach to analysing how these workers are excluded from existing social protection while experiencing precarious working conditions. Similarly, static approaches are found in discussions on class such as the 'class of uniformities in life changes' (Goldthorpe), 'occupational structure and relations' (Wright), work logic (Oesch), 'welfare state effect' (Esping-Andersen), and the effect of institutions on the structuring of dual labour groups (the dualisation thesis). However, given the different mobility patterns from Fordism-based class theory and various precarity in flux, the degree of class closure is highly uncertain. Therefore, the criterion of life changes and the identification of multiple sources of class formation are crucial to studying stratification patterns in an evolving post-industrial society. Thus, a static picture of 'precarious work' may be misleading. The intersection of melting labour and institutional inconsistency places groups at risk and creates a niche for a new group of precarious workers to emerge. However, it remains unclear if they form a new class structure that can be classified as a precariat.

The next avenue of research involves exploring the contribution of the varieties of precarity to the class discussion. Examining the mobility patterns of precarious workers in the melting labour era becomes a new research agenda for understanding class dynamics. The concept of mobility detection among various precarious workers can provide insights into the formation of class boundaries where precarity persists across generations. Melting labour serves as an analytical framework that helps outline the emerging class structure. Melting labour is an analytical prism that establishes the contours of an emerging class structure. However, confirming the mobility patterns of precarious workers can reveal a new class structure in the post–industrial and digital economy era. Notably, depending on the presence or absence of institutions that are consistent with changes in the work form and workplace, mobility patterns may differ, and the class structure of each country may vary. Ultimately, further analysis of the mobility of various precarious workers can also explain the difference in power between classes according to the role of institutions. Further research is required to examine whether this flux of melting labour confirms the end of classes or harbours the main springs of new regimes of class formation.

The book discussed the increasing pressure on the Korean welfare state due to societal changes and the rise of melting labour. It explains how policy drift can arise when policy makers fail to adapt to new labour market contexts, resulting in institutional inconsistency and weakened social protection frameworks.

The book's analysis of the intersections between institutional protection and melting labour in the Korean context can serve as a valuable case study for other countries undergoing similar changes in the nature of work and the workplace. The challenges faced by precarious workers in Korea, as illustrated by the case studies, are not unique to that country, and the analysis can provide insights into how to address these challenges in other contexts. Moreover, the concept of melting labour can be applied more broadly to describe the diverse types of work and workplaces that blur the boundaries of traditional 'standard' work, particularly during times of industrialisation. As such, the book's reform principles for addressing fundamental issues of social security can also be adapted and applied to other countries facing similar challenges. Ultimately, by examining the experiences of precarious workers in Korea and the implications of institutional protection and melting labour for their work, the book can contribute to the ongoing global conversation on how to create more secure and equitable working conditions for all.

In the context of institutional drift and precarity, it's worth noting that institutional reform can be a potential solution. But how does the presence or absence of an updated welfare state influence the mobility patterns of precarious workers? The new class structure of each country can differ based on how 'loser groups' mobilise their political resources. Upgrading the old welfare state may contribute to the mobilisation of such groups to increase their political resources, thereby leading to gradual change. Factors like skill, education, dependency on benefits and social protection coverage can impact mobility patterns. Therefore, analysing the absence and presence of welfare institution reform can help determine whether a class closure exists for precarious workers or whether it's just a temporary fix for the digital economy. This can eventually explain the difference in power between new classes and the quality of life of precarious workers in the melting labour era. Though it's challenging to predict precisely when the window of institutional reform will be opened, the forging method is straightforward. It's crucial to establish labour and social protection legislation that ensures universal institutional protection for all workers (OECD, 2017, 2018a) in the era of melting labour.

Notes

Chapter 2

[1] All statistical data referring to KOSIS (Korean Statistical Information Service) have been obtained from http://kosis.kr/.

[2] Insurance planner, construction equipment engineer, workbook teacher, golf caddy, courier engineer, exclusive quick service engineer, loan recruiter, credit card recruiter, surrogate driver, visiting instructor, visiting salesperson, rental product visiting inspector, home appliance installer and freight owners.

[3] In the survey, in response to a question targeting those who have worked for income in the last three months at the time of the survey, 'Are there any jobs that use online platforms such as websites or mobile phone apps to find customers or jobs?', those who answered 'Yes' and gave the name of the app or website, that is, the people who sought work through the platform, comprised 7.64 per cent (about 1.38 million) of the total employed (24 million people) aged 15 to 64 in 2020.

Chapter 3

[1] This subsection presents major results of the study led by myself together with my colleague Kim Seung-sup. See Lee S.Y. and Kim S.S. (2015) for more details on survey results.

Chapter 4

[1] This subsection presents some of the major results of the study led by myself and colleagues EunJi Kim and Goeun Park. For more information and detailed results, see Lee S.Y. et al (2017b).

Chapter 5

[1] This subsection presents selected major results of the study led by myself and colleagues Hyojin Seo and Koeun Park. For more information and detailed results, see Lee S.Y. et al (2018).

[2] This subsection presents some of the major results of the study led by myself and colleague Cho Hyukjin. For more information and detailed results, see Lee S.Y. and Cho H.J. (2019).

[3] CSR (call centre representative or customer service representative) is a type of call centre worker who handles inbound or outbound communication with customers through various channels like phone, live chat, email or letter. They may receive calls or make calls, depending on the nature of their job responsibilities.

Chapter 6

[1] This subsection presents some of major results of the study led by myself and colleagues Kyoung-jin Park and Gyu-hye Kim. For more information and detailed results, see Lee S.Y. et al (2019b).

Chapter 7

[1] In December 2019, Delivery Hero (DH), the operator of Yogiyo, took over Baedal Minjok. However, it was announced that the two platform companies would not merge together, operate independently as before (Yonhap News Agency, 2019).

[2] This subsection presents some of the major results of the study led by myself and colleagues Seung-ho Baek and Jae-wook Nahm. For more information and detailed results, see Lee S.Y. et al (2020a).

References

Ahn J.H. (2014). Bargaining structure and class section formation of indirectly-employed contingent workers in urban railway. *Korean Association of Labor Studies*, 20(3), 67–104.

Ahn J.Y. (2015). The gap in working conditions and structure of original subcontracting in automobile and shipbuilding industries. *Labor Review*, 126, 38–49.

Assemblyman wung rae Noh (2020). *Special employment type industrial accident compensation protection status*. Press release.

Assemblywoman Hye-young Jang (2020). *Non-wage workers such as special employment, freelancers, and platform labor increased by 2.13 million over the past five years*. Press release.

Baek S.H. (2005). A comparative study on the institutional complementarities in coordination of the sphere of distribution and production: Focus on the determinants of income inequality. *Korean Journal of Social Welfare*, 57(4), 91–118.

Baek S.H. (2014). Class and precarious work in Korean service economy. *Korean Social Policy Review*, 21(2), 57–90.

Baek S.H. and Lee S.Y. (2014). Changes in economic activity, skills and inequality in the service economy. *Journal of Asian Sociology*, 43(1), 35–58.

Bauman, Z. (2000). *Liquid modernity*. Cambridge: Polity.

Beck S.H. (2014). Class and precarious work in Korean service economy. *Korean Social Policy Review*, 21(2), 57–90.

Beck, U. (1992). *Risk society: Towards a new modernity*. London: SAGE.

Blank, R.M., Danziger, S. and Schoeni, R. (2006). *Working and poor*. New York: Russell Sage Foundation.

Böheim, R. and Mühlberger, U. (2009). Dependent self-employment: Workers between employment and self-employment in the UK. *Zeitschrift fur Arbeitsmarktforschung*, 42(2), 182–195.

Bonoli, G. (2006). New social risks and the politics of post-industrial social policies. In K. Armingeon and G. Bonoli (eds), *The politics of post-industrial welfare states: Adapting post-war social policies to new social risks* (pp 3–26). London: Routledge.

Bonoli, G. (2012). Active labour market policy and social investment a changing relationship. In N. Morel, B. Palier and J. Palme (eds), *Towards a social investment welfare state?* (1st edn, pp 181–204). Bristol: Bristol University Press.

Chae Y.J. (2015). Normalization of dirty work by job crafting: College janitors' identity construction. *A Study on the Human Resources Organization*, 23(3), 7–41.

Cheong H.J. (2019). A new approach to estimating the size of special type workers. *Employment Labor Review*, 88, 1–11.

Cho D.M. (2007). Working-living conditions of subcontracted cleaning workers. *Catholic Journal of Social Science*, 23, 5–41.

Cho D.M., Cho G.B., Choi H.I., Sim J.J., Kim K.S., Hwang S.O., Chung H.J., Lee N.S., Kim G.S., Song Y.H. and Noh S.C. (2015). *A survey on the human rights status of non-regular workers in the private sector: Focusing on special-type workers*. Seoul: National Human Rights Commission of Korea.

Cho D.M., Chung H.J., Hwang S.W., Lee N.S., Nam W.G., Kim G.J., Lee S.H., Song M.S., Cho H.J., Jang H.E., Hwang S.O. and Hong C.G. (2018). *Survey on labor rights of indirect employment workers*. Seoul: National Human Rights Commission of Korea.

Cho J.M. (2015). *A study of occupational practice and identity of freelancers in local broadcasting stations: Focusing on the broadcasting of freelancer Jeonbuk province*. Jeonju: Chonbuk National University.

Cho S.K. (2007). Outsourcing and indirect discrimination in women's jobs. *Korean Association of Women's Studies*, 23(2), 143–176.

Choi C.W. (2017). Political economics of platform capitalism: Commodification of social life and the future of labor. *Cultural Sciences*, 92, 48–73.

Chosun Ilbo (2020). Forty-six reinstated Ssangyong Motor laid-off workers, and despite the management's paid leave policy, 'Going to the factory on the 7th as scheduled'. *Chosun Ilbo*. https://www.chosun.com/site/data/html_dir/2020/01/06/2020010603131.html

Doeringer, P.B. and Piore, M.J. (1971). *Internal labor markets and manpower analysis*. Lexington: Heath.

Emmenegger, P. (2009). Barriers to entry: Insider/outsider politics and the political determinants of job security regulations. *Journal of European Social Policy*, 19(2), 131–146.

Emmenegger, P., Häusermann, S., Palier, B. and Seeleib-Kaiser, M. (2012). *The age of dualization: The changing face of inequality in deindustrializing societies*. Oxford: Oxford University Press.

Eom E.H. (2007). Issues and challenges of non-regular workers: Focusing on the Non-regular Workers Protection Act. *National Policy Study*, 21(2), 71–105.

Esping-Andersen, G. (1990). *The three worlds of welfare capitalism*. Princeton: Princeton University Press.

Esping-Andersen, G. (1993). *Changing classes: stratification and mobility in post-industrial societies*. London: SAGE.

Estevez-Abe, M. (2008). *Welfare and capitalism in postwar Japan*. New York: Cambridge University Press.

Eun S.M. (2011). Changes in Japan's employment strategy: Temporary employee and the second social safety net. *International Journal of Japanese Sociology*, 4, 48–79.

Eurofound (2018). *Employment and working conditions of selected types of platform work*. Luxembourg: Publications Office of the European Union.

European Parliament (2017). The social protection of workers in the platform economy. Study for the EMPL Committee, IP/A/EMPL/2016–11, Brussels.

Fachinger, U. and Frankus, A. (2015). Freelancers, self-employment and the insurance against social risks. *The Handbook of Research on Freelancing and Self-Employment*, 135, 135–146.

Fersch, B. (2012). 'German angst' vs 'Danish easy-going'? On the role and relevance of insecurity and uncertainty in the lives of freelancers in Denmark and Germany. *Sociology*, 46(6), 1125–1139.

Friedman, G. (2016). A worker without an employer. *International Labor Brief*, 14(9), 9–18.

Garben, S. (2017). Protecting workers in the online platform economy: An overview of regulatory and policy developments in the EU. European Risk Observatory discussion paper [Article]. European Agency for Safety and Health at Work.

Geum J.H. (2004). Female labor market, sexual discrimination, occupational segregation, crowding hypothesis, dual structure. *Korea Review of Applied Economics*, 6(3), 259–289.

Gold, M. and Mustafa, M. (2013). 'Work always wins': Client colonisation, time management and the anxieties of connected freelancers. *New Technology, Work and Employment*, 28(3), 197–211.

Goodman, R. and Peng, I. (1996). The East Asian welfare states: Peripatetic learning, adaptive change, and nation-building. In G. Esping-Andersen (ed), *Welfare states in transition: National adaptations in global economies* (pp 192–224). London: SAGE.

Gordon, D.M., Edwards, R. and Reich, M. (1982). *Segmented work, divided workers*. New York: Cambridge University Press.

Gorz, A. (1999). *Reclaiming work: Beyond the wage-based society*. Cambridge: Polity Press.

Green, F., Krahn, H. and Sung, J. (1993). Non-standard work in Canada and the United Kingdom. *International Journal of Manpower*, 14(5), 70–86.

Gwak S.S. and Park M.J. (2013). Ssangyong Motor Incident: Diagnosis of cause and seeking alternatives. *Labor Review*, 97, 20–33.

Hacker, J.S. (2004). Privatizing risk without privatizing the welfare state: The hidden politics of social policy retrenchment in the United States. *The American Political Science Review*, 98(2), 243–260.

Hacker, J.S. (2006). *The great risk shift: The assault on American jobs, families, health care, and retirement and how you can fight back*. New York: Oxford University Press.

Hall, P.A. and Soskice, D. (2001). *Varieties of capitalism*. Oxford: Oxford University Press.

Hankyoreh (2018). All 119 people fired from Ssangyong Motor will return to the Pyeongtaek Factory. https://www.hani.co.kr/arti/society/labor/862091.html

Harris, S.D. and Krueger, A.B. (2015). A proposal for modernizing labor laws for twenty-first-century work: The 'independent worker'. *The Hamilton Project,* Discussion Paper 2015–10.

Heo H.J. (2016). *The cruel history of modern Joseon.* Seoul: Humannitas.

Houseman, S. and Osawa, M. (2006). Nonstandard employment in developed economies: Causes and consequences. *Industrial & Labor Relations Review,* 59(2).

Huws, U., Spencer, N. and Joyce, S. (2016). Crowd work in Europe: Preliminary results from a survey in the UK, Sweden, Germany, Austria and the Netherlands. FEPS Studies.

Hwang J.W. (2009). Characteristics of freelance labor and policy response. *Labor Review,* 6, 55–66.

Hwang J.W., Kwon H.J., Kim Y.M., Park J.S. and Nam J.R. (2009). *A study on freelance employment relations: Focusing on film and IT industry.* Sejong: Korea Labor Institute.

ILO (2003). *The scope of the employment relationship.* International Labour Conference 91st Session Report. Geneva.

ILO (2016). *Non-standard employment around the world.* Geneva.

ILO (2017). *Dependent self-employment: Trends, challenges and policy responses in the EU.* Geneva.

ILO (2018). *Digital labour platforms and the future of work: Towards decent work in the online world.* Geneva.

ILO (2019). *Extending social security to workers in the informal economy: Lessons from international experience.* Geneva.

ILO and OECD (2018). Promoting adequate social protection and social security coverage for all workers, including those in non-standard forms of employment. Paper prepared for the EWG meeting, 20–21 February.

Industrial Accident Compensation Policy Division of the Ministry of Employment and Labour (2019). *Analysis of industrial accidents in 2019.* Seoul: Ministry of Employment and Labour.

Jang J.Y. (2019). *An integrated labor market policy paradigm for the resolution of the labor market dual structure.* Sejong: Korea Labor Institution.

Jang J.Y. (2020a). *Employment safety net in the digital age: Focusing on responding to the spread of platform labor.* Sejong: Korea Labor Institution.

Jang J.Y. (2020b). Size and characteristics of platform workers. *Employment & Labor Brief,* 104. Korea Labor Institution.

Jang J.Y. and Lee H.G. (2019). *The prospect of platform workers protection system: Focusing on the protection of labor law and the application of social security system.* Sejong: Korea Labor Institute.

Jang J.Y. and Park C.I. (2019). Social insurance blind spot: Employment insurance and industrial accident insurance. *Labor Review*, 176, 9–19.

Jang J.Y. and Hong M.K. (2020). Employment insurance for a national employment safety net. *Labor Review*, 183, 72–84.

Jang J.Y., Kim G.J., Park E.J., Lee S.Y., Lee C.S. and Jeong S.G. (2017). *New job types and policy responses in line with the development of digital technology*. Sejong: Korea Labor Institute.

Jang J.Y., Lee H.G., Cho I.Y., Park E.J. and Kim G.J. (2020). *Employment safety net in the digital age*. Sejong: Korea Labor Institution.

Jeong E.H. (2001). How to view the size of non-regular workers: Related to the debate over the size of non-regular workers. *Labor Society*, 56, 91–103.

Jeong E.H. (2002). Inequality in labor market and inequality within organizations: A study of wage inequality in the 1990s in Korea. *Korean Journal of Sociology*, 36(6), 1–25.

Jeong E.H. (2013). Formation of labor classes and alternative welfare models in the era of non-regular employment. *Economy and Society*, 98, 351–356.

Jeong E.H. and Jeon B.Y. (2001). Changes in the Korean wage structure in the 1990s: Is the internal labor market weakening. *Economy and Society*, 52, 156–183.

Jeong H.J. and Jang H.E. (2018). *A basic study for estimating the size of workers in special types of work*. Sejong: Korea Labor Institute.

Jeong I.H. (2001). How to view the size of non-regular workers: Related to the debate over the size of non-regular workers. *Labor Society*, 56, 91–103.

Jeong I.H. (2013). Formation of labor classes and alternative welfare models in the era of non-regular employment. *Economy and Society*, 98, 351–356.

Jeong M.K. (2007). The historical formation of the developmental production and welfare regimes in Korea. *Korea Social Policy Review*, 14, 256–307.

Jeong Y.H. (2013). The history, reality, and direction of the struggle for the minimum wage. *Contingent Labor*, 99, 24–29.

Jung E.H. (2015). Wage inequality in Korea in comparative perspective. *Korean Journal of Sociology*, 49(4), 65–100.

Jung H.J. (2019). A new approach to estimating the size of special type workers. *Employment Labor Review*, 88, 1–11.

Kalleberg, A.L. (2000). Nonstandard employment relations: Part-time, temporary, and contract work. *Annual Review of Sociology*, 26, 341–394.

Kalleberg, A.L. (2003). Flexible firms and labor market segmentation: Effects of workplace restructuring on jobs and workers. *Work and Occupations*, 30(2), 154–175.

Kalleberg, A.L. (2009). Precarious work, insecure workers: Employment relations in transition. *American Sociological Review*, 74(1), 1–22.

Kalleberg, A.L. and Vallas, S.P. (2018). Probing precarious work: Theory, research, and politics. *Research in the Sociology of Work*, 31(1), 1–30.

Kalleberg, A.L., Hewison, K. and Shin, K.-Y. (2021). *Precarious Asia: Global capitalism and work in Japan, South Korea, and Indonesia.* Stanford, CA: Stanford University Press.

Kang H.A. (1996). A comparative study on women's labor policy in Korea and Japan. *Modern Social Science Study,* 7(1), 273–303.

Kang S.B. (2011). Working conditions of cleaning service industry. *Labor Review,* 79, 92–108.

Kang S.T. (2014). Informal employment and labour law. *Labor Law Research,* 36, 147–178.

Katz, L.F. and Krueger, A.B. (2016). The rise and nature of alternative work arrangements in the United States, 1995–2015. *NBER Working Paper Series, 22667.*

Kazi, A.G., Yusoff, R.M., Khan, A. and Kazi, S. (2014). The freelancer: A conceptual review. *Sains Humanika,* 2(3), 1–7.

Kenney, M. and Zysman, J. (2016). The rise of the platform economy. *Issues in Science and Technology,* 32(3), 61–69.

Keum J.H. (2000). Changes in the women's labor market and policy direction. *Regulatory Study,* 9(2), 157–185.

Kim C.S. (2019). *A survey on the human rights situation of platform workers.* Seoul: National Human Rights Commission of Korea.

Kim, D.H. (2018). *History of welfare capitalism in Korea.* Seoul: Seoul National University Publication and Culture Center.

Kim G.H., Lee S.Y. and Park S.J. (2020). Between 'employment' and 'unemployment': A qualitative study on youth turnover. *Korean Social Policy,* 27(4), 49–85.

Kim H., Lee S.H., Park S.H., Kwon S.J., Kim K.M., Park S.M. and Jeong W.S. (2009). *Evaluation and implications of labor-management relations in 2009.* Seoul: Ministry of Employment and Labor.

Kim H.K. (2008). A study on the labor market system for economic growth and social integration. *Labor Policy Review,* 8(3), 93–124.

Kim J.J. (2013). Labor process and status of call center counselors. *Labour Society Bulletin,* 172, 112–129.

Kim J.J. (2018). Employment status and alternatives for freelance in Korean society. *Gyeonggi-do Youth Freelance Support Ordinance Plan Forum.*

Kim J.J., Park G.S. and Yoon, J.H. (2018). A plan to create quality jobs through the establishment of a public employment corporation. *FKTU Research Center Series of Research,* 5, 1–216.

Kim J.J., Shin W.J. and Kim Y.W. (2021a). Digital platform labor status and characteristics II: Web-based, regional-based scale and actual conditions. *Issue Paper,* 5, 1–35.

Kim J.J., Shin W.J., and Kim Y.W. (2021b). Status and characteristics of digital platform labor II: Web-based, regional-based scale and actual conditions. *Korea Labor and Social Research Institute Issue Paper,* 5, 1–35.

Kim J.S., Kang M.J. and Jeong H.O. (2005). *Characteristics of female non-regular workers and policy tasks*. Seoul: Korea Women's Development Institute.

Kim J.Y., Kwon H.J., Choi G.S., Yeon B.R. and Park B.G. (2018). *Estimation and characterization of platform economy workers*. Eumseong: Korea Employment Information Service.

Kim M.S. (2006). A critical review on the profiles of Korean female labor force: 1960–2000. *Korea Journal of Population Studies*, 29(1), 133–156.

Kim N.G. (2012). The reformation way of redundancy dismissal system from the view point of Ssangyong motorcar case. *Labor Law Review*, 33, 247–291.

Kim P.H. (2010). The East Asian welfare state debate and surrogate social policy: An exploratory study on Japan and South Korea. *Socio-economic Review*, 8(3), 411–435.

Kim S.H. (2015). A study on the trends of gender wage gap in Korea. *The Review of Social & Economic Studies*, 28(3), 113–148.

Kim S.H., Lee J.A. and Jeong J.Y. (2013). The mutual construction of aged women workers and the low wage work: The study on gender and age discrimination and occupational segregation of aged women. *Labor Policy Study*, 13(3), 59–90.

Kim S.Y. and Kim Y.M. (2015). Working experiences of cleaning workers. *Korean Journal of Occupational Health Nursing*, 24(3), 183–193.

Kim T.H. and Kim K.H. (2022). *Social Research Methodology*. Seoul: KNOU Press.

Kim W.S. and Shi S.J. (2020). East Asian approaches of activation: The politics of labor market policies in South Korea and Taiwan. *Policy and Society*, 39, 226–246.

Kim Y.C. and Kim J.H. (2006). *Qualitative Research Methodology*. Yongin: Muneumsa.

Kim Y.H. and Lee S.Y. (2014). Analysis of the 'time selective job policy': A comparative study on South Korea, Netherlands and Germany. *Korean Association of Social Policy*, 21(3), 93–128.

Kim Y.J. (2004). *Industrial accident status report of in-house subcontractors in the shipbuilding industry*. Seoul: Assemblywoman Kim Young Ju Office.

Kim Y.O. (2010). The gender pay gap in managerial positions. *The Journal of Women and Economics*, 7(2), 1–24.

Kim Y.S. (2014). Issues and alternatives: Results of the employment type disclosure system for non-regular workers at large companies with 300 or more employees. *Labor Society*, 178, 82–98.

Kim Y.S. (2016). Size and actual condition of non-regular workers. *Korea Labor Institute* Paper, 9, 1–35.

Kim Y.S. (2017). Assessment model for industrial accidents prevention policy. *Journal of Applied Reliability*, 17(1), 38–49.

Kim Y.S. (2019). The size and status of non-regular workers: The National Statistical Office's additional survey on economically active population. *Korea Labor and Social Research Institute Issue Paper*, 17, 1–36.

Kim Y.S. (2020a). Laborers' images in the era of platform capitalism. *Korean Journal of Urban Studies*, 18, 117–146.

Kim Y.S. (2020b). Size and status of non-regular workers: Statistics Korea, results of 'additional survey of economically active population'. *Korea Labor Institute Issue Paper*, 20, 1–33.

Korea Occupational Safety and Health Agency (2017). *Announcement of the 2016 survey results on the calculation of integrated statistics on original and subcontract industrial accidents.* https://www.kosha.or.kr/kosha/report/pressr eleases.do?mode=view&articleNo=336844&article.offset=10&articleLi mit=10&srSearchVal=%EC%8B%A4%ED%83%9C%EC%A1%B0%EC %82%AC&srSearchKey=article_text

Korea Women's Development Institute (1992). *A survey on women's employment*. Seoul: Korea Women's Development Institute.

Korean Jobs Committee (2020). *Report on the results of the 16th Job Committee Meeting*. Press release.

Kroon, B. and Paauwe, J. (2013). Structuration of precarious employment in economically constrained firms: The case of Dutch agriculture. *Human Resource Management Journal*, 1(24), 19–37.

Kwon H.J. (2005). Transforming the developmental welfare state in East Asia. *Development and Change*, 36(3), 477–497.

Kwon H.Y., Kwon H.J. and Kim Y.M. (2016). Continuation and cracking of categorical inequality in university cleaning service work organization. *Korean Association of Employment and Labor Relations*, 26(2), 111–139.

Kwon J.Y. (2012). Miracle of Warak Center: Hugging 'Warak' your difficulties. *The Journal of Localitology*, 8, 211–234.

Kwon K.W. (2007). Do you dream of being a freelancer. *Today's Literature Criticism*, 213–225.

Laparra, M., Barbier, J., Darmon, I., Düll, N., Frade, C., Frey, L., Lindley, R. and Vogler-Ludwig, K. (2004). Managing labour market related risks in Europe: Policy implications. *Final Report ESOPE-Project*.

Lee A.Y., Hwang N.H., Yang J.S. and An Y. (2019). *Analysis of the poverty status of self-employed households and social security policies*. Sejong: KIHASA.

Lee B.H. (2004). Comparative study of labor disputes in the period of restructuring: The cases of Hyundai motor and power generation companies. *Korean Journal of Labor Economics*, 27(1), 27–53.

Lee B.H. and Yoon J.H. (2001). The conception and categorization of non-regular labor. *Industrial Labor Study*, 7(2), 1–33.

Lee B.H., Kang H.Y., Kwon H.J. and Kim J.S. (2006). *Employment relations and labor issues in call centers*. Sejong: Korea Labor Institute.

Lee G.C. (2009). *The history of national health security*. Paju: Yangseowon.

Lee H.S. (1984). *Analytical framework of labor market structure*. Paju: Bobmunsa.

Lee H.Y. and Yang J.J. (2017). Who are the outsiders in the South Korean labor market? *Korean Policy Studies Review*, 26, 65–104.

Lee J.A. (2013). Performance of overwork and wage determination. *Economy and Society*, 97, 226–251.

Lee J.H. (1992). An empirical study of Korea's dual labor market. *Korean Journal of Labor Economics*, 15, 37–75.

Lee J.H. (2008). Discriminatory effects of occupational sub-categorization system in Korean financial sector. *Economy and Society*, 80, 165–194.

Lee S.G. (2015). Employment structure and employment change of the original subcontractor. *Labor Review*, 125, 56–66.

Lee S.G. (2018). Digitalization in work and changing of workers' status. *Journal of Business Administration & Law*, 28(3), 181–215.

Lee S.R. (2013). Freelancers treated as workers, self-employed. *International Labor Brief*, 11(12), 1–2.

Lee S.R., Kim S.S., Hwang J.W., Park M.J. and Shin H.G. (2013). *Labor and risks of freelancers: Policy tasks for establishing a social safety net for freelancers*. Sejong: Korea Labor Institute.

Lee S.S. (2011). Looking back on the struggle of cleaning service workers in Hongdae. *The Radical Review*, 48, 149–158.

Lee, S.S.-Y., and Baek, S.-H. (2014). Why the social investment approach is not enough: The female labour market and family policy in the Republic of Korea. *Social Policy & Administration*, 48(6), 686–703.

Lee S.Y. (2011). The shift of labor market risks in deindustrializing Taiwan, Japan, and Korea. *Perspectives on Global Development and Technology*, 10(2), 241–269.

Lee S.Y. (2016). Institutional legacy of state corporatism in de-industrial labour markets: A comparative study of Japan, South Korea and Taiwan. *Socio-economic Review*, 14(1), 73–95.

Lee S.Y. (2018). A comparative study on unemployment insurance, social assistance and ALMP in OECD countries. *Korean Association of Social Policy*, 25(1), 345–375.

Lee S.Y. (2019). The era of unstable youth labor. *Hwanghaemunhwa*, 103, 20–43.

Lee S.Y. and Kim S.S. (2015). Ssangyong Motors layoff and dual labour market in Korea. *Korean Association of Social Policy*, 22(4), 73–96.

Lee S.Y. and Kim K.T. (2017). A qualitative study on the poverty process of sick workers. *The Korean Social Security Association*, 2017, 819–820.

Lee S.Y. and Cho H.J. (2019). A qualitative research on the precarious employment relations and social security experience of customer service center subcontracted workers. *Korean Social Security Studies*, 35(2), 1–34.

Lee S.Y. and Kim Y.H. (2020). Female outsiders in South Korea's dual labour market: Challenges of equal pay for work of equal value. *Journal of Industrial Relations*, 62(4), 651–678.

Lee S.Y., An J.Y. and Kim Y.H. (2016). Why women remain outsiders: A comparative study of labour market in Korea and Japan. *Korea Social Policy Review*, 23(2), 201–237.

Lee S.Y., Baek S.H. and Kim Y.Y. (2017a). *Korea's precarious worker.* Seoul: Hummanitas.

Lee S.Y., Kim E.J. and Park K.E. (2017b). Subcontracting workers outside of Korean social safety net: A case study of subcontracting workers in Ulsan shipbuilding industry. *Social Welfare Policy*, 44(2), 111–143.

Lee S.Y., Seo H.J. and Park K.E. (2018). Why are cleaning workers precarious? Subcontracted female cleaning labour and fictional Korean social protection. *Labour Society Bulletin*, 24(2), 247–291.

Lee S.Y., Baek S.H. and Kim Y.Y. (2019a). Korean dual labour market and dualized old-age income security: Simulation analysis of pension reform combinations. *Journal of Critical Social Policy*, 63, 193–232.

Lee S.Y., Park K.J. and Kim G.H. (2019b). A qualitative study of young freelancers' experience of work and social protection system in South Korea. *Journal of Critical Social Welfare*, 64, 181–239.

Lee S.Y., Baek S.H. and Nahm J.W. (2020a). Labour process in South Korean platform labour market and its mismatch with social protection system. *Korean Journal of Labor Studies*, 26(2), 77–135.

Lee S.Y., Beak S.H., Kim T.H. and Park S.J. (2020b). *Status and implications of employment safety nets in major countries.* Seoul: Audit and Inspection Research Institute.

Lee Y.J. (2014). *A study of the job satisfaction and ways to mutual cooperation between public TV announcer and broadcaster freelance.* Seoul: The Graduate School of Konkuk University.

Lee Y.J. (2017). A study on the definition of 'employee' on social insurance. *Social Security Research*, 33(3), 139–167.

Lee Y.S. (2015). The reality and dreams of cleaning workers. *New Radical Review*, 65, 222–224.

Lenaerts, K., Beblavý, M. and Kilhoffer, Z. (2017). *Government responses to the platform economy: Where do we stand?* Brussels: KEPS.

Manyika, J., Lund, S. and Bughin, J. (2016a). *Digital globalization: The new era global flows.* New York: McKinsey & Company.

Manyika, J., Lund, S., Bughin, J., Robinson, K., Mischke, J. and Mahajan, D. (2016b). *Independent-work-choice-necessity-and-the-gig-economy.* New York: McKinsey & Company.

Media Today (2015). The 28th victim of Ssangyong Motor's dismissal … It's my second time this year. *Media Today.* http://www.mediatoday.co.kr/news/articleView.html?idxno=122973

Media Today (2018). Ssangyong Motor's weight of death and ease of power. *Media Today.* http://www.mediatoday.co.kr/news/articleView.html?idxno=144080

Ministry of Employment and Labor (2022). *Platform worker size and work status in 2022*. Eumseong: Korea Employment Information Service.

Ministry of Trade Industry and Energy (2021). *2020 shipbuilding industry order, the world's No. 1*. https://www.motie.go.kr/motie/ne/presse/press2/bbs/bbsView.do?bbs_seq_n=163698&bbs_cd_n=81&currentPage=1&search_key_n=content_l&cate_n=&dept_v=&search_val_v=VLCC

Moon J.H. (2014). Redundancy dismissal caused by international transfer of manufacturing facilities – in case of Cort, Cortek companies. *Public Interest and Human Rights Law Review*, 14, 3–48.

Mühlberger, U. and Pasqua, S. (2009). Workers on the border between employment and self-employment. *Review of Social Economy*, 67(2), 201–228.

Muntaner, C. (2018). Digital platforms, gig economy, precarious employment, and the invisible hand of social class. *International Journal of Health Services*, 48(4), 597–600.

Nahm J.W. (2020). *A study on guaranteeing social rights of platform workers*. Sejong: Krivet.

Nahm J.W. (2021). A study on the labor situation and job satisfaction of platform workers. *Labor Policy Study*, 21(2), 101–133.

Nam K.M. and Bang H.S. (2012). Experience of social workers' case management for the elderly at home. *Korean Social Welfare Administration*, 14(4), 363–394.

National Human Rights Commission of The Republic of Korea (2006). *A survey on the human rights status of cleaning workers*. Seoul: National Human Rights Commission of the Republic of Korea.

National Human Rights Commission of The Republic of Korea (2008). *A survey on the human rights status of call center telemarketers in women's non-regular workers*. Seoul: National Human Rights Commission of the Republic of Korea.

National Pension Service Compilation Committee (2015). *National pension statistical yearbook*. http://www.riss.kr/link?id=M14038404

Noh B.H. (2009). A study on the dismissal for managerial reasons. *The Journal of Labor Law*, 16, 51–89.

OECD (2017). *Concept paper: Future of work*. Paris: OECD.

OECD (2018a). *Good jobs for all in a changing world of work: The OECD jobs strategy*. Paris: OECD.

OECD (2018b). Promoting adequate social protection and social security coverage for all workers, including those in non-standard forms of employment. Paper prepared for the EWG meeting, 20–21 February.

OECD (2019). *Employment protection legislation index*. Paris: OECD.

OECD (2020). *Employment proctection legislation database*. Paris: OECD.

OECD (2022). *Decline ratios of gross earnings*. Paris: OECD.

Oesch, D. (2006). *Redrawing the class map: Stratification and institutions in Germany, Britain, Sweden and Switzerland*. London: Palgrave Macmillan.

Olasunmbo Ayanfeoluwa, O. (2018). Subcontracting systems and social protection in the informal building construction industry in Lagos, Nigeria. *Journal of Construction Business and Management*, 2(1), 10–19.

Park C.I. (2018). Labor status of special type workers: Focusing on 9 jobs covered by industrial accident insurance. *Labor Review*, 160, 7–28.

Park C.R. (2020). Measures to strengthen the social safety net for low-income small business owners: Introduction of national pension insurance premium support and expansion of employment insurance premiums. *Issues and Discussions*, 1664.

Park J.S. (2014). *The structural transformation of the internal labour market and the risk transfer of occupational accidents and diseases*. Seoul: Yonsei University Graduate School.

Park J.Y., Yoon J.H. and Kim S.S. (2016). Massive layoff and health: A study in SsangYong motor workers. *Health and Medical Sociology*, 41, 61–97.

Park O.J. (2016). Cleaning-contract women workers' working conditions and experiences. *Korean Association of Women's Studies*, 32(2), 217–251.

Park O.J. and Sohn S.Y. (2011). In-between job experience of women converted from irregular worker to unlimited worker: Focused on clerical and sales work. *Korean Association of Woman's Studies*, 27(1), 75–115.

Park S.E. (2015). Job characteristics and job-related emotions and attitudes of call center counselors. *Yonsei Business Review*, 52(1), 21–54.

Park S.J. (2022). A comparative study on welfare regime and production regime considering the dual structure of the labor market. *Social Welfare Policy*, 49(1), 121–156.

Peng I. (2012). Economic dualization in Japan and South Korea. In P. Emmenegger, S. Häusermann, B. Palier and M. Seeleib-Kaiser (eds), *The age of dualization: The changing face of inequality in deindustrializing societies* (pp 226–247). Oxford: Oxford University Press.

Pierson, P. (2001). *The new politics of the welfare state*. Oxford: Oxford University Press.

Piore, M.J. (1980). Economic fluctuation, job security, and labor-market duality in Italy, France, and the United States. *Politics & Society*, 9(4), 379–407.

Polanyi, K. (1944). *The great transformation*. New York: Farrar & Rinehart.

Prenovitz, S. (2021). What happens when you wait? Effects of social security disability insurance wait time on health and financial well-being. *Health Economics*, 30(3), 491–504.

Rifkin, J. (1995). *The end of work*. New York: Putnam.

Rodgers, G. and Rodgers, J. (1998). *Precarious jobs in labour market regulation: The growth of atypical employment in western Europe*. Geneva: International Labour Organization.

Rueda, D. (2005). Insider–outsider politics in industrialized democracies: The challenge to social democratic parties. *American Political Science Review*, 99(1), 61–74.

Rueda, D. (2006). Social democracy and active labour-market policies: Insiders, outsiders and the politics of employment promotion. *British Journal of Political Science*, 36(3), 385–406.

Ryu G.S., Kang S.H. and Kim D.G. (2017). *A study on the improvement of private income security system for self-employed*. Seoul: Kiri.

Saint-Paul, G. (1996). *Dual labor markets*. Cambridge, MA: MIT Press.

Sargeant, M. (2009). Health and safety of vulnerable workers in a changing world of work. ADAPT Working Paper, 27 November, 101.

Schmidt, F.A. (2017). *Digital labour markets in the platform economy*: Mapping the political challenges of crowd work and gig work. Berlin: Friedrich-Ebert-Stiftung.

Scholz, T. (2016). *Platform cooperativism: Challenging the corporate sharing economy*. New York: Rosa Luxemburg Foundation.

Seo J.H. (2015). Non-standard employment's precarious work. *Labor Policy Study*, 15(1), 1–41.

Seo J.H. and Lee J.S. (2015). An causal mechanism analysis to the effect of the labor market structures by industry on precarious work in service sector. *Korean Journal of Social Welfare Studies*, 46(1), 283–314.

Seo M.K. (2009). *Phenomenological study on the employment experience of pre-elderly women in Korea*. Seoul: The Graduate School of Ewha Womans University.

Seoul (2018). Survey on 'freelance work environment' in Seoul. Press release.

Shin S.J. (2013). Justification of layoffs. *Journal of Labour Law*, 46, 337–340.

Skocpol, T. (1985). Cultural idioms and political ideologies in the revolutionary reconstruction of state power: A rejoinder to Sewell. *The Journal of Modern History*, 57(1), 86–96.

Srnicek, N. (2017). *Platform capitalism*. Malden, MA: Polity.

Standing, G. (2009). *Work after globalization*. Northampton, MA: Edward Elgar.

Standing, G. (2014). *A precariat charter: From denizens to citizens*. London: Bloomsbury Academic.

Statistics Korea (2008). *Household income and expenditure survey*. Daejeon: Statistics Korea.

Statistics Korea (2016). *Korean economically active census supplemental census August, 2016*. Daejeon: Statistics Korea.

Statistics Korea (2018). *2018 August national survey of economically active population*. Daejeon: Statistics Korea.

Statistics Korea (2019). *Korean economically active census supplemental census August, 2019*. Daejeon: Statistics Korea.

Statistics Korea (2020). *Korean economically active census supplemental census August, 2020*. Daejeon: Statistics Korea.

Statistics Korea (2021). *Korean economically active census supplemental census August, 2021*. Daejeon: Statistics Korea.

Statistics Korea (2022). *Korean economically active population survey*. Daejeon: Statistics Korea.

Sung J.M. (2020). What if overcoming the corona virus does not lead to deepening inequality. *Labor Review*, 184, 34–47.

Taylor-Gooby, P. (ed) (2004). *New risks, new welfare: The transformation of the European welfare state*. Oxford: Oxford University Press.

Thelen, K. and Mahoney, J. (2015). Comparative-historical analysis in contemporary political science. In J. Majoney and K. Thelen (eds) *Advances in comparative-historical analysis*. New York: Cambridge University Press, pp 3–36.

Vosko, L.F. (2006). *Precarious employment: Understanding labour market insecurity in Canada*. Montreal: McGill-Queen's University Press.

Wayne, S.J. and Green, S.A. (1993). The effects of leader–member exchange on employee citizenship and impression management behavior. *Human Relations*, 46(12), 1431–1440.

Webster, E., Lambert, R. and Bezuidenhout, A. (2008). *Grounding globalization: Labour in the age of insecurity*. Cambridge, MA: Blackwell.

Weil, D. (2014). *The fissured workplace: Why work became so bad for so many and what can be done to improve it*. Cambridge, MA: Harvard University Press.

Weil, D. (2015). *Fissured workplace: No company for you*. Seoul: Hwangsojari.

Won S.J. (2013). *Social welfare history community*. Goyang: Gongdongche.

Yonhap News (2020). Excludes workers' compensation insurance for couriers. Employers force … National Inspectorate Points pouring out. *Yonhap News*, 15 October. https://www.yna.co.kr/view/AKR20201015074951530

Yoon J.D. (2008). *The role of social insurance and labor unions*. Sejong: Korea Labor Institute.

Yoon J.D., Kim S.H. and Jr, P. (2008). *Social insurance and the role of trade unions*. Sejong: Korea Labor Institute.

Yoon S.J., Yang G.W., Chae Y.J. and Kim H.R. (2012). Dirty work and identity: Job crafting of college janitors. *Korean Academy of Management*, 2, 1–30.

Yoon Y.S. and Chung H.J. (2016). New forms of dualization? Labour market segmentation patterns in the UK from the late 90s until the post-crisis in the late 2000s. *Social Indicators Research*, 128, 609–631.

Index

References to figures appear in *italic* type;
those in **bold** type refer to tables.